Demon in the Box

DEMON IN THE BOX

Jews, Arabs, Politics, and Culture in the Making of Israeli Television

TASHA G. OREN

RUTGERS UNIVERSITY PRESS
New Brunswick, New Jersey, and London

Library of Congress Cataloging-in-Publication Data

Oren, Tasha G.
    Demon in the box : Jews, Arabs, politics, and culture in the making of Israeli
television / Tasha G. Oren.
        p.   cm.
Includes bibliographical references and index.
    ISBN 0-8135-3419-4 (alk. paper) — ISBN 0-8135-3420-8 (pbk. : alk. paper)
    1. Television broadcasting—Israel.   I. Title.
    PN1992.3.I75O74   2004
    384.55'095694—dc22

                                                                    2003020098

A British Cataloging-in-Publication record for this book is available from the
British Library

Manufactured in the United States of America

This book is dedicated in loving memory of Dr. Sarah Oren, who first showed me how ideas can make a world.

Contents

Acknowledgments

I and this project have benefited from the assistance and support of so many extraordinary people along the way that writing a single acknowledgments page that marks their contribution with mere mention is woefully inadequate. In Madison, where this project was first conceived, I am indebted to Julie D'Acci, whose guidance, support, and careful reading brought this work into being. I also thank Michele Hilmes, John Fiske, Hemant Shah, Vince Kepley, Dan Marcus, Jason Mittell, Shari Goldin, and Amy Seaham, who offered helpful suggestions and much-needed support. I am especially grateful to Henry Jenkins at MIT for his mentorship and extraordinary generosity. In Israel, Vered Molocho and Vardit and Israel Shreberk went well beyond the calls of duty and friendship; Tzvi Oren, Dan Trainin, and Paula Dub also gave selflessly of themselves and deserve thanks here. I thank the staff of the Israeli Broadcast Authority Archives in Jerusalem for their valuable assistance and for access to their film and document collection; to the Tel Aviv University library, the David J. Light Law Library, the Beit Ariela library, the Knesset archive, the Widener Library at Harvard University, and the *Ha'aretz* newspaper for their kind reprint permission. I am also grateful for the travel grant from the University of Wisconsin in Madison for my initial research trip, and for a generous research fellowship from the graduate school at UW–Milwaukee, which allowed me to return to Israel and complete the research for the final three chapters of this book.

At the University of Wisconsin in Milwaukee, I was fortunate to find a community of scholars, friends, and students who've made my working life a privilege and a pleasure. Thanks go out to the Department of Journalism and Mass Communications and the Department of English for their gracious support. I am especially grateful to the Center for Twenty-first-century Studies for the gift of a wonderful year I spent writing this book as a fellow there. Thank you, Kathleen Woodward, Kristie Hamilton, Dan Sherman, Carol Tennessen, Maria Liesegang, and the entire center staff (past and present) for making such an ideal environment for research, writing, and intellectual fellowship. Special gratitude goes out to my fellow fellows at the center, especially Lane Hall, Jennifer Jordan, Denis Provencher, Mark Netzloff, and Amanda Seligman, for their enthusiasm, brilliance, insightful comments, and raucous camaraderie.

I am grateful and indebted to Patrice Petro for her extraordinary support, guidance, friendship, intelligence, and bottomless enthusiasm; these have nourished me through this project and since. Karen Riggs and Mia Consalvo stoked the fire daily, and I have been so very lucky to have them as colleagues, readers, and cherished friends. Thanks to Pat Mellencamp, Sandra Braman, Mat Rappaport, Marilu Knode, Toby Miller, and Peter Paik for giving so generously of their time and their gifts; to Shilpa Dave and Leilani Nishime, who've taken on extra burdens at the final stretch and cheered me on; and to Leslie Mitchner, Bobbe Needham, and everyone at Rutgers University Press for all their work and for believing in this project from the start.

Finally, I thank my parents, family, and friends, who helped sustain me while suffering both my obsessions and my neglect, and of course, Stewart Ikeda, who has been a true partner in this endeavor: my most exacting reader, demanding interlocutor, fierce critic, and loving husband.

An early version of chapter 3 ("The Belly-Dancer Strategy") was published in *Media, Culture, and Society* 25, 2 (March 2003).

Demon in the Box

INTRODUCTION

Television simply scared them. . . . How do you harness such a creature from
the start?

—Tsvi Gil, *House of Precious Stones*

In 1952, NBC president David Sarnoff sent word to David Ben-Gurion,
the first prime minister of the four-year-old nation of Israel, offering to
help the new Jewish homeland—and its army—establish a television
broadcasting system.[1] The leading U.S. broadcast network even offered
to help fund-raise for the endeavor in exchange for a hand in future
programming. Ben-Gurion's reply was terse and unequivocal: Israelis
were people of the book, the prime minister fired back. They had no
use for television.

In light of the near-global rush to television that would characterize the Fifties, such a blunt refusal may have taken the Americans by
surprise, but it typified an approach to the new technology by those
Israelis who had bothered to notice it.[2] For them, television was an
anti-intellectual and antieducational pursuit that would corrupt the
socialist state and interfere with its emerging national culture.[3] As one
Knesset member would later offer, "Television is an expression of a consuming, passive man, a man who buys his life, . . . who needs only to
receive."[4]

Sixteen years would pass between this short correspondence and
the introduction of a general-television service to Israel. In these years,
the new nation would be transformed from an eccentric collection of
refugees, fervent idealists, and seasoned guerrilla fighters to a powerful
state riding a wave of international admiration, with its own refugee
camps and a legacy of pride and shame that would dominate its politics

and shape its future. Television's place in this history, however, has rarely been explored. My aim in this book is to provide, not a full and comprehensive history of Israeli television in total, but rather an Israeli history *through* television. In what follows, I take up specific moments as case studies in television's formative two decades to argue for the medium as a central force in shaping discursive formations and popular knowledge, *not* in its representational capacity but in its role as an object of fantasy and projection.

This approach yields a kind of reciprocal dialogue among different cultural and political discourses, a multivocal conversation that reveals broadcast history, as Michele Hilmes has argued, to be a social practice grounded in culture rather than in electricity.[5]

Although the state of Israel came into existence a mere twenty years before its first national television broadcast, the medium's relatively late arrival was galling to many commentators who watched as, one by one, Arab nations erected television broadcasting transmitters all around Israel's borders.[6] This was not just a matter of pride and technological competition: Arab broadcasts could be received in Israel and were watched regularly by Arab Israelis and Arabic-speaking Jews. More than any other, this concern would ultimately tip the scales in favor of television as Israel emerged from the Six Day War a Middle Eastern powerhouse and an occupying force.

Yet, television in Israel has a long, convoluted, and often perplexing prehistory. The phantom of television haunted public and political debates for a full decade before Israeli television's inauguration, then continued to be the focal point of debates over representations of the nation and its history for a decade more. During this turbulent period—and through political shake-ups, social and economic transformations, two major wars, ongoing hostilities with their Arab neighbors, and the devastating outcome of the 1967 occupation—Israelis, ostensibly arguing over a communication technology, were in fact debating the very foundations of their national project. First as an imagined technology (what I will call "telespeculation") and then as the "real" of a domestic broadcast service, the idea of the medium facilitated a unique form of public discursive engagement that served to define official priorities, articulate ephemeral values, and debate an ongoing national transformation.

How does a broadcasting system fit into a nation's history? What is its relationship to the forces and ideas that shape a self-defined society? In its representational capacity, textual production, and cultural intervention, television is obviously a central cultural mechanism whose conventions, narratives, and industrial norms become part of a national, and increasingly global, currency. But what of television as an institution? As a technology? And, perhaps most pressingly, what about television as a mode of information and a way of thinking? In beginning with a "prehistory" here, I want to trace the path of Israeli television to its very source: back beyond the point of origin of the first transmission, where a particular media system begins, to a moment when it is first conceived as a possibility. As I will show, this path is neither isolated nor fortuitous but stretches along well-traveled ground. More than a history of a single institution, what results is a trek through intersections that reveals the development of television as formed in the convergence of various political and social forces. Further, it demonstrates the bidirectionality of such a construction: First imagined by and for ideological and political forces, television also served to define and shape such forces, along with public ways of knowing and understanding them.

Since discursive analysis and cultural critique operate primarily within a process of textual interpretation, I take up policy debates, government discussions, and official correspondence about television, as well as press coverage and public and industry responses to these debates, as a semi-unified textual entity. As we shall see, each series of debates was brought about by particular sea changes in Israeli politics, and with each new current, the idea of television was swept up in a fresh wave of predictions, hopes, and anxieties. As a broadcast history, this work sets out to examine these waves, both as discrete discourses about television and as complex historical moments that implicated television in a larger struggle—accounting for the forces that animated the course of television's history, and that ultimately "invented" it.

With official and popular texts as my primary informants, the book's focus is on the conversations, arguments, fantasies, and conceptual understandings television has facilitated throughout this period. In gauging which and how such notions were expressed and popularly received, absence is of equal import—not only in terms of the absence of "actual" television, but also in the absence of particular voices from the debate. As we will see, Arabs and Eastern immigrants consistently occupied a central place in much of the television discourse (as primary target audiences, as particularly vulnerable would-be viewers, and as threats to a unified national culture). Yet, in the public sphere of radio and newspapers or in the official sphere of law and policy discussions, their voices were rarely heard. It is in these pronounced absences in the context of struggle and transformation that television history emerges as a lens through which social, ideological, and cultural patterns reveal themselves with a particular clarity.

In one of the earliest critical engagements with television, Raymond Williams urged against an artificial separation between technology and the society in which it develops, calling on historians to restore an account of intention into the narrative of technical development so that it is understood as institutionally embedded, and fostered within preexisting purposes and practices.[7] Recent historical engagements with television, as well as with other technologies, have widely taken up this approach, exploring media technologies not as forces that spring up unexpectedly to reshape their surroundings but as calculated responses to existing conditions and particular aspirations. Scholarship informed by cultural studies, policy research, and the recently emerging field of Internet studies has further emphasized that historical accounts of technology are incomplete without the examination of such developments as dynamic and ongoing processes forged at the meeting place between innovation, official intent, economic and political realities, and popular practice.

The process that brought Israeli television to life offers an exceptionally cogent example for such an intentional, translucent technology, since television's ability to address specific national and social needs was the sole impetus for its consideration, evaluation, and institution. Indeed, the Israeli government's central role in television's introduction and the relative absence of profit-motivated industries from the process makes this approach an (initially) ideal fit, as political and ultimately ideological motivations took precedence over economic ones in the efforts to shape television and press it into service as a cultural institution.[8]

However, the ultimate failure of these forces to fully control and delimit the shape that television would take in the Israeli case illustrates the important limits of such intentionality. In part, this failure points to the lack of cohesion in the processes of power—themselves mutable and subject to historical and internal shifts. Further, it reveals the always present gap between expectations of effect and the messy realities of practice, taste, and popular circulation.

Tony Bennett argues that the creation of another cultural institution, the public museum, exemplified the "development of a new 'governmental' relation to culture," where products deemed "high culture" were utilized for social management.[9] Official display, as Steven Mullaney and others have pointed out, not only denoted what was culturally worthy, but also helped define the "public" to which it was addressed.[10] These "governmental" attentions (or, as Toby Miller termed them after Foucault, "technologies of governance"), then, were equally engaged in delimiting a sanctioned national culture and a "proper" public as citizenry.[11] As I will show in what follows, television technology was conceived to operate in much the same way in the Israeli case (down to the understanding of programming as "displays"), as interested governmental factions worked to enlist it in a grander process of cultural production: a process that sought to define a nationally appropriate and culturally unified Israeli public. In this, Israeli television was far from unique.[12] Yet, what I stress here is the role of television as an idea and a conceptual site of articulation that, in the Israeli case, operated largely (and perhaps primarily) outside the logic of programming per se. In thinking about the role of television, I draw from works that stretch the notion of the medium beyond its utility as a conduit for programming. Particularly instructive here are Thomas Streeter's important analysis of how classical liberalism and ideas about markets, audiences, and broadcasting technology underpinned policy and legal structures that shaped U.S. broadcasting as a private corporate system; Lynn Spigel's outstanding work on the constitutive implications of television in postwar U.S. discourses about the home, family, and gender; and Anna McCarthy's illuminating exploration of television's site-specific function in public spaces.[13] These works, among others, contribute to our understanding of television not only as an institution and a source of information and cultural narratives, but also as a formative presence in ideas about everyday life.

Israeli television, as a concept, an idea, and a plan, was made and remade many times over before a single broadcast was ever transmitted. Each time, television was proposed as a solution to a particular problem and conceived to operate in accordance with particular national preoccupations that arose from Israel's predominant ideological investment in cultural unity, border security, and its relationship to its Arab neighbors. The precise formulations of these preoccupations—and thus television's implication in them—would shift repeatedly in the two decades I cover here. Yet, as I will argue, the essential, locally constructed understandings of the technology—its conception as a solution to, and its implication with, anxieties about Israeli culture, security, and politics—would remain the same. Further, the deployment of such telespeculating logic facilitated the distinct expression and conjoining of these national anxieties in significant and consequential ways.

In part, then, this book dwells on (largely unfulfilled) official expectations and strategic maneuvers, as culled from personal and public

accounts, official government documents, discussion minutes, correspondence, and legal interventions. As I will show, these institutional
plans and official definitions were remarkably successful in circum-
scribing the discursive field in which television was discussed and conceived. What's more, they effectively and permanently penetrated the
social realm well beyond the narrow sphere of broadcast policy.
Namely, as television was implicated in the Israeli state project, primary
national concerns were defined *in terms* of broadcasting, offering a rare
and lucid glimpse into the anatomy of such definitions and their significance to the Israeli project. Here I argue that television's ideological
utility was never as potent in Israel as in the decade before its actual
birth.

In addition to such top-down accounts, however, I pay particular
attention to public responses and participation in these debates, illustrating the degree to which these (and the actual service) eschewed
some elements of television's intended deployment while embracing
others. The conclusions I come to in observing the expansive quality
of the conversation over television, its capacity to invoke, absorb, and
refresh old anxieties in recombinant ways and reflect them publicly
back, extends beyond the historical moment, technological particularity, and national framework I focus on here. Taken together, the case
studies herein suggest that technological developments in general—
and television in particular—are not impersonal, "naturally" evolving,
or completely pliable. Rather, television is necessarily a compound
concept (a cultural network of meaning making, a daily practice, a
technology, and a legal and economic institution) whose presence in
our daily lives derives its power precisely from the ambiguity of its
realm of influence.

A few words on translations, assumptions, and omissions. The story of
Israeli television lacks an important aspect in many telecommunication histories—invention. On its surface, it is a bureaucrat's narrative
and a story whose twists, turns, and moments of tension depend
wholly on legal and policy contentions—hardly the stuff of riveting
drama. Unlike early telecommunication histories—rife with stock elements of tenacious inventors, unscrupulous operators, prophetic
managers, and fateful accidents—"second-tier" telecommunication
histories of nations that adopted television after its initial period of development must contend with a foreignness already embedded in the
system, in its institutional structure, in its preferred textual traditions,
and, it seems, in the signal itself. In this sense, such histories, for many

nations, include the process of re-invention: ridding television of its foreign tinge (a deeply contradictory story that intercedes in the usual tale of globalization's sweep) and fashioning the signal as local, specific, and—in a national sense—useful.

As a book about encounters over television's representational capacity, translation is already at the heart of *Demon in the Box*. Inasmuch as this is an account of television's becoming, it is also the story of its conceptual translation and actual transformation from words to the audio-visual, from governmental to private and popular, from imagined to actual, and from global to national (and back again).

One of the most interesting and productive tensions in the telespeculations about the technology and its Israeli translation was its simultaneous imagining as (foreign) progress and (domestic) degeneration. Far from indicating Israeli unease with modernity or technology at large (no such tension existed in the Israeli embrace of computer technology, for example), apprehensions over television—its immediate scent of foreignness and passivity, its American legacy and Arab preexistence—were rather an indication of Israeli ambivalence about cultural exchange in the first era of underpoliticized leisure. The process of introducing television into Israel was in large part a discursive—as much as a technological—endeavor of translation and adaptation. Repeatedly, Israel was defined as a "special case" with particular needs, an extraordinary set of viewer populations, and unique values and cultural aspirations.

In my own process of translating these debates into English, and casting them into a narrative and flow of interrelated and specific meanings, I encountered a particular problem of translation politics. Surely familiar to all who traverse linguistic borders, the process involves the discovery—mundane as it is in retrospect—that language carries its own geography intact. In the case of Hebrew—tied, as it is, to the longing of people, nation, and place—one finds the specificity of location and association encompassing. The word for a "national population" (*Leum*) folds within it the understanding of "nation" (*Ooma*) and the ethnospecific origin of "people" (*Aam*). "Country" (*Eretz*) contains the feel of the "land" underneath one's feet (*Aretz*), while "state" (*Medina*) conveys the commanding sense of "order, law, and judgment" (*Din*). Used interchangeably, the semiotic looseness and intermingling of these signs in everyday speech presents a compound coexistence that is difficult to capture in translation. Such too was the task for Israelis themselves in their effort to define and adapt television.

Following Thomas Streeter, we can think of government actors in broadcasting establishment and policy engineering as an interpretive community that shares, as Streeter notes, relatively stable, agreed-upon meanings for imponderables that may otherwise be open to a wide variety of interpretations.[14]

Although much of what follows necessarily engages with the notion of cultural and national identity, I want to avoid reifying this concept outside of its usefulness as a collective of thought and a "handle concept" produced with and through official discourses about television's utility. Whereas exploring notions of identity (both collective and private) as expressed in the practices of culture—the relationship between the content of people's lives and the content of a people's life, as Virginia Dominguez has put it—is a worthy project, it is not my aim here.[15] Rather, I focus on national and cultural identity in the Israeli case as largely formal concepts through which culture (and text) are presumed to work and what they are perceived to evoke.

Similarly, I want to distinguish my use of "imagining" in the national context with the well-known and widely influential work of Benedict Anderson and his concept of imagined nation.[16] Unlike Anderson, whose concern was with the readership itself, in its imagined sense of kinship through literary address, my focus here is on official imagining: not by the reader outward, but as a top-down assumption about a reader-perceived sense of collective kinship. I am less interested in the actual success of television (or its various texts) to grant such collective community status to its joint readership than in the assumption that it did, and in the efforts to direct and shape such would-be responses. Jonathan Boyarin's observation about the opportunities offered by cultural studies is helpful in this context: "Cultural studies offers a way out of the schizoid disciplinary dilemma of trying to squeeze the Jews into definitions as a historical or a cultural people. . . . Writing theory out of a primary interest in Jewish life in turn offers an opportunity to uncover unsuspected links among knowledge, culture and power."[17]

Finally, my aim in this book is to illustrate a set of arguments about media through a historical examination, and to this extent, the Israeli example serves as a convenient case study. However, I also endeavored to make this close examination specific and narratively cohesive—worth telling in its own right. Even as my methodology and the set of interlocking assumptions and critiques employed throughout stem from my own investment in media theory, policy, and cultural studies,

I have chosen to let these implicitly undergird my account while high-lighting specific—and lesser known—Israeli engagements.

The creation of Israeli television and its subsequent development is explored here in two parts and through six consecutive stages (and chapters), each defined by a government debate and a public scandal. These two parts represent successive periods in the history of Israeli television—first imagined and then real. While both are about the discourses that surrounded broadcasting, part 1 focuses on the development of television as an idea and part 2 explores the "real" of television's early presence in Israel and the process of its introduction and cultural integration into Israeli daily life. The first three chapters (part 1) are organized as a "prehistory," tracing the developments of television-related discourses, spotlighting several proposed models and experimental plans for a television service, and examining the surprisingly potent role of the still-absent technology in Israeli political and cultural imagination. Throughout this period (1956 to 1968), television existed largely as a structuring absence—an empty and thus infinitely flexible sign—that facilitated its discursive implication in Israel's most immediate preoccupations.[18] Two basic concerns thus dictated future understandings of broadcasting: cultural integration and security.

In chapter 1, I show how official and popular attitudes toward broadcasting were shaped by a particular history that pre-dated the creation of the Israeli state and trace how interrelated preoccupations and anxieties first evolved to conceive the idea of television—and simultaneously began the process of defining national problems and their hierarchical value through a broadcasting logic.

Crucial to this process were economic and ideological shifts marked by the transition from agricultural settlements to an urban middle-class life, and concurrent demographic changes in the mid- to late 1950s, following immigration waves from eastern Europe, the Middle East, and North Africa. Ethnic tensions in the diversifying Israeli society, emerging definitions of leisure and entertainment, and the appearance of television sets—and Arab programming—in Israeli homes combined here to form official responses to social and cultural tensions that introduced "cultural integration" as a central preoccupation. This notion first produced broadcasting as a possible solution to a national problem.

The etymological origin of the word "culture" has long fascinated theorists, as it so plainly reveals its ideological connection to both organic growth and cultivation through active tending.[19] Moreover, as

Halton notes after Herder, "culture" and "colonize" share a root origin, implying not only a willful self-transformation but also an institutional foundation.[20] Thinking through these trajectories of definition here reveals how Israeli television was initially conceived literally as a culture machine: a transformative technology that would use culture as a cultivating—indeed, civilizing—force. Moreover, this logic not only equated assimilation with national unity, but also saw both as pivoting on cultural preferences, quite separate from considerations of imposed social hierarchy, political representation, or economic inequity.

Chapter 2 details the process by which television became both a legitimate subject of debate and the object of political anxiety. Framing television as a technological solution to a national problem forced the Knesset (Israel's parliamentary governing body) to articulate and debate the young country's unique character and needs. This not only produced conflicting definitions of national values and priorities, but also defined "proper" Israeli television (and culture) in opposition to U.S. commercial mass broadcasting and Arab cultural influences. Along with accounting for the "politicization" of the television debate—and a detailed analysis of its controversial relationship with radio—this chapter examines both the first Israeli industrial efforts to introduce entertainment television, and the first government attempts to control and restrict receiver ownership. All three cases illustrate how a nonexistent television service came to be endowed with enormous political significance.

As the television debate begins in earnest in 1962, official understanding of and projections about the technology preclude mass broadcasting or popular entertainment in favor of a narrowcasting model that took up particular "problem" populations (Eastern immigrants, youth, resident Palestinians, and Arab spectators) as targeted viewers. Notable in this context is the proximity of, and nearly collapsed distinctions between, the cultural anxiety the television debate provoked and the political interests, priorities, and ideological concerns it raised and reinforced. As a fitting illustration of Foucault's formulation of discursive technology—here applied, and worked through, the relatively novel technology of broadcasting—Israeli television, while at the center of the debate, was only tangentially its object.

For Toby Miller, public policy functions to produce a cultural subject in four ways: "the ethically incomplete subject in need of training into humanness; the national public in need of a dramatological mirror in which to recognize itself; the politically incomplete public subject in need of democratic training in citizenship; and the rational, consuming subject in need of alignment with this public citizen."[21]

As I chronicle in this chapter, policy arguments and early attempts to institute television as a national technology precisely paralleled these categories. Further, the relationship between these rhetorical constructions of specific publics and the definition of television as a national utility was a circular one: Neither could exist without the other.

Government attempts to fight the proliferation of TV sets introduced competing assessments of television as an insubordinate technology whose signal could not be easily controlled. Another definitive struggle ensued when a foreign patron emerged, promoting a particular type of television and threatening to sever the familial ties between it and radio. The contest over television's technological derivation became the flash point for a larger debate over its "nature," pitting proponents of the evolutionary and predetermined view of the technology against those who regarded it as flexible and "neutral." This debate was formative not only for television itself, but also for projections of national goals and their encounter with international norms.

Most important, I show how the rhetorical tensions between "natural" and "neutral" understandings of technology were most instrumental in their definitions of audiences. In addition to debating television's threats and merits in terms of national challenges, official television rhetoric facilitated the classification of various population segments in a hierarchy of cultural vulnerability and "fitness." In this sense, early television discourse would have a lasting impact on understandings and formal articulations of social tensions well beyond the broadcasting context.

In chapter 3, I turn to public responses, expectations, and other "telespeculations" that characterized popular discourses about television. These existed alongside official debates about the technology and intensified as the Israeli government finally expressed its full support for general television, and a vision for its introduction. In all, the examples in this chapter focus on the question of control and authority, as television's yet unknown structure oscillated among proposed public, private, and governmental versions.

This chapter's latter half recounts the creation of an educational service, the first experimental broadcasts, and the impact of these developments on the television debate and the burgeoning retail industry that quickly followed. Early advertising campaigns reveal the degree to which government plans to narrowcast messages to problematic audience segments conflicted with both public and industrial expectations for television. Further, as television's introduction appeared a virtual certainty by the mid-1960s, government focus again shifted to target Arab audiences, both within and outside Israel's borders. In this sense, the initial model of cultural reform within Israel gave way to a self-representational model of cross-border political communication addressed to a presumed hostile audience.

The next three chapters (part 2) account for television's formative decade and focus on public scandals that situated television at the center of fundamental controversies about religious identity, censorship, popular entertainment, and political representation. In chapter 4, I argue that the Six Day War and its immediate consequences—particularly for Palestinians in the occupied territories—was the definitive factor in the final establishment of an Israeli television service. In tracing this process and the government's early attempt to introduce a principally Arab-language service (targeted first at Palestinian viewers), I show how previous imagined incarnations of television, the successful deployment of wartime radio, and the military effort to direct and shape international media reports about the war paved the way to a definition of television that essentially ignored Israeli citizens as primary viewers. Even as it finally "really" appeared, Israeli television was still immured in competing utilitarian models of national reform and political utility. As this chapter illustrates, Israeli television, as a debatable concept, becomes a kind of repository for specific nationalist aspirations.

Chapter 5 examines the controversial process of the institution of a full weekly television schedule. This case study illustrates how growing tensions between a secular majority and an Orthodox, politically powerful minority exploded in a confrontation over Saturday programming. As this episode demonstrates, the discursive role of television not only was defined to suit a particular problem, but also worked in circular fashion to shape and delimit (and here, inflame) public engagement with the issues at hand. In this sense, television—as both a domestic technology and a tax-supported institution—functioned here to define the religious/secular discord as a conflict over governance and a clash of values between individual rights and collective Jewish identity.

Chapter 6 similarly focuses on a single foundation-shaking controversy that played out through television. It differs from the previous chapters, however, in that it concerns a specific text, the short story "Hirbat Hizaa," and its adaptation to television in 1978, just as Israel's first right-wing government ascended to power under Menachem Begin. The story of a young Israeli soldier's breakdown as he is forced to evacuate an Arab village during the 1948 pan-Arab-Israeli war, "Hirbat Hizaa" has been a well known and celebrated work of fiction since its publication in 1949. This semi-autobiographical recollection by Israeli author S. Yzhar not only describes the young protagonist's guilt and shame at his own action, but also goes further to indict Israeli wartime conduct, equating the weight of the Palestinian experience with that of the Jewish Diaspora. The television adaptation of the story and the struggle over its proposed airing became one of the most explosive episodes in Israeli television history. The so-called *Hirbat-Hizaa* affair served to highlight television's role in disturbing the complex interdependence of historical narratives, political ideology, and public consensus over memory in Israel's formative years.

Along with the political upheaval that came in its wake, the film also left Israelis wondering about the fundamental difference between literary and cinematic representations of history: Why would such a brutal critique, so celebrated on the page, be so reviled when filmed? How does the word, transcribed into the televised image, lose its authorial singularity to become an accusation of national culpability?

In the most potent revelation of television's ideological dimension, the *Hirbat Hizaa* affair exposed the shortcomings of the medium's role as a direct communication "pipeline" between the viewer and the state. The controversy, as played out in the wake of the election and the start of peace negotiations with Egypt, forever changed perceptions of television as unproblematically corresponding to a national imagination, and shattered the appealing official fantasy that anchored proper citizenship in its place on the living-room couch.

This book aims to provide a multidimensional view of both broadcast history itself and, through it, Israeli culture and politics in the decades that saw the development of the nation's electronic broadcasting system. As one central theme, this approach illustrates how the still-unresolved Palestinian/Israeli conflict dominated the very definitions of media, self-expression, cultural identity, education, and entertainment in Israel. The accompanying structuring anxieties over internal cohesion and external security extended beyond institutional and programming considerations to the very definitions of popular Israeli culture.

Whereas basic preoccupations (politics, security, cultural and religious identity, and Arab-Israeli relations) informed the discourse of television, the resulting definitions circulated back into the public sphere and gained wide currency beyond their utility in the media context. Thus, tracing the popular debates, political struggles, and public scandals that surrounded television's formative years presents a unique opportunity to examine, in distilled form, the negotiations over Israeli national identity, ethnic culture, and international politics. In total, this process demonstrates how media history can provide a portal into the knotty processes and intricate social narratives that together fabricate the disorderly concepts of nation, ethnicity, and culture. Moreover, tracing these debates reveals a new functional dimension for media technologies, lived not in the "real" of circuitry, image, transmission, and reception, but in popular and official imaginations, where complex social, political, and cultural forces can gain materiality and cohesion through their reduction to the constructed, local, and very human logic of technology.

PART ONE

TELESPECULATIONS

Debating Israeli Television

MERE GLINTS AND REFRACTIONS

1

The Uses of Prehistory and the Origins of the Television Discourse

We will take care that this instrument is provided for, that it is loved and taken care of, and will not be thrown to commercial dealings but used as a great and important instrument for the nation's education, enlightenment, and its elevation to a higher standard.

—Ytzhak Ben-Aharon

There is no country in the world that does not curse the day when it let television have a foothold.

—Menachem Parosh

GOOD FOR THE PEOPLE

At the time of NBC's initial proposal, the idea of an Israeli television service would have seemed both fantastic and laughable to most Israelis.[1] Perceived primarily as an empty leisure activity, the technology was a luxury Israel could scarcely contemplate in its present reality. Yet the swift and unambiguous rejection of television by Ben-Gurion's government was motivated by more than a conviction about its frivolity: For Israel's bookish leader, as for many public figures, the very nature of television—particularly in its U.S. incarnation as commercial entertainment—presented an essential incongruity, even a threat, to the bedrock vision of the fledgling Jewish state. The presence of television was simply inconceivable within the fresh Zionist dream of nation building or the harsh reality of border guarding. Television, for Ben-Gurion, could serve no constructive role within the Zionist project, and, having no useful benefits for the Israeli worker-soldier-pioneer, it was merely an unwelcome distraction that would soften ideological resolve, distort the spirit, and alienate the Israeli citizen from social activity and political participation.

Compounding the opposition to television on ideological grounds, religious leaders worried about the adverse effects of electronic media on religious observance (imagined as much more damaging than the already controversial radio broadcasts), and educators, politicians, and other public figures warned of television's negative effects on youth. By the Sixties, sensational statistics about U.S. crime and violence were repeatedly invoked as evidence of the medium's influence on juvenile delinquency and antisocial behavior. By 1962, when Israeli television first appeared as a realistic possibility, the range of arguments against it spanned the general (television will corrupt the young and impressionable) to the local (it will rob Israelis of community activities and isolate them); the ideological (television will foster materialism and greed) to the cultural (Israelis are too smart and intellectually advanced for television); and concerns over Judaism (television will destroy the very essence of Jewish tradition) to anxieties over masculinity (it will "soften" soldiers, rendering them weak and passive).

In so articulating this spectrum of threats, early arguments against television precisely reflected the primary anxieties against which Israeli nationalism strove to define its citizenry. By 1962, the first generation of Israeli-born teenagers presented parental and official authorities with the first challenge to heretofore unquestioned nationalist ideology, as Israeli culture in the first postcolonial period was forced to develop an identity that reached beyond the Jewish struggle for a homeland. New material possibilities threatened its socialist roots and collective identity as diverse communities redefined themselves around political affiliation, social interaction, tradition, work, and recreation.

For most opinion makers, television was a leisure technology associated with rich and secure countries, those whose citizenry had time to kill, and nations with too many amusement parlors and precious few libraries. For the benefit of mere entertainment, it presented myriad potential disasters; even if Israel could afford the expense, the real price was too high to contemplate.

Since Israel's formation in 1948, the country was wholly absorbed in the difficult task of creating a national infrastructure, all the while beset by continuous internal and external pressures. Arab-Israeli hostilities persisted, accompanied by outbursts of violence and cycles of border infiltration and retaliation. The nation struggled to absorb new immigrants who often arrived at the rate of twenty thousand a month, more than doubling the national population in six years, while its democratic structure weathered an unstable political system beleaguered by fierce enmity. The debate over home broadcasting would not start in earnest until its proponents could put forward a tangible advantage for its introduction. In 1952, when Sarnoff extended his proposal, television offered no such utility; a technology without purpose or benefit, it was dismissed out of hand.

Still focused on its immediate survival, the country made do with its radio service, Kol Israel (Voice of Israel), which operated through the Office of the Prime Minister and the Israeli Defense Force's (IDF, or Tzahal, in Hebrew) radio station. Kol Israel provided continuous news, mostly classical and Israeli folk music, and a few talk and entertainment programs. The more amateurish Galei Tzahal (the Tzahal channel) offered programming by and for soldiers.

Aside from the ideological opposition to television and its general low priority for the fledgling state, the government's lack of experience in instituting national communication or media services was another impediment. Due to Palestine's status as a Turkish and then a British colony, early Jewish populations, living mostly in Zionist agricultural settlements (*yeshuvs*), had already established communication channels that served the growing Jewish community. Hebrew newspapers were published in Palestine as early as 1918, and most party and independent newspapers with a Jewish readership (three daily independents; four party journals; one Arabic newspaper; and three foreign-language papers, in English, Hungarian, and German) were firmly established before the creation of the state.[2] Similarly, PBS (Palestine Broadcasting Service), a radio service founded under the British Mandate, had been operating since 1936, with programming in English, Hebrew, and Arabic. Jewish underground broadcasts began in 1940, partly due to the growing needs of the Jewish settlements and as a response to increasing censorship by the British service.[3] By 1945, the underground Voice of Israel—Kol Israel—was broadcasting regularly, supplemented by three other, smaller, underground stations that gave voice to various factions within the Jewish nationalist movement.

Like radio and the print media, film exhibition and production (although scarce) were also installed well before the creation of the independent state. Perhaps due to early European and U.S. filmmakers' interest in Palestine in general and Jerusalem in particular (both the Lumiere brothers and Thomas Edison's crew shot films in Palestine at the turn of the century), films were screened there as early as 1900. A Jewish-owned movie theater was inaugurated in Jerusalem in 1908 and in Tel Aviv in 1914.[4]

As a ruling body, the Israeli Knesset had not yet instituted any mass-communication technology, finding all in place by the time it took office at the founding of the state in 1948. This point was stressed later, in a protelevision editorial that skewered the government for its excessive hand-wringing over television:

It seems that we Israelis were in luck since, when the state was established, there already was a radio station and the public and its leader were already accustomed to the reality of radio . . . and there was no discussion over its necessity and the need for its development. If the invention of radio were late by a few decades, we would be facing today the question of whether to create a broadcasting station or give up this "luxury" since in many countries it has shown itself as an element whose influence is not the best, and maybe even negative, on youth. We would surely be witnessing the same argument over radio that has gone on in recent months regarding television.[5]

Whereas government officials may have worried about television's effect on culture, its political opponents regarded television with even greater suspicion. Although Israeli radio now programmed music, entertainment, and news, its pre-1948 roots were resolutely grounded in broadcasting's political utility as an outlet for the Jewish resistance against the British authorities. Indeed, Kol Israel heralded Israel's birth when it carried Ben-Gurion's proclamation of state independence on May 14, 1948. Since this first national broadcast, Kol Israel had remained a government-operated agency. Many members of the smaller opposition parties wryly took to calling Kol Israel "Kol Mapai" (the voice of the ruling Mapai Party) and often complained that their own points of view were excluded from news coverage and commentary. In 1952, one Knesset member argued that such an arrangement was incompatible with Israel's democratic aspirations:

> The broadcasting service is a public service, whose function is to serve the public and all citizens in the state. . . . This is the view in every democratic state, whether radio services are passed to private companies—as it is done in the United States—or are publicly held without governmental or partisan dependency—as it is done in England. Only in totalitarian states is the broadcasting service tied in with the information services of the government, and is, in actuality, one of the tentacles the government uses to spread propaganda.[6]

Nonplused by this attack, Prime Minister Ben-Gurion replied: "I too agree that [the broadcasting service] is a public service. But I think that [you] would agree with me that the main servant of the public in this state is the government. The government serves the public each day, and the public must and is entitled to know what the government is doing."[7]

"And thinking," he might have added. As communication analysts Dan Caspi and Yechiel Limor have observed, the government's close supervision over radio stemmed from the unquestioned belief that communication media were essential tools for maintaining political power and ideological consensus.[8] The same leadership, all veterans of the Zionist national underground, were accustomed to secrecy and the use of selective information as radio propaganda. This approach, ingrained through the practice of anticolonial struggle, was reinforced by a supreme regard for security and a conception of each Israeli as a potential soldier and an active participant in the nation's fight for survival. Indeed, Ben-Gurion's stance toward media can be succinctly summarized in his pronouncement that "I don't know what the people think is good, only what is good for the people."[9] In tandem with this attitude, born of the underground, was the perception that "leaking" information out to the public was a betrayal, even a treasonous act that might imperil the Zionist cause. Despite independence, the political hierarchy maintained an attitude of siege, demanding absolute loyalty and tight political control, abetted by both Israel's precarious security and internal political rivalries.

The government's chokehold on Kol Israel would be challenged repeatedly in the decade to come and was significantly reduced with the creation of the semi-independent Israeli Broadcasting Authority in 1965. However, the prevailing attitude that defined broadcasting as a technology in the service of the state anchored all future debates and steeled opposition to television outside the Labor-led coalition.

Operating first as part of the internal information service and then directly out of the prime minister's office, Kol Israel was allotted an annual budget that covered both its production expenses and personnel salaries. This arrangement, although increasingly controversial, still granted radio the status of a governmental agency. Unlike the U.S. and British models, however, television in Israel was not immediately perceived as the structural—or natural—progression of radio. Moreover, similarly financing television seemed prohibitively costly, and the only available alternative, a commercial model, with a market-driven mass media, was simply anathema. The shift that would introduce television into the mainstream of public debate was initiated, like virtually all changes in Israeli history, with military action.

A NATION AMONG OTHER NATIONS: ISRAEL AFTER OPERATION KADESH

As violent clashes with Jordan and Egypt intensified throughout the Fifties, Israel took advantage of growing tensions between Egypt and the French and British over control of the Suez Canal. Working with active assistance from France and tacit agreement from Britain, Israel launched Operation Kadesh in October 1956, an offensive that pushed Gamal Abdel Nasser's Egyptian forces out of the Sinai and the Gaza Strip, opening the passage to ships in the Gulf of Aqaba through the

Strait of Tiran. The Sinai campaign had far-reaching consequences for Israel. The deployment of U.N. Emergency Forces in the region provided a buffer zone between Israel and Egypt in the Sinai and Gaza Strip; the Gulf of Aqaba was open (and would remain so for the next eleven years), making possible a trade relationship between Israel and the East and stimulating the Israeli economy. The young state also received generous loans from the World Bank and increased support from the United States following its retreat.[10]

Despite some misgivings over Israel's collaboration with the French and the British—one politician would lament that Israelis "appeared before the whole world as tools of the imperialists"—Operation Kadesh greatly increased Israeli morale and military confidence and significantly improved the nation's standing with Europe and the United States. Following the Sinai operation, Israel experienced a period of growth and stability that launched it into a new era. With the immediate security concerns somewhat eased and the economy finally bearing fruit, the old pioneer-soldier was becoming a citizen.

Israeli society was stabilizing in the late 1950s, absorbing new immigrants and slowly taking on the characteristics of a sovereign state. As Israelis moved from fledgling farms to bustling cities and from sing-alongs around a campfire watch to the safety and comfort of avenue cafes, a demand for leisure grew, along with an industry to provide it. The transition of cultural practice into the mundane register of everyday life prompted its own set of anxieties. In 1962, the powerful Histadrut coalition, the national Israeli workers' union, held a series of talks and published pamphlets on "the problem of leisure." One pamphlet described modern leisure as a "neglected but pressing problem . . . that will grow more essential in the years to come."[11] Free time and its management, one author insisted, was a political issue that demanded the attention of the state. It was a mark of poverty for Israeli civilization if "the simplest of people cannot . . . fill their time with worthy content."[12]

Since, by this logic, social developments stemmed from cultural cultivation, a common rhetorical convention rapidly evolved that coupled culture and national politics, and designated cultural consumption as an arena for "citizen training." Such an approach, while hardly novel, was exceptionally compelling in the Israeli case, since immigration was so central to the experience of nation building, and the absorption of diverse populations into a collective citizenry so prominent a goal. This discursive suture delimited the accepted parameters of cultural activity, branding it as necessarily prosocial and "beneficial." What's more, by identifying culture as a national project (and thus linking it with the two other dominant priorities, immigration and Arab/Israeli relations), this mode of address institutionalized such common euphemisms as "cultural standards" in a discourse of growing anxiety over the transition from ideological community to civil—and increasingly consumer—society.

The discursive relocation from leisure to culture necessarily emphasized the public and collective as the sites of experience and discouraged the very understanding of culture that emerged in the private market: that of restful, distracted pleasure and individual entertainment. Further, by posing cultural consumption as a transformative social process toward a shared communal identity, the discourse produced a hierarchy of cultural values and yielded diversity of practices as an impediment to progress. The conspicuous absence of television and its capacity for a mass national address would emerge from this very discourse to form the first argument in its favor. Even Ben-Gurion, who remained suspicious of television, began a qualified retreat from his earlier position when, on a 1960 trip to France, he was urged by his assistant to watch a television documentary. With the aid of a microscopic camera, the program presented a close-up look at life inside a beehive. Perhaps moved by the exhilarating scenes of collective labor, Ben-Gurion was fascinated. "How did they manage to get into the hive? Look . . . what a wonder, you can see everything. I had no idea that such things can be shown, and in such an educational and enlightening way. Amazing, just amazing!"[13]

Ben-Gurion's encounter with television was no longer extraordinary. New immigrants to Israel were arriving with television sets among their possessions and, as economic conditions for the Israeli middle class improved, many began traveling abroad and returning with purchased sets. Much like the early radio amateurs of U.S. broadcasting, hobbyists engaged in "fishing" for foreign broadcasts using sets purchased in Europe and North America. Early enthusiasts formed a "television club" in Tel Aviv, met for joint viewing and discussion of programs, and produced signal guides to monitor reception ("Saudi Arabia—weak, Napoli—weak to medium, Damascus and Cairo—medium to strong").[14] Some set owners even wrote to various Knesset members and to the prime minister himself, urging the creation of television in Israel and complaining about the unavailability of sets. "In Israel," wrote Y. Browner, president of the Israeli Television Club, to Teddy Kollek, then deputy director of the Prime Minister's Office, "as in any other democratic country . . . a citizen should be able to buy a television set at any store."[15]

In 1957, reports circulated that an unnamed U.S. company had offered to invest in Israeli commercial television. The paper *LaMerchav* claimed on April 9 that the government had demanded a part in the venture and finally turned it down, leaving the Americans to turn to Arab countries (who could possibly use the stations for "anti-Israeli propaganda"). Along with offers from NBC and CBS, foreign proposals included patronage from the Jewish-American Congress, the Scottish Broadcasting Consortium, and even an offered donation—hastily rejected—from the German Social-Democratic party.[16] Proposals came from domestic sources as well. The joint organization of Israeli theater owners, in an attempt to minimize competition, came forward to offer its services in the creation and management of the Jewish small screen, citing their experience as exhibitors. An Israeli appliance company, Amkor, suggested a joint television project with the government or a private enterprise in 1956.[17] And in 1960, Ben-Gurion was approached by Menachem Aviv, a radio pioneer whose work was acknowledged by the prime minister after the War of Independence. The president of the Israeli radio club, Aviv was a friend of Vladimir Zworkyn and his host when the television inventor visited Palestine in the Thirties. A long-time television enthusiast, Aviv even built an experimental model of a television station prior to the state's independence.[18] His proposal sketched out an educational-television service run jointly by a commit-tee (45 percent university and school representatives, 45 percent government representatives, and 10 percent for Aviv himself). In ex-change, Aviv would build and install a television service that would reach most of the nation.[19]

The official reply to all such overtures was courteous indifference. On their own, these expressions of interest did nothing to change govern-ment perceptions of television as a pernicious technology that would only corrupt the young, erode Israeli values, and endanger cultural stan-dards. However, as the rhetorical linking of culture and national better-ment brought new focus on radio, critical attention fixed on broadcasting as the current "cultural instrument of the nation," and Israel's premier political body found itself increasingly in conflict over radio's program-ming. The essence of the argument lay in the medium's great potential: "The broadcasting service must be an instrument of culture and educa-tion for the public," declared one politician in 1959; "incredible powers lie in this institution. It is a shame to use it for idleness."[20]

Few in the Knesset questioned the notion that "raising" public tastes and molding national character was part of the state's official charge. And for most, Kol Israel was ideal for the task of transmitting and promoting culture—thus shaping the ideal Israeli listener-citizen. Unsurprisingly, politicians often relied on their own tastes and cultural consumption to "test" the appropriateness of programming: "I'm not saying that all of the radio must be to my liking, . . . I'm saying that the radio must satisfy the minimum that is acceptable to a cultured person. First and foremost, it must be on such a level that a person of proper cultural stature will enjoy the program."[21]

The ubiquitous construction of the maxim "proper culture" was rarely defined but served as the perfect euphemistic device that assembled destabilizing elements within Israel's cultural aspirations and self-representations. One Knesset member referred to popular foreign music as one component of the undesirable "low standard" of programming that afflicted Kol Israel. Another commended Kol Israel for providing entertainment—thus stopping Israelis from listening to Arab stations—but also accused the service of becoming "too light" and adapting itself to "the atmosphere of the street."[22] A few others argued for more classical music and for programs of political, science, and art education. Yet programming was mostly tied to Israel's special needs as a new state with an ethnically diverse populace that must forge a worthy, shared culture. Criticizing the large bulk of broadcasting time dedicated to music and entertainment, one speaker argued that it's "just too much during this time of diasporic integration." Israel was unlike other nations, in both its needs and its character:

> What people have so many problems to solve like our people? And we are, after all, people of the book. In every country we are in the intellectual stratum, we are the intelligentsia, the learned and educated, . . . able to digest spiritual and educational matters a little better. . . . I can appreciate the positive, artistic, educational and entertaining value of music for the nation in general and the individual music lover, . . . I just demand appropriate proportion. . . . In this regard, the radio is dragged down to the taste of the man in the street, instead of serving as a guide to educate and refine his taste.[23]

The growing consternation over radio's role in Israel's cultural life is instructive here since it provides the foundation for the burgeoning debate over television and its perceived contribution to Israeli cultural life. However, it also grants us a glimpse into the operation of the term "culture" within a national context. As MK (Member of Knesset) Greenburg's comments about "appropriate proportions" reveal, the very category of culture was troubled by an internal contradiction: The legacy of Jewish culture, a tradition of learning and intellectual pursuits, was defined as somehow "inherent" to Jewish life—and so, presumably, to Israeli cultural life. However, the repeated calls for radio to partake in national cultural instruction and resist the tastes of "the street" exposed such cherished characteristics as less than natural. This tension, far from eroding the evocative force of the term "cultural standards," reinforced an accepted link between appropriate tastes and particular populations. If unworthy idleness and commercial culture posed a threat to a changing Israel and precipitated a debate over cultural standards, these concerns were only amplified when directed toward Israel's most pressing problem, the ethnic diversity of its immigrant population.

As the Israeli engagement with the project of a national culture encountered the problematic reality of ethnic difference, broadcasting increasingly appeared at the center of a constellation of notions about education, difference, culture, and mass influence. By the early 1960s, the "problem" of cultural integration was approaching urgent dimensions in the official imagination.

BETWEEN CULTURE AND THE DESERT:
THE "IMMIGRANT PROBLEM," THE RADIO SOLUTION,
AND THE RISE OF THE CULTURAL EDUCATION DISCOURSE

> The indispensable job ahead is to raise the level of education and culture of what are known as the "Oriental communities . . . to reach a certain measure of homogeneity between the different parts of the nation.[24]

The new focus on culture had to do not just with the growing economic possibilities of the citizenry, but, more important, with its changing demographics. Following Operation Kadesh, Israel experienced a dramatic upsurge in immigration; between 1956 and 1957, the country received 125,000 new immigrants, a majority of whom came from North Africa and Egypt. This first wave was followed by 43,000 Polish, Hungarian, and Rumanian Jews in 1958 and 1960, and another 194,000 immigrants between 1961 and 1964, mostly from Iran, Morocco, and Algiers.

The country's makeup was changing; Ashkenazi Jews (ethnically European Jewry, primarily from Germany, Russia, and Poland), who previously constituted the overwhelming majority among Israelis, were rapidly losing their majority status, with Sepharadic Jews (North African and Middle Eastern Jewry) making up nearly equal parts in the Jewish population of Israel by 1961.[25] Economically, however, the picture was much different. As Israel was industrializing and experiencing considerable economic growth, its original egalitarian vision was rapidly fading. With a growing and visible middle class on one hand, and an influx of poor immigrants on the other, an economic gap was widening, with the upper 20 percent of the population earning more than 40 percent of the national income and the bottom 20 percent earning approximately 5 percent.[26] These differences were most pronounced in urban areas, where Ashkenazis thoroughly dominated top earning brackets, managerial positions, elite professions, and government offices.

For the new immigrants—most of them poor and vocationally unprepared for life in Israel—the economic inequities and practical segregation they faced was compounded by a teacher shortage, substandard "temporary housing" in hastily erected transition camps and remote development towns, and an overwhelming unease in a homeland where they were regarded largely as a liability. Hindered by disadvantage and discrimination, many of the new "oriental" immigrants grew frustrated, while all around them the press and the Knesset (both institutions in which they had virtually no representation) obsessively mulled over the "problem of integration" and "cultural reform."

The educational and economic gap between Ashkenazi and Eastern immigrants was nationally expressed not only as a concern on the level of culture and national unity, but was also explicitly linked to Israel's national security and superiority over its Arab neighbors. To this point, Yosef Almogi, a leader in the powerful Histadrut workers' organization and the ruling Mapai Party, argued that Eastern immigrants should receive more support from social programs, for fear of Israel's deterioration both socially and politically: "Israel is a poor country. And precisely because we are poor we must have a certain minimum standard of living unless we're prepared to drop to the level of our Arab neighbors—and that we are not willing to do. . . . Even our military superiority over the Arabs comes from our technical skills and our advanced system of education, our better diet, the superior environment we're able to provide our children. We can't give all that up. If we did, we might go under."[27]

As Almogi's speech reveals, much of the Ashkenazis' attitude toward the Eastern immigrants stemmed not only from their cultural difference in general—a difference couched in familiar colonialist terms of Western cultural and intellectual superiority—but particularly from their perceived kinship to "backward" Arab culture.

This attitude was symbolically reenacted as a kind of "tension between culture and the desert," in Nurit Gertz's words. As Gertz argues, the narrative construction of the Israeli warrior as representative of the West in a battle with a cruel and primitive East gained purchase during the 1948 independence war as a way to mitigate Israel's complete political and cultural isolation in the Middle East. Such a cultural association with the West helped "rescue the Israeli from his 'Jewish fate': the fate of a persecuted and despised minority."[28] Thus, through the continuous evacuation of the Orient from both the narrative of Israeli progress and national identity through culture, the Israeli national psyche exorcised its anxiety over isolation by maintaining an allegiance to Europe and the West. This ironically ahistorical approach to Zionist ideology has been described by Amnon Raz-Krakotzkin as Israel's "negation of exile," a stance which, he argues, functioned as a foundation for Israeli collective identity.[29] Ella Shohat has similarly described this process of cultural erasure: "The paradox of secular Zionism is that it ended a Diaspora, during which all Jews presumably had their hearts in the East—a feeling encapsulated in the almost daily repetition of the ritual phrase 'next year in Jerusalem'—only to found a state whose ideological and geopolitical orientation has been almost exclusively toward the West."[30] The economic acceleration of the late Fifties only accentuated the virtual apartheid developing in the new nation. As Howard Sachar argues, native (Sabra) and Western (Ashkenazi) Israelis, growing increasingly obsessed with the fear of Levantinization and shaken by the changing face of their Zionist utopia, had begun to question the spartan values and the communal ideals that structured Israeli ideology in its first decade.[31] Turning away from agricultural settlements, many migrated to urban centers and joined the metropolitan middle class, further accentuating the sharp dichotomy between the establishment and the new, "backward Orientals."

These developments, along with blatant discrimination in housing, jobs, and education, contributed to brewing ethnic tensions and led to exasperation and occasional eruptions of rage. The most famous was the Waddi Salib uprising of North African immigrants in 1959. The uprising began as a barroom brawl and escalated into a clash between police and the Moroccan community after a patron was shot by the authorities. In the ensuing demonstration, the police, the party headquarters, the labor union club, and the dilapidated shops and cafes in the center of the impoverished neighborhood all became targets of the crowd's anger and frustration.

The mass protest received wide coverage in the Israeli press and succeeded in focusing new attention on the plight of North African immigrants. A government committee was appointed to investigate the cause of the violent incident and, in the course of the hearings, witnesses recounted their daily encounters with prejudice and exclusion. The committee report made few practical recommendations but did acknowledge the profound psychological damage inflicted on the Moroccan immigrants, whose cultural rejection and isolation was particularly crushing since it echoed their experience with French colonial culture. As Howard Sachar recounts, the plight of Moroccan immigrants was exacerbated by a cruel irony: Despite their perceived cultural affinity with the French colonial authority, they were largely excluded by the cultural elite because of their Jewishness, only to arrive in the Jewish homeland and be disdainfully regarded for their "Arab-ness."[32]

More than any other incident in Israel's first two decades, the Waddi Salib rebellion came to represent the ugly, ruptured center of the national dream of unity. In an article that called for an antidiscrimination law to protect Eastern minorities, Joseph Yambor made mention of several historical and contemporary "African Jews" who were prominent outside of Israel. "If [such a figure] were to come to Israel," Yambor sardonically observed, "he would have been sent to live in Waddi Salib." Arguing that the ethnic divide must be healed through both a physical and a vocational integration, Yambor concludes: "Waddi Salib exists at the heart-of-hearts of the nation. It exists in poverty and in inhuman conditions; it exists in the place where there is abjection and dilapidation and so endless bitterness. Is it our will to commemorate this shame and perpetuate it to the entire nation?"[33]

As contemporary critics Yagil Levi and Yoav Peled point out, these ethnic tensions represented a challenge to the political system directly and threatened the interests of the Israeli establishment—middle- and upper-class European veterans, known as the founding generation, who controlled the government through the Mapai (labor) Party.[34] The Waddi Salib incident made the deep rift between the Ashkenazi and Sephardic communities impossible to ignore, especially since its implications were articulated in terms not only of national cohesion but also of Israel's sheer survival as a besieged state surrounded by enemies.

Here Israel's cultural aspirations for both distinction and unity drew strength and relevancy from their association with concrete concerns over geographical borders and national difference. As Daphna Golan observes, Israelis took on the pioneer perspective of a frontier society, paying acute attention to their own unique identity in direct opposition to that of the nations that surrounded them: "Israel, cramped within such narrow borders, feels that it is all border, that it is in a permanent state of siege, that 'the whole nation is an army.' Thus it has become a society with very little tolerance for the difference of the other."[35] Its engagement in repeated and violent encounters with its neighbors further served to enforce group identity and emphasize unity as essential to self-preservation, and the project of healing the ethnic divide within Israel was seamlessly conflated with the goal of cultural integration.

As much recent scholarship on national formations and cultural production emphasizes, discursive constructions of culture and the project of nationalism are inextricably linked in the matrix of collective identity. However, it is important to note the particular strategic deployment of this framing in the Israeli case: By articulating the ethnic divide as a problem to which cultural assimilation was the ready solution, the threat to the fundamental political structure was cast out of the debate in favor of a discourse of individual reform.

With its obvious Western-colonial inflection, this understanding of culture was especially problematic in its Jewish incarnation. As Shlomo Fisher argues, such a model, and the premise of the collective that structures it, is readily comprehensible only within the tradition of European Jewish history. As Fisher suggests, secular Zionism—which developed in eastern Europe at the turn of the century—was informed and thoroughly infused by European nationalist movements and the general tenets of liberal humanist thought. As such, it perceived the collective as a unit through which the individual's universal needs are met. With such constructions of liberal nationalism, Zionists sought to "overcome their placement in the margins, dictated by their Jewishness, and join the center arena of a humanist, universalist history."[36]

By contrast, Jews living in Islamic countries, whose identities were conceived in opposition to Islam (which placed emphasis on religious identity and practice), were also profoundly shaped by their home countries' domination by colonial interests. Thus, the Eastern notion of the collective was developed on a foundation of extreme particularity, not of universalist aspiration, and of identity through community, local tradition, and faith, not through political and nationalist structure. For Middle Eastern and North African Jews, this approach coalesced around a strong emphasis on religious practice and tradition.

These converse attitudes, in Fisher's formulation, stem from the profoundly different Western and Eastern encounters with nationalism and modernity. However, their cultural manifestations, in the eyes of the Israeli Western establishment, further rendered the Eastern immigrants' reliance on tradition a "backward" rejection of progress and evidenced their cultural inferiority. This attitude is manifest in a 1961 editorial of the daily Al Hamishmar that describes the "problem of closing the gap over the formation of Israel's image and culture." Challenging commonplace attitudes, the polemic argues against the establishment's seeming desire to erase "Oriental culture," urging instead its recognition as a legitimate ethnic difference within Israeli cultural expression. Yet the author's description reenacts the same dichotomy that sets Western culture as forward thinking and "Oriental culture" as resistant to change and "frozen in the past":

The deepest gap is between the Oriental and Islamic-country tribes (ethnic groups) and the Ashkenazi tribe. Culture stands against culture. The Oriental culture—based on traditional life, in which cultural and economic contributions are slow—struggles against a dynamic culture which breaks barriers, that does not know a moment's rest or satisfaction, that strives endlessly to conquer new grounds in science, technology and economics. In comparison, Oriental culture sticks to its fixed tradition and does not [change] to catch up and minimize the gap between it and the achievements of Western culture.[37]

The portrayal of Eastern Jews as passive, recalcitrant and bound by tradition further endowed modern Western culture with maturity and foresight, and thus with the authority and responsibility to nudge and coax the fractious "Orientals" forward. In so doing, it fortified the existing distribution of political power and granted legitimacy to the solutions it pursued.

What had come to be known as "the education gap" was indeed real for the thousands of poor children who made up the majority of the new Eastern immigrants. Teacher shortages and underfunding in immigrant communities resulted in substandard education in immigrant communities, while a de facto segregation system in urban centers (enacted through testing children as a condition for admission) perpetuated further disparities. However, the discourse of education implicated the adult population as well in a none-too-subtle infantilization, expressed through concepts of uplift, cultural standards, and teaching respect for institutions: "Among our public, there is not so small a segment who, in terms of their political and social education, are still of childhood age. We must teach them to build the state and respect its principles and to change their attitude toward State institutions in general."[38]

The preoccupation with the compound concept of culture and education, and its imbrication with national identity and politics, thus produced broadcasting as the ideal arena for such a project, and politicians repeatedly called for radio to take a more active role. "What have you done to help speed up integration? To remove the obstacles of conflict?" one Knesset member demanded of radio in 1959. Calling for more Eastern-culture programming, the MK urged radio to "fulfill its role and bring up the good and beautiful in their [Sepharadic Jews] culture, so that they are understood and are brought closer, diminishing the distance that the cursed Diaspora has created."[39]

Kol Israel did run various foreign-language broadcasts, mainly news and Hebrew lessons, for immigrant groups. Yet most arguments

in the Knesset surrounding Kol Israel's role in assimilating the new immigrants were less concerned with giving access to alternative voices
on the national broadcast service than with radio's role in the cultural
education of newcomers. The culture argument framed the immigrants' lack of "proper" education as the reason for their "cultural
inferiority" and presented education as a solution. In turn, cultural
standards were proffered as the antidote for any integration difficulties
the new immigrants experienced—or indeed posed. Culture, in this formulation, became the hook by which social and economic standards
would be hauled upwards, and broadcasting emerged as an ideal instrument for such heavy lifting.

Radio, as one politician saw it, was "a tool for the education of society in Israel, . . . educating the tribes [ethnic groups] about good citizenship in our land by bringing to its citizens the best of our land."[40]
Another MK defined the broadcast service in terms that easily combined leisure, cultural standards, and the education agenda. Radio, he
argued, must "educate the listening public . . . to morality, to decency,
and normal, wholesome social life. Every radio program, be it a skit, entertainment, or story, requires an educational inspiration. The listener
should receive something, to learn something from every program, to
broaden his knowledge and his cultural standard."[41]

By the late Fifties, official fixation on broadcasting as a cultural delivery system par excellence lent it new gravity by fitting it into a
"problem-solution approach." This stance provided the foundation for
the future debate over television, but first, it made the idea of television
newly palatable and worthy of contemplation.

One of the earliest documented considerations of an Israeli television service came from Hannoch Givton, the news head of Kol Israel and its future manager, who traveled the United States in 1959 to
study the issue. As this first official communiqué makes clear, Givton
found the U.S. system useful primarily as a cautionary tale. In a
lengthy report sent to the embassy and the Prime Minister's Office,
he lamented that the U.S. notion of "public interest" is "whatever interests the public." To avoid such a profit-driven system, with its obvious effect of trivial mass-appeal entertainment, Givton concluded
his report with a practical proposition for compromise: "When considering the creation of an Israeli television service, it will not be a
Utopian effort to try and create a system that, despite its base on
commercial interests and partial private investments, will remain under the final supervision of a public body. Such a system will be able
to . . . provide a comprehensive service of education, culture, and entertainment [and] . . . will play a role in the integration of the het-

erogeneous population of Israel, and in the education of a new generation."[42]

Givton's letter provides an instructive glimpse into the imagined utility of an Israeli television service along with its already-assumed funding structure. Most notable is Givton's early attempt to negotiate the inherent contradictions of institutional control in a hybrid system. Whereas he dismisses the U.S. commercial system as fundamentally opposed to the ideological underpinnings of Israeli broadcasting, Givton— surely motivated by his experiences at government-controlled Kol Israel—also avoids an explicit government involvement, steering discussion toward a supervisory "public body." Television is proposed as a national technology and a system of "public service"—contrasted with the U.S. model of "public interest." However, at the heart of Givton's report is an endorsement of television, framed, as his final sentence makes clear, by its utility as a social apparatus that aids in the education and integration of new immigrants. Here, the idea of television finally finds its purpose: to address, and even "fix," the acutely perceived cultural gap between the Ashkenazi elite and the Sephardic immigrants.

SIGNAL CROSSING: ARAB BROADCASTS AND THE ISRAELI SET

> The ether is the joint property of all nations and countries. We cannot, nor do we wish to, shut it down.[43]

As the foregoing summary illustrates, official emphasis on the realm of culture and the national charge of fostering it adroitly employed the Israeli preoccupation with the nation's "special circumstance" to interlock cultural tastes and preferences with the most vital aspects of Israeli national survival. Simultaneously, it successfully muted arguments that linked ethnic tensions and difference to political, social, and resource inequities. Most immediately, it eschewed the questions of institutional change or any redefinitions of Israeli self-representation in light of its changing demographics and infusion of varied cultural practices. However, the focus on culture was more than a mere "displacement" of politics; with the growing prominence of broadcasting technology in the anxious debate, programming itself became an ideologically charged minefield, particularly in terms of national distinction and audience allegiance.

The role of broadcasting in maintaining a "cultural distance" from Arab countries was made explicit in one Knesset member's comments on the difference between Kol Israel and Radio Ramallah, a nearby Arab station: "[W]e often hear the reasoning: if we don't give these things to

listeners, they'll listen to radio Ramalah. I say, it is better that they listen to radio Ramalah. Let them enjoy broadcasts from Ramalah and
Beirut, all the while knowing that these programs are unworthy and
that Kol Israel has rid itself of them. *That* is educational.[44]

Coinciding with the awakening interest in educational programming, the gradually increasing presence of television sets in Israeli
homes became an additional facet of the burgeoning discourse over
television. This inducement, too, was born of anxiety. The reception of
Arab programming in Israel was patchy and sporadic; nonetheless,
with the Egyptian signal available mainly the south, Syria's broadcast
visible in the northeast, and Lebanon's programming faint but de-
tectable in most of the north and along the coast, the possibility of an
Arab "telepenetration" caused great consternation in the Israeli Prime
Minister's Office. Apprehension over "thousands of Israeli families
[with] sets whose antennae point toward Beirut, Cairo and Alexandria"
steadily increased, with rumors that the Arab League was planning to
erect a giant broadcasting tower on Hermon Mountain with one of its
antennae pointed toward Tel Aviv.[45] Others spoke of Jordan's intention
to create a television service—whose proximity to Israel would make its
broadcasting readily available to any Israeli with a TV receiver. Whereas
the idea of "counterstrike programming" would not arise until 1966, as
Israeli-Arab tensions worsened and anti-Israeli broadcasts became routine (see chapter 4), imagining that Jewish families spent their nights
watching Arab broadcasts disturbed many politicians, who especially
feared the broadcasts' adverse influence on Arab-speaking Israelis.

As a result, immigrants who arrived in Israel with televisions were
heavily taxed (the import fee often exceeded the cost of the set), and as
the number of receivers in Israeli households grew from fewer than a
thousand in 1960 to an estimated twenty thousand in 1965, an additional annual tax of fifty lira—about seventeen dollars in 1962—was
levied for each receiver, for no service at all, in an attempt to discourage
set ownership.

For some observers—and many set owners—the small but steady
trickle of television sets into Israel signaled another stage in the reluctant but nonetheless inevitable plodding toward local television. For
others, however, Israeli access to Arab programming only compounded
arguments against any television service—and the subsequent mass influx of receivers. A commonly expressed scenario linked its introduction to a substantial increase of Arab anti-Israeli messages: "Television
in Israel could open the nation's gates to hostile propaganda. Even today, Arab television stations disseminate poisonous diatribes against Israel. And today, there are television sets in many Arab and Jewish

households; . . . still, they do not receive this hostile propaganda to the same degree they would if there was television in Israel." Television, this author warned, was a much more potent propaganda tool than were radio, print, or film because of its ability to manipulate visual montages and fabricate "the ultimate counterfeit," a lie much more seductive and persuasive than "the gray truth."[46]

Similar fears were expressed in the Knesset a few months later:

> Supporters of television explain that the installment of our own television will prevent those who have a television receiver from listening to Cairo, Beirut, or Damascus. This, too, is unclear. Are we to install programming 24 hours a day? And if we do have a television service, can we supervise [and] ensure that [viewers] do not tune in . . . for hours, to the programs of the Arab states that spread hate and poison against us? Instead of a few hundred receivers owned today—on which Arab broadcasts are available—there will be thousands and soon more. Is there a factor worse than this, in our situation with our neighbors?[47]

This new problem of "electronic trespassing" added yet another dimension to the developing definition of television in the national context. The original objection to television's introduction as an empty, passive leisure activity still held sway for some opinion makers, yet television's use as a cultural delivery system for immigrants and a public-relations arm for the government was now joined by the new notion of television broadcasts as a factor in international politics. For good or ill, the technology threatened any state's ability to contain and delimit information; inversely, it bestowed such border-crossing powers on any nation that possessed it.

Israel was no stranger to the uses of broadcasting outside its borders; Kol Israel had been broadcasting to Europe, America, and Africa for years with programming designed for the Jewish Diaspora. Nor was the government blind to the possibility of broadcasting into enemy territories, as MK Emma Telmi explicitly noted in a 1959 speech that stressed the power of radio and its primacy over newspapers. Telmi's description is interesting since her argument for keeping Kol Israel a government agency delineates the very grounds on which the utility of television would now be debated: "We've all learned to appreciate [radio's] power in anxious times when worry filled the heart. . . . It supported the people and lifted the morale; . . . it informs the illiterate, broadcasts in every language, it penetrates without passport, stamp or permit, the walls of enmity, [and] travels on the border between friend and foe. . . . It shapes public opinion. . . . It educates and guides in art, in the kitchen, in politics, in fashion, in prayer and in sports. Is it any wonder it is a state instrument?"[48]

Telmi's characterization does more than address the broadcasting signal as a manifestation of the nation's will materialized in the ether. With its mixture of information, entertainment, propaganda, and religion, and its easy slippage between official and informal matters, her description associates the function of a national broadcasting service with all aspects of public and private life, all the while arguing for the state's necessary position as overseer of such functions. Here, daily activities—sports, cooking, and prayer—are easily juxtaposed with both domestic and international politics, illustrating the degree to which national interest (and, consequently, involvement) was seen to infiltrate all aspects of everyday life: a formulation amplified by the logic of broadcasting, particularly its domestic presence, mobility, and ubiquity.

This linkage points to the substantial stakes in national broadcasting for the political forces responsible for its institution. Broadcast technology's casual presence and reliability as a site of address helped define not only programming but also listeners themselves as active participants in the nation's formation and maintenance.

This context saturated all aspects of the television debate: its benefits and dangers evaluated on the collective level of the nation, its fitness contingent on its utility. With this underlying vision, television's incarnation as a mobile, explicitly international element, able to travel unhindered through borders and facilitate a cross-national encounter within the domestic space, only served to further thrust the "television problem" into the political realm and bind it to government machinations.

Similarly, for some, the idea of a "Jewish television service" inflamed the imagination and led to misconstructions of the technology, where the signal of this "radio with pictures" (envisioned as an extension of the shortwave transistor) would emanate from the Holy Land and reach a Jewish Diaspora all over the world. One advocate implored Ben-Gurion to create an Israeli television, "[i]f not for the Israeli citizens, then for the citizens of the world. . . . We have plenty to say and show to the Jewry of the world. It is easy to imagine the joy of those Jews who heretofore were not allowed contact . . . to see our wonderful country."[49]

This position, uninformed as it was by the realities of technology, did articulate an important element in the structure, or grammar, of the television argument. According to it, television's use fell into two distinct categories: the internal needs of the state (cultural cohesion, immigrant integration, education) and the developing notion of communicating the nation outside its own borders. As these lines of argument evolved in the mid-Sixties, they would repeatedly coalesce and bifurcate according to political circumstances. In the early Sixties, Israel's preoccupation with immigration and education dictated the primacy of the domestic broadcasting model meant for internal consumption. As tensions with Israel's Arab neighbors intensified, television's imagined address would undergo a radical shift; still envisioned as a state apparatus, it would become a forum for the nation to address itself, collectively, to others.

In 1962, the Israeli government would reluctantly begin the process that would eventually produce a television service. However, domestic pressures from some industry and public sources, along with gentle prodding from U.S. and European parties, did not, by themselves, provide the catalyst for this change in attitude. As this chapter demonstrates, the mold television would be expected to fill, as a utility, was cast long before its material introduction into the public realm. In the same year, an initial exploratory committee would cautiously recommend the institution of television, setting off a series of public and political deliberations, yet the terms for debate were already in place, delimiting all discussions of television along particular strategies of containment.

It is, perhaps, a significant irony that this television history should begin with its rejection and progress through a "rebranding" that would cast a troublesome popular technology in the mold of ideological utility. Meaningfully absent, television hovered just above the debates over culture and broadcasting, becoming progressively more conspicuous with the arrival of Israeli receivers. It is precisely through this absence that the link between technology and ideology was made manifest, providing a window onto the process of discourse formation. These rhetorical syntheses of meaning would prove crucial not only to television's subsequent history, but also to the ongoing Israeli preoccupation with borders, cultural unity, and ethnic difference.

Befitting this controversial beginning, the government's response to the infiltration of television sets into Israeli homes was to tax their owners while offering no programming. Although the policy's aim was to discourage set ownership, the ironic result was that viewers paid the Israeli government for the privilege of watching enemy broadcasts. Television, it seemed, presented a thorny political dilemma. For a small minority of set owners, the ghostly absence of local programs, among the din of debate, was itself a signal that spoke volumes.

2

BROADCASTING THROUGH
THE BACK DOOR
Three Models for Israeli Television

We fear and have no trust in those who would implement television.
—Menachem Perosh

Why doesn't Israel have television? You are so much more photogenic than me.
—General De Gaulle to Prime Minster Ben-Gurion, September 1962

On a typically sweltering mid-June evening in 1962, a crowd of Israelis in sandals and shorts gathered to watch Toscanini conduct the NBC orchestra on a flickering monitor in a Tel Aviv park.[1] Those closest to the towering antenna, which resembled a diminutive version of the Eiffel Tower, could peek into the adjacent glass-encased structure to take in the rows of lighted buttons, dials, and the thick black electric cords that snaked between heavy instruments. Inside, technicians enwrapped in cumbersome headphones smoked furiously as spools of film spun slowly on the console. Across from the control room, curious onlookers could watch the studio being prepared for an upcoming live broadcast. Glaring lights turned on and off again, chairs moved into place, a heavy camera rolled forward, a nervous director bit his lips. But for all the fuss inside the impromptu studio, and all the curious attention from just outside its transparent walls, the would-be debut of Israeli television went on with relative efficiency and unremarked-upon success.

The year 1962 was a watershed for Israeli broadcasting. A burgeoning conversation over television was spurred on by new international attentions and seething internal political tensions. Broadcasting was suddenly the subject of intense debate and scrutiny that began with a government scandal and ended in the creation of the Israeli Broadcast Authority three years later. In the thick of the debate, a television prototype was unveiled, right in the middle of a Tel Aviv park. In every way, this "first television experiment" posed an alternative to the dominant model of broadcasting; it was private, international, and entertaining—and was completely and resolutely ignored. The path to this broadcast, the cause of its near-total obscurity, and the countermodels of television that emerged in 1962, are the subjects of what follows.

STICK AND CARROT: THE EXPERTS STEP IN

June of 1961 saw the publication of a preliminary report by an international committee of experts on the advisability of a television service in Israel.[2] As media insider Tzvi Gil described it, the Cassirer Report used a "stick and carrot" approach to press for television. The carrot, as many Israeli television proponents had already argued, was television's potential role in helping to integrate new immigrants, diminish differences among ethnic groups, and contribute to educational and cultural values. The stick, too, was by then old news: Hostile neighbor countries already had television broadcasts, and it behooved Israel to catch up quickly.[3]

The "stick and carrot" incentives recommended by the report fit snugly into the (external) threat and (internal) benefit rationale that guided early debates about television in the post–Operation Kadesh period. If nothing else, the opinions of international experts helped legitimize the problem-solution approach to television, solidifying an understanding of the technology in terms of challenges to national integrity.

Imagining television as a facilitator for the advancement of national/cultural goals—an understanding of broadcasting that was commonplace in public service models such as the BBC and most European state-owned systems—helped cast the medium as an "official" technology directed for the collective public good. In turn, it granted television an air of political potency and power of influence that was all but unquestioned.

In the Israeli case, however, directing the television discourse along the well-worn grooves of the nationalistic rhetoric of service and sociopolitical utility not only enforced a particular conception of the medium and channeled television into a narrow rhetorical corner, but also remade local articulation of priorities in the shape of a transmission technology.

This careful and constricted prescription for television's use effectively foreclosed certain possibilities for debate over its future; aside from pejorative references to "low-quality" programming and

"corrupting" influences, a productive discussion of television as an entertainment or news medium was wholly absent from the official debate. Despite a developing leisure industry in Israel, entertainment—as
diversion—was carefully extracted from the larger concept of culture
and spiritual and intellectual growth. Thus, the notion of another technology that delivered entertainment into the domestic space quickly
became the province of television's opponents, who used the billy club
of empty, coarse, and morally suspect entertainment to beat back
claims for television's purported benefits.

The evacuation of entertainment from conceptions of television is
particularly noteworthy since issues of morale—especially in time of
war—were so salient in the elevation of culture on the Israeli national
agenda. Radio had been singled out and praised for its ability to raise
morale in times of crisis, as much of the pre-1960s conception of the Israeli people as pioneer-protectors of a besieged land was expressed in
cultural memory through morale-boosting rituals of comedy and song.
However, as I argue throughout, notions of cultural consumption became increasingly entangled with anxieties over cultural decline, particularly in association with a growing minority of non-European
immigrants. These anxieties produced a dichotomy that formally resembled a high/low delegation of cultural value, only with much
higher stakes. Animated by a nationalist discourse that linked culture
to the Zionist project and to Jewish survival, the widening "cultural
rift" in Israel stood for a separation more essential than "mere" markers
of class or ethnicity: It threatened the very foundation of Israeli identity and, by extension, of statehood.

An Israeli follow-up committee—known as the Avidor Committee,
after Moshe Avidor, head of the Education and Culture Office—generally supported the findings of the Cassirer Report but was divided on its
implementation, with six of the twelve members citing cost as a pro-
hibiting factor. Despite the split over feasibility, the committee's report
highlighted remote agricultural settlements as primary beneficiaries of
a would-be Israeli television. These settlements were inhabited mostly
by new immigrants, sent there as part of the government's attempt to
disperse poor immigrant populations out of the cities. Reasoning that
poor North African and Moroccan immigrants would gravitate toward
the city and create impoverished "ghettos," the government instituted
a "ship-to-village" policy in 1954 designed to settle new immigrants directly into agricultural farms and development towns. Such villages—
set in clusters of three or four, and often populated by a single ethnic
group—provided housing and social services to the immigrants while
effectively segregating them from the increasingly urban Ashkenazi

elites. By 1959, more than 75 percent of all North African immigrants were living in farm collectives or development towns.[4]

Emphasizing an educational gap between development-town immigrant children and Israeli-born city kids, the committee suggested that "the possibility of television is of great importance to the 900 agricultural settlements, especially to the immigrant population within them." Television offered an educational boost to students, along with cultural programming that would aid in immigrant integration and furnish a connection with the rest of the country.[5] In line with television's envisioned use for education and national unity, the Avidor Committee categorically rejected a commercial structure for the service, recommending a public municipal system instead. A compendium recommendation for a noncommercial public television followed in early January from the director general of the Education Ministry.[6] Notably, the report concluded by suggesting the creation of a joint directorial committee that would supervise both television and radio.

Television, it seemed, was finally conceived, yet a paternity debate of sorts soon erupted. The proposition that television was a "sister medium" to radio appeared to place responsibility for its nurturance with the government—specifically, the Prime Minister's Office (where Kol Israel was housed). Compounding Ben-Gurion's outright resistance to television, and the common objections to the cost of the enterprise, were fears within the cabinet that television would prove a "potent outlet for anti-establishment oratory."[7] The reverse anxiety—that television would soon become an official mouthpiece for the political elite—preoccupied the opposition. Thus, by 1962, television had gone through an ironic conceptual turnaround: If before it was too trivial a medium for serious government involvement, it was now too potent to tender for government interests. The notion that Israel should move to introduce a television service enjoyed no consensus, yet a new focus on the relationship between broadcasting and government contributed to a reorientation of the argument by adding institutional structure to the list of concerns for both supporters and opponents. As one editorial noted: "[A]nyone sensitive . . . to the democratic conditions in the nation should know that leaving an instrument with such awesome influence as television in the hands of the government could, in time, put an end to public life."[8] Beyond the still-raging argument about programming and cultural effects, the new emphasis tightened the links between culture and politics in the discursive field of broadcasting by aligning the medium's power of influence with questions of source, interest, and

means of production. This notable shift, however, was only a byproduct of a fundamental change taking place in radio.

By the early 1960s, Ben-Gurion's government was rocked by a series of
political scandals that undermined the old leader's hold on his party
and severely damaged his public image. The controversy began with a
feud between Ben-Gurion's Labor Party (Mapai) and Pinchas Lavon, a
union leader and a former defense minister. Lavon had been forced to
resign when an investigation found him responsible for a botched military operation. Disgraced, Lavon reemerged a few years later charging
that he had been the victim of an elaborate cover-up by senior Ben-
Gurion protégés. The ensuing public battle between Lavon and Ben-
Gurion, and the accusations that the prime minister exercised extreme
pressure on Kol Israel regarding reports on the matter, raised new questions about objectivity and journalistic freedom within the radio-
service. Under the strain of public scrutiny, the Mapai Party was
splintering; "the Old Man" appeared to be on his way out, and burgeoning party rivalries were blooming into full-fledged power struggles.
In this contentious climate, the government responded to the ferment-
ing criticism about its media handling with capitulation, initiating the
process of moving Israeli radio from the Primer Minister's Office and establishing it as a semiautonomous body. Practically, the move would
entail the creation of a new public agency, the Israeli Broadcasting Authority (IBA), and the formation of a set of laws and policies that would
govern the agency, provide for its government funding, specify its
managerial structure, and ensure its independence from direct government control. Subsequent accounts often regarded the broadcasting
law as part of the evolution of Israeli democracy, yet the events leading
up to the IBA's creation belie such smooth narratives of "natural" development. Moreover, these events offer new insight into the "backroom" rationale that accompanied decisions over television's future.

Despite Ben-Gurion's notoriously possessive stance toward Kol Israel, it was the prime minister himself who submitted the proposition
of the law for government discussion. For the beleaguered leader,
readying to announce his resignation from the post he had held since
the nation's birth, relinquishing government control over radio was far
from voluntary but appeared to be a "scorched-earth" tactic. "You cannot imagine how Ben-Gurion's people took advantage . . . of the fact
that radio was subordinate to them," Levi Eshkol, Israel's next prime
minister told a reporter years later. The emancipation of radio, Eshkol
argued, was the result not only of public criticism, but also of a reluctant surrender of leadership. As Eshkol saw it, the IBA law was Ben-

Gurion's way of ensuring that no other prime minister would ever wield or enjoy the same power over Israeli broadcasting. "I know . . . that they began thinking of changing the status of radio only when they knew he would retire; . . . suddenly they became great Democrats, . . . they wanted to keep the seats and take away my influence on the radio, since only they understood the power there was in controlling [it]."[9]

Emboldened by the sudden attention to broadcasting, supporters of television marshaled the two committee reports to champion the medium, especially as a public institution that would help unify the country, close the education gap, and "disseminate culture" throughout Israel.[10] Alarmed by the staid air of utility that was gathering around considerations of the technology, television's opponents countered publicly: Teacher's groups warned about television's deleterious effects on concentration and learning; religious groups campaigned against the technology as a further secularization of Israeli culture; and owners of movie theaters protested the possible demise of their livelihood with the introduction of "home screens."

Most pundits and opinion makers, however, were wholly preoccupied with the possible restructuring of Kol Israel and its detachment from the Prime Minister's Office. As Knesset members and a committee of artists and public figures debated the issue behind closed doors, the Israeli independent press was virtually united in its support for the institution of a BBC-style, state-supported but sovereign broadcasting agency.[11] And as discussions over the broadcasting law heated up, television, with its problematic allegiances and suspect morphology, was left to simmer on a back burner. Yet it soon emerged again, not as the sober vehicle of cultural reform and national policy, but as a summertime curiosity of international dimensions.

THE FUTURE PAYS A VISIT: TELEVISION, THE INTERNATIONAL SIGNAL, AND THE PROBLEM OF SPECTATORSHIP

During the winter and spring of 1962, as hearings over the creation of the IBA noisily continued in the Knesset, the issue of television service was sluggishly tossed about from one committee to another. With few advocates, no one to foot the bill, and a general confusion over the coming changes in the structure of broadcasting, the future of an Israeli television service appeared far from certain. Despite this torpid pace, one Israeli company—assisted by European and U.S. interests—was doggedly pursuing the development of television-set technology for an Israeli market.

Amkor, a leading Israeli appliance company, had been studying television since 1956, even after its original proposal for a partnership with Ben-Gurion's government was rejected. Unhindered by government disinterest and by some public criticism—one editorial indirectly targeted the company, stating that "outside the circle of commerce with direct interests who stand to profit from erecting broadcasting stations, productions of sets, and television commercials, all other responsible sources object to [television's] creation"—the company continued to research and develop television technology.[12] Through its radio division, Amkor-Amron, the company had been preparing to lead the way in a domestic television market, sending company trainees to the United States and Europe and investing in a television prototype for the Israeli market.

Joining forces with mostly British backers, Amkor announced its plans to build and operate a temporary television studio to be unveiled at the international Tel Aviv Eastern Fair in the summer of 1962. Anticipated by one paper as "surely one of the central fair attractions," the television exhibit was planned as an elaborate effort by Amkor to acquaint an Israeli public with the wonders of television, flex its technical muscle, and presumably, generate excitement at the prospect of an Israeli service.[13] The sneak peek the company was preparing was to be the debut of live Israeli broadcasts and the public's first encounter with television from all over the globe.

The International Eastern Fair of 1962 was a month-long extravaganza unprecedented in Israel's history. Primarily a trade show, the fair drew participants from more than thirty countries and from seven hundred local industries, displaying their wares in specially built national pavilions across fifteen kilometers of park grounds in Tel Aviv.[14] The fairgrounds also enticed audiences with widely publicized attractions such as the custom-built cable car, performances by the Israeli symphony orchestra, amusement park rides, fashion shows, ice-dancing spectacles, and, of course, the first-ever live television station.[15]

Marking its exhibition center, Amkor erected a temporary control room and a television studio. The glass-encased structure allowed visitors to witness technicians, camera crews, and production staff bring the hazy notion of Israeli television to life, if only fleetingly. A crowd watched the production of a live broadcast whose programming included appearances by journalists reporting on local news events, musical performances by Israeli artists, welcome addresses by representatives from various participating nations, and a public-participation quiz show.

In addition to live shows, taped international programs were specially imported from Europe, the Americas, and Japan in a wide variety of subject offerings. Sport events from Chilean football to Japanese judo tournaments, performances by classical musicians such as Yehudi Menuhin and Arthur Rubinstein and by popular singers like Yves Montand, taped tours of famous museums, footage from the U.S. space mission, and other international fare were broadcast on monitors positioned all over the fairgrounds.[16] In the first incarnation of a television lineup, Amkor ran daily ads in various papers that detailed that evening's airing. Nightly broadcasts ran from eight to eleven, typically beginning with a roundup of local news—presented jointly by Amkor and the news daily *Ha'aretz*. These were followed by a classical concert, a popular international musical performance, a filmed visit to a museum or a sports contest, an interview with a local public figure, and, to end the evening, a roundup of international news broadcasts, filmed and flown in daily from London.[17]

The exhibit was also to debut a new Israeli film, *In the Footsteps of the Past*, which documented an archeological exploration team and the finding of valuable Bible-era scrolls and artifacts. Perhaps the irony of the film's subject matter was not lost on the exhibit's organizers; the discovery of remains from a Jewish cultural past was to be broadcast electronically by the very medium deemed dangerous to the country's Jewish cultural future.

As a commercial endeavor, the exhibit sought to present television as an electronic cornucopia and a gateway to the rest of the world that was capable of the immediacy of radio, the spectacle of film, the live excitement of the stage, and the informative reach of the print press. Significantly, the program devoted little time to practical discussions of education and civic responsibility, choosing to position its cultural offerings on the same level as soccer games and news broadcasts. This was not the service envisioned by a government committee or championed by a handful of politicians. Amkor's artificial window into Israel's would-be television future was a global spectacle of popular enchantment.

Amkor's expensive and ambitious endeavor proved a qualified technological success. Despite a blown electric circuit that disrupted programming on opening night by plunging the Amkor station and a full quarter of the grounds into darkness, the subsequent nightly programs ran with relative smoothness and attracted large crowds of onlookers. However, as a cultural or political intervention into the fate of television in Israel, the project met with scant success. Unlike RCA's unveiling of television at the 1939 World's Fair in New York City, Amkor's 1962 exhibition inspired little excitement and even less media attention. In part, such a response may have been expected, since broadcasting technology itself was no longer the fresh and wondrous development it had been two decades earlier. The mere fact that instantaneous electronic transmission of image and sound was possible surprised few visitors—although many were curious to witness such transmissions for the first time. Nevertheless, Amkor's experiment, as an event, was doomed to obscurity, a self-contained moment in pretelevision history, a bubble of technical possibility in a sea of unyielding official regulation, doubt, and resistance.

RCA's 1939 television debut had served to mark the beginning of America's television age and a regular, albeit limited, supply of programming already in the works—a process interrupted by the breaking war but resumed in its wake. With a commercial foundation and a private management structure already in place, the moment of its first 1939 World's Fair exhibition inaugurated television into U.S. cultural life with the certainty of a fait accompli. By contrast, Israeli television's first demonstration at the International Fair in 1962 could just as well have been its last, with no such certitude, economic feasibility, or institutional foundation to support it. Its appearance did not so much herald the coming of a video age as offer a momentary diversion of amusing novelty.

Such an unpromising environment can, in part, account for the one-time broadcast's lackluster reception by the print media. Among the dozens of articles that heralded the coming of the fair and reported on the goings-on once it opened, very few even bothered to mention Amkor's television station. Even *Ha'aretz*, cosponsor of the nightly local news broadcast, ran only two brief stories that referenced Amkor's broadcast exhibit, and just one photograph of the studio itself—the only one to appear in any major daily. Most stories that did mention the television debut made do with merely a fleeting allusion to television as part of the attractions lineup. In part, such editorial snubs were due to a profound ambivalence—and often hostility—in the papers' newsrooms toward the idea of television, yet the casting of Amkor's television as a public recreation activity rather than a technological advancement was also a factor.

The positioning of Amkor's television as mere temporary entertainment with no long-term consequences is primarily evident in the advertising campaign for the fair: In a widely circulated poster that promoted the fair and the June 7 opening-night activities, Amkor's television appears third in a seven-item list of attractions: a first-ever Israeli cable car (the top attraction in all subsequent reports), an orchestra performance in an outdoor amphitheater, a fashion show, a Ferris wheel, an ice rink, and a cabaret act. Each event was accompanied by an iconic drawing that was consistently used in subsequent print ads for the fair. Along with dancing figures on skates, a minimalist rendering of an orchestra performance, and a cable-car station sketch, the television item is illustrated not with a drawing of a television set, a camera, or a studio, but with one of a large, crowded public space flanked by a huge, towering antenna and a stagelike transparent box (presumably a representation of the studio).

Primarily, such a representation placed the television studio within the larger category of a temporary attraction, akin to the Ferris wheel and fashion show, and apart from any association with the trade exhibition itself. Further, it moved television away from its domestic association, relocating the television experience into the public sphere and a central, geographical location—configured here as the site of communal spectatorship, a "special event" like a live performance or an amusement park ride. As such, Amkor's television exhibit bore little resemblance to the concept of television as a permanent fixture in Israeli life (or a tool for targeted domestic outreach), as the subject of debate within the echelons of power, or even a first step in a would-be process of investment and development.

On July 12, about a week after the fair, newspaper headlines announced the world's first successful television broadcast via satellite. News of the U.S. Telstar satellite and Russia's plans to launch a similar broadcast satellite fed speculations about "global broadcasts" that were strikingly reminiscent of Amkor's international television experiment.[18] Television, it appeared, would soon outgrow its local-signal limitation, stretching out to envelop the world in an electronic blanket of simultaneous broadcasts. Such imagery of uniform programming, although wildly speculative, was a far cry from the national specificity that even television proponents conceded was an absolute necessity for Israeli television. The launching of the satellite and its first successful transmission to Europe—and later back again—were regarded by the Israeli press as major stories, worthy of front-page attention. These reports may have impressed readers with their account of growing technological sophistication and television's global reach, yet few were moved to advocate for Israeli television in light of the news.

Reporters' professional hostility goes only so far in explaining the tepid response to Amkor's television effort. Similarly, the fair's atmosphere and function as a public event and a trade show does not fully account for television's overall casting as a one-time public attraction, rather than as a model prototype. Ultimately, understanding the generally underwhelmed response requires a broader examination of the television discourse in Israel as it evolved in 1962—out of concerns over immigration and Arab broadcasting.

AIRTIGHT BORDERS: ARAB VIEWERS AND TELEVISION REGULATION

[Television] has great influence, especially on the Arab minority in our midst, but it also influences the Jewish populace. Maybe from this consideration, it would be good to educate the citizen through our television and not through hostile television?[19]

The mere fact that Arab countries had implemented television technology and Israel had not was, in itself, of no great concern to most commentators. Rather, anxious attention was paid to the slow but steady emergence of the television set as a desirable commodity and a conduit for Arab broadcasts into Israeli homes. The concern surrounded television's simultaneous ability to define and violate national borders through (Israeli) spectatorship of (enemy) foreign broadcasts.

In an attempt to fight the illicit spread of receiver ownership, the government increased the import tax on each set, yet the number of television households continued to grow, reaching an estimated ten thousand in 1962. Sets were also making appearances in public places, not only in Arab villages and immigrant development towns—where the cost of individual sets may have been prohibitive for many poor residents—but also in urban centers like Tel Aviv. One columnist described how a once-struggling Tel Aviv eatery owner cultivated a perpetually full dining area by keeping his clientele enraptured with Arab television and the promise of an always upcoming belly-dancing program.[20] The appearance of such reports in the spring of 1962 was quickly followed by the announcement of new television regulations.

By May of 1962, reports of the imminent debut of Amkor's television at the Eastern Fair were interspersed with news of a government crackdown on "illegal" sets. In addition to the existing import taxes on receivers from abroad, the new regulation required each set to be officially licensed by the post office. No explicit connection was ever drawn between the unveiling of Amkor's television project and the growing government wariness over sets, yet the thematic link between the two was difficult to miss since newspaper articles about these items appeared together, sometimes side by side. To the Israeli reader, unaccustomed to seeing the word "television" in news headlines at all, the sudden juxtaposition of technological fanfare with governmental stricture broadly hinted at stirrings of anxious authority.

Terms of the licensing requirement—penalties of large fines or six-months' incarceration, and seizure of the offending receiver—made plain the extent to which the presence of television sets in Israel was perceived as a threat. Eligibility requirements further revealed the heart of that threat as a grave national security concern, demanding that all license applicants produce proof of citizenship. Moreover, the set owner was "forbidden from revealing or recording—or allowing another to reveal—an image or information that has been unintentionally received and was not the type of picture or information for which . . . the use of television receivers has been allowed." Such information was not be repeated to anyone but a state official, a governmental body, or a certified court.[21]

Decried by many commentators as arbitrary and legally unfounded, the new regulation—struck down by an Israeli court soon after its passage—in all its paranoid flair, cast the technology as a double political threat: an electronic gateway that made Israel vulnerable to hostile infiltration from without and to security leaks from within. The cryptic warning about "unintentionally received" information appeared to portray television technology as a wild, unharnessed force capable of compromising national security through the dissemination of restricted information. Whether such compromising leakage was the deliberate product of Arab broadcasting intervention or haphazard—an unanticipated byproduct of a promiscuous technology impervious to border defenses and information control—the Israeli citizen was directly implicated in the eventuality of such a security breach. The regulation appointed each "head of household," the licensed owner of a receiver, as a kind of technological border guard of Israeli security. Television technology and the mere practice of viewing it were here again impregnated with political significance.

If the notion of Israeli families settling down to an evening of enemy-nation telecasts inspired concerns about the effects of anti-Israeli propaganda on morale and the cultural allegiances of Arab-speaking Israelis, even more worrisome was the overtly political consequences of seditious materials on a non-Jewish population. As legal analysts pointed out, the requirement of presenting one's Israeli passport for daily services and licenses was an unusual measure, especially since Israeli law did not require residents to be citizens and conferred rights to both Jewish and Arab Israelis on the basis of residency. Yet, in its language and restrictions, the regulation invoked a shadow world of breached security and national containment, positing the technology as a potential weapon—dangerous in some hands, and for some viewers.

Further, this threat was constructed as inherent to the technology (a sieve that allowed information to seep into one's living room at any time), to its program content (anti-Israeli propaganda would stream into the home), and to its audience reception (the cultural and political allegiances of viewers). To that extent, the government's attempt to tie licenses to financial means, national loyalty, and citizenship represented certain television viewers as more susceptible to the political threats of the set than others, and Arab noncitizens most susceptible of all.

Whereas most Arab residents of Israel did obtain the status of Israeli nationals by 1962, the process was clearly devised to benefit Jewish immigrants. As Howard Sachar documents, the 1952 Nationality Law specified four means by which citizenship could be granted: birth, immigration, residence, or naturalization. These four categories appeared inclusive, yet a maze of regulations made such conditions of residency or birthright difficult for Arab residents to prove, and clearly—deliberately—favored the Jewish population.[22]

Since no clear borders between Palestine and neighboring Arab lands were enforced at the time of the British Mandate, many Arab farmers simply crossed these borders and settled in Palestine with no official citizenship papers. Similarly, refugees driven off their land during the 1948 war who returned later were also excluded from official residency status under the 1952 law. These discriminatory measures were criticized by both Arabs and Israelis and were not rigorously enforced, allowing a majority of Arabs to circumvent the regulations and obtain national status in Israel by the late 1950s. However, the exclusionary nature of such citizenship requirements was likely recalled by the fresh insult of television regulations. Such an attempt to bar Arab viewers from owning a television was clearly futile, yet it targeted the very portion of the population already most disenfranchised and deemed most likely to seek out and be swayed by anti-Israeli messages.

Anti-Israeli propaganda directed toward Israel's Arab minority was no mere flight of national paranoia. As a typical article in the popular national daily *Yediot Ahronot* reported, Egypt and Syria regularly directed broadcasts to Israeli Arabs, addressing them as "[o]ur dear brothers, sons of a robbed Palestine," and promising a coming attack of Arab forces that would free them from their "Zionist captivity."[23] This rhetoric, and the attention paid to it by the Israeli press, served to heighten the already acute Israeli concerns for security and to further cement the association between broadcast technology and political incitement. Apprehension over such cross-border propaganda escalated to alarm as unofficial surveys estimated that nearly two thousand sets—close to a third of all sets in operation within Israel in 1962—were Arab owned.

As many commentators emphasized, Arab viewership was often a social activity, making the sum of actual viewers of Arab programming much larger than the number of sets. No other apparatus, it was further argued, was as successful in creating a sense of affinity and kinship between Israeli Arabs and Arabs in enemy countries. The snug discursive coiling of Arab cultural programming, TV set proliferation in Israel, immigrant integration, Arab-Israeli viewing habits, and national security was quickly becoming received common sense. "The matter of television, too, has turned into a war of survival between us and the Arabs, as if this is the deciding element between us and those who seek our destruction," observed one commentator in a rare critique of the prevailing view. "All this loud talk of television as part of national strategy, . . . the explanation given in high talk on the dangers of propaganda from Arab stations, . . . is a stinging insult to the Israeli public; . . . providing film and theater to distant villages is not what guides supporters of television, but some unusual national strategy: not Nasser's missiles guide us, . . . but belly-dancing on Beirut television."[24]

The licensing regulation's precondition of citizenship and implicit prerequisite of national loyalty appear, in retrospect, to have been potent illustrations of government anxiety, down to their impossible enforcement. Yet, the threat of television, as envisioned by the architects of such attempts at legal constraints, followed the already established pattern underlying broadcasting discussions that emphasized targeting another specific group—Eastern immigrants—for cultural refinement and education through television.

Whether for education or espionage, assimilation or propaganda, television's power was presumed to reside in its capacity to reach, isolate, "transport," manipulate, and indoctrinate very specific audience segments. In effect, this presumption all but defined official imagining, expectations, and discussions of projected strategies for the medium. Rhetorically, then, the technology emerged not as a utility whose power rested in a format of mass transmission, but rather as a tool of specific, localized address. Thus Israeli television was imagined not as *broadcasting* at all, but as a model of carefully targeted *narrowcasting*. Moreover, official preoccupation with the signal's careful containment and the dangers of cross-national transmission fortified the logic of narrowcasting by associating its alternative with cultural contagion and security hazards.

In the face of such quickly reifying formulations—and their enthusiastic endorsement by television proponents—Amkor's free-flowing vision of global inclusion and popular appeal, and Telstar's reminder of the approaching possibilities of transnational broadcasting, may very well have been the strongest arguments *against* television in the summer of 1962.

The month-long television experiment—an indiscriminate mix of local and international programs with an emphasis on entertainment, sports, and popular interests, bookended by local and world news— directly contradicted the image of television promulgated by its government supporters. Unlike the narrowcasting instrument of national interests, or the problem-solution model for education and Israeli cultural cohesion, Amkor's television celebrated local immediacy and popular tastes, bound up in global interconnectedness. Aside from the daily news show, local performances, and public-participation programs that drew on the specific experience of the fair, most of Amkor's lineup consisted of international offerings, emphasizing a "window on the world" experience that eschewed a specific Israeli context in favor of foreign mass entertainment. Aside from the suspect "attraction" quality of this content, the very ease with which the prototype embraced cross-border access and invoked the porous character of television played directly into the anxious visions of a leaky, capricious medium that haunted the official discourse of the period. For proponents of the medium, who fought to cast television as an appealing solution to national ills, Amkor's populist experiment must have seemed more a nuisance than a boon.

Despite its frosty reception, however, the Eastern Fair ultimately did signal the start of a new phase in Israeli broadcast history—albeit serendipitously.

THE "KNOWN BENEFACTOR": TELEVISION FINDS A PATRON

Those who plan the creation of television will forgive me, but bringing in television under the pretext of education is false and ridiculous to the core. Television and learning are two opposites.[25]

I wonder how such an automaton, an instrument that can contain whatever one wishes, could be a target for such rage.[26]

From all aspects—educational, religious and humane—we completely reject the installation of television of any kind since it is a cancer that destroys the learned life.[27]

Following the 1962 fair, Amkor announced that it would be ready to supply the Israeli consumer with affordable television receivers three to four months after the government approved the creation of an Israeli service. An article that surveyed the progress concluded that "quietly, preliminary technological and scientific conditions have been created that will make the founding of television possible in Israel in a very short time, once the question is put on the table."[28]

In the aftermath of the Cassirer Report's recommendations, follow-up endorsements, and the support of government officials—such as Ben-Gurion's chief of staff, Teddy Kollek; Minister of Culture and Education Abba Eban; and Israeli radio official Hannoch Givton—the question of television was gaining a semblance of respectability. Proponents found new willingness among Knesset members to discuss television's educational properties and local options for overcoming the attraction of Arab broadcasting. As many supporters argued, Israeli television of "the proper level" would attract Israeli viewers by offering quality programs. If Arab television threatened immigrant assimilation, Israeli broadcasts could offer programs that targeted the same immigrants and promoted cultural absorption. Where Arab television offered propaganda and distraction, Israeli television would offer education and intellectual betterment. For all these possibilities, however, a lack of acceptable funding sources relegated the argument to largely theoretical exchanges. Not that there was a lack of willing sponsors: Twenty separate international offers to finance an Israeli service passed through the Prime Minister's Office, yet all proposed a direct commercial model, a programming exchange, or other organizational demands that conflicted with the strictly educational and cultural model—the only model that would withstand official scrutiny.

In the fall of 1962, however, an unexpected offer jump-started the idea of an Israeli television service. On September 9, a government spokeswoman indicated the shift by saying that "because television has been generating waves, the government has decided . . . to examine the problems associated with its founding in Israel."[29] The "waves" over television were generated by an unlikely source: Baron Louis De Rothschild, an English millionaire and a longtime patron of scientific and educational projects in Israel. The baron, commonly referred to as "the known benefactor," announced his readiness to invest in the creation of an Israeli educational-television service. The Rothschild fund, it was proposed, would finance broadcasting facilities and establish educational programming for twenty schools during an experimental phase, allowing the Israeli government ample time to evaluate the benefits of such a project and decide whether it would be interested in continuing the service at the end of the experimental two- to three-year term.[30] As Rothschild repeatedly emphasized, he had no interest in conventional domestic telecasting and objected to any association with mass media per se or with Israel's general broadcasting service, Kol Israel.

Reportedly, the early September Knesset discussion of the baron's patronage offer was marked by a friendly and surprisingly calm atmosphere, due in part, as one columnist speculated, to the temporary absence of Ben-Gurion, "who is known to fiercely oppose the creation of television."[31] At the meeting, Eban informed the Knesset that many who opposed the Avidor Committee's protelevision conclusion did so on a financial basis and had, since Rothschild's announcement, retracted their objections.[32] Whereas opponents reasoned that television would artificially raise the standard of living and cause "wild competition and snobbism," proponents—led by Eban—extolled educational television's contribution to the integration of new immigrants and warned against complacency in the face of a growing Israeli populace already watching Arab television.[33] For all the new relevance Rothschild's education plan injected into the television discussion, opponents and supporters alike still recognized the issue of Arab programming as a potent and effective reasoning strategy, since it solidly linked television with national security, thus propelling it up the list of national priorities. As before, anxiety over corruption and materialism dominated arguments on the antitelevision side; opponents balked at the suggestion that television could add to Israel's cultural life and argued that instituting television would "open the nation's gates to hostile propaganda" and pose a serious "danger to social life in Israel, . . . creat[ing] a two-tiered social system of those who own a television set and those who don't: the arrogant and the deprived."[34] Yet concerns over immigrants and Arab viewers proved most effective as counterarguments. "Reality has set in," wrote one commentator immediately after Eban's Knesset announcement: "Television sets adorn many households in Israel today, especially in places closest to the border. Because of this, and for many other reasons, television's antagonists have turned to champions."[35] Ben-Gurion, who was on a diplomatic trip to Scandinavia at the time of the Knesset meeting, mocked the idea that television could somehow improve Israel's cultural potential. However, the Old Man appeared ready to admit defeat. "I'm fighting a losing battle," he remarked, conceding that despite his opposition he was sure that television would be established in Israel in a year or two.[36] According to newspaper reports in September, the prime minister's opposition to television was flagging in the face of pressures within his own cabinet. "He yielded," wrote one disapproving columnist. "In the question of television he surrendered, and with him, we all surrender. The Baron will foist television on us."[37]

In early October 1962, the national daily *Ha'aretz* noted that "the argument over the institution of television has been significantly amplified in the past few weeks."[38] Coverage of Rothschild's proposal was accompanied by related stories of Israeli industrial readiness, foreign pressure by European and U.S. companies, and speculations over the feasibility and cost of an Israeli broadcasting service. As opposing pro- and anti-television officials were locked in a near stalemate over its institution, life on the ground was rife with the evidence of a television invasion: "Across Israel," observed one columnist, "television sets pop up like mushrooms with every new day."[39]

By late September, the government had increased the tax on televisions again, and, on November 5, a widely publicized police action had seized numerous television receivers from cafés in the Tel Aviv–Jaffa area for failure to pay tax. A subsequent investigation revealed an organized black market of television sets, some fraudulently sent to Israel from Cyprus and others purchased by new immigrants—exempt from the purchasing tax—and sold to café owners. At the same time, commentators called attention to a new feature in the Israeli landscape: hundreds of antennae poised on rooftops as if to advertise the illicit pleasures contained in the apartments below. A testimony to the continuing spread of sets, these reports also reignited fears over what Israelis were watching: "It is clear that every such antenna represents a very dangerous phenomenon: inside the apartment there sits a whole family, friends and relatives, and together they feast their eyes on television—Arab television. As is known today, this has turned into a social occasion in certain places; . . . many in Israel understand Arabic, and a large part also comes from a cultural background like the one that typifies Egyptian or Lebanese television." In accordance with the discursive framing of television anxieties, support for television was thus couched in the rationale of national security: "No wonder that the security forces began looking worriedly and with doubt at the growing antennae. And it is no wonder that the army supports the idea of instituting television. Supporters of television claim that if television in Israel was of a proper level, none would tune in to broadcasts from Alexandria."[40]

In tandem with government attempts to fight the illicit spread of receivers, notices appeared daily in local papers advertising "television installation experts" who, more often than not, had "just returned from training" abroad.[41] By mid-October, ads for the Israeli Institute of Technicians regularly advertised classes in electronics, television, and radio technology, and featured a photo of a white-coated engineer gazing intently at a television set. In an odd confluence of official resistance, entrepreneurial zeal, and popular interest, television seemed both certain and questionable, instantly available and years out of reach.

"Rothschild Is Ready to 'Push the Button' and Start Educational Television in Israel," announced a breezy headline in *Ma'ariv* on

November 2, 1962. Days later, *Yediot Ahronot* reported that Ben-Gurion and Rothschild's representatives had reached an agreement on the structure of the educational project and named the general manager of the Education and Culture Office to head an eleven-member management committee. The committee would include only two of Rothschild's people and feature a majority of government representatives. To maintain its educational mission according to Rothschild's condition, the agreement resolutely stated, the educational service would carry no news broadcasts, "since [such broadcasts] could be interpreted as inappropriate."[42]

Publicly, Rothschild expressed sensitivity to the concerns of opposition members who worried not only about television's overall effects, but also, as one Knesset member put it, about its "purely foreign element."[43] In an interview with *Ha'aretz*, Rothschild's representatives were even more forceful in their emphasis on "education in the narrow sense of the word," stressing that lessons in mathematics, languages, and biology would have preference over "low-priority" subjects such as social sciences, philosophy, and society. The baron further underscored that there would be no instruction in religion and politics, and no inclusion of current affairs.[44] Rothschild and his advisors were, it appeared, keenly aware of the potential for controversy in all manner of broadcasting, and the proposal was carefully tailored to avoid any tinge of politics or ideology—down to the exclusion of most humanities from the educational program schedule.

PUBLIC RADIO AND "PRIVATE TELEVISION":
RADIO, TELEVISION, AND THE BATTLE OF ORIGINS

Like Kol Israel's news director, Hannoch Givton, who had argued for a municipal television service since 1959, the Cassirer Report, the Avidor Committee, and the director general of the Education Ministry all rejected a commercial broadcasting structure in favor of a public municipal system. The education official had gone further, recommending a joint directorial body that would supervise general Israeli broadcasting of both television and radio. By mid-1962, as plans for the creation of the Israeli Broadcast Authority were already underway, television's spot under the IBA umbrella seemed assured. However, as Tzvi Gil documents, an ideological struggle soon ensued over the relationship between Kol Israel and the future organization of television.[45] The very strategy that sought to advance the cause of television by highlighting its educational and cultural narrowcasting abilities had distanced the technology from radio. In 1962, mounting pressures to separate the radio service from government supervision expanded that gap, focusing attention on radio as a mass journalistic medium by forcefully distinguishing between a responsibility to inform and the shady penchant for influence.

With the logic of television wholly reliant on just such a claim of affect, and on an ideological unity no longer tolerable in radio, the broadcasting systems were forced into rhetorical dissonance. Such discord in perceived purpose and effect stood to sever any structural connections between radio and television, and to facilitate the creation of two broadcast systems: the IBA, a semi-independent radio agency, and a government television service that could at any time revert to the prime minister's control. Concern for a potential schism between broadcasting parts was further magnified by Rothschild's resolve to isolate his television project from general broadcasting in name and affiliation. Distressed over this possible development, Givton retaliated with a long letter to the Office of the Prime Minister arguing that "all over the world, television has organically grown from radio," and that the two media share a similar role in society. "A wise, central management of both media together promises flexibility and a rational utility for both." Using the BBC as a primary model, Givton made a case for the financial benefits of keeping radio and television under one management, and ended with a plea that made plain the news manager's fears for Israeli radio: "Even after television, primary broadcasting—in terms of the length of programs and their scope—will remain that of the radio. We must take special caution, then, not to damage radio broadcasting for television. I can foresee no other option than the destruction of Kol Israel and the dispersal of its most senior workers if Israeli television is delegated to a different body."[46] For virtually all of Kol Israel's staff, close kinship between television and radio seemed essential for IBA's survival. The appearance of a television patron was promising at first, yet the proposal that directly disdained any family resemblance between the two media not only threatened radio but also raised a new problem of allegiance for television supporters.

Rothschild's reason for avoiding organizational ties with the established radio service was never clearly articulated. However, it is safe to assume that the fund saw its instructional, student-targeted television as incompatible with the journalistic mission and mass entertainment programs of Israeli national radio. For Rothschild and his supporters, the fund offered a chance to radically reimagine television as an educational tool apart from the polar, nearly global, conceptions of popular-entertainment vehicle or state megaphone. Rothschild's goal required a conception of the technology as a tabula rasa, free of public expectations and unsullied by institutional ties. As the prehistory of Israeli television has shown us thus far, such wishful thinking was not just too late, but was part of the very technological imagination that had spurred Israeli telespeculations nearly a decade earlier. Thus, Rothschild's proposal for a "new" television resonated with supporters precisely for its fit with earlier conceptions that stressed narrowcasting and influence for the novel, Israel-specific promise of television.

The fund's reluctance to associate its television plan with Israeli radio may also have been grounded in the efforts to keep the project free of political wrangling and unwelcome critiques of partisanship. Kol Israel's status as an agency of the Prime Minister's Office, paired with an increasingly high number of controversial broadcasts and cries of bias (growing ever more shrill with the Lavon affair revelations), made an association with Kol Israel a potential liability. What is more, the anticipation that Kol Israel would soon be set free from the prime minister's direct control made its future uncertain and volatile. Indeed, some within Kol Israel suspected that it was this very prospect of independence from government control that made Rothschild wary of linking his project's fate—and favor—with a potential outsider.

Less charitable observers speculated that it was precisely those government ties that Rothschild covertly courted, preparing his service as an eventual mouthpiece for government propaganda. Whatever the motivation, Rothschild's tenacity and the government's apparent acceptance of the condition fueled suspicion and anger within the ranks of the radio service.

Kol Israel saw itself deliberately barred from what it perceived to be the natural evolution of Israeli broadcasting toward a general-television service. Its hopes to direct television's inauguration in Israel were being thwarted just as Rothschild's plan specified it was under no obligation to hire any Kol Israel employees. One radio manager angrily described reading the proposal: "I was shocked; . . . there was enough in that report to sneak television into the nation by some back alleyway."[47]

For other commentators, the exclusion of the would-be public broadcasting agency raised troubling questions in light of Israel's past attitudes toward broadcasting: "Who will guarantee that this television will remain 'educational'? And what is the difference between 'formal education' and 'education to good citizenship' that could slide into 'explanation' (*hasbara*) that all over the world is nothing but a polite term for propaganda?"[48]

Rothschild's representative was indignant in the face of such claims, insisting that it was precisely general, public, or political broadcasting that the baron wished to avoid. "We were told that the introduction of an educational television will speed up the establishment of a general television service to Israel," he wrote in an angry letter to Ben-Gurion. "Rothschild has no interest in general television. Our only concern is education."[49]

Despite government assurances that it would include Kol Israel's interests in the negotiations with Rothschild, reports soon surfaced that a scheduled hearing on the institution of television included no apparent change in the Rothschild position over Kol Israel's exclusion. In response, the radio service stepped up its efforts, and the matter soon turned from an internal conflict to a public quarrel.

Television was coming, and, Kol Israel workers feared, radio would be abandoned—or pushed—to a quiet death just as it was about to declare its long-awaited independence. "Had Teddy Kollek and the rest of the 'Television Prophets' decided to forsake radio to its fate?" demanded one letter to the editor of *Ma'ariv*. The writer went on to critique the hasty investment in television while "it is well known to all listeners . . . that Kol Israel programs are produced in disgraceful conditions, and with mostly old and outdated equipment."[50] Like many other critiques, the letter based its argument in a comparison of Israel with "all advanced nations," reinforcing the notion that Israel's broadcasting development either eluded the natural process of modernity or was planned deliberately to hasten Kol Israel's demise. As accounts of clashes between Kol Israel workers and government officials filled the dailies, *Yediot Ahronot* reported that a government decision to approve television was "unavoidable," although the Knesset would attempt to come to an agreement with Kol Israel before finalizing the project. The first phase of programming would, according to the report, begin with twenty to thirty schools in the Tel Aviv area by the end of 1964.[51] Kol Israel representatives sent an urgent message to Ben-Gurion, imploring him to hold off on his decision about television and threatening a general strike. Rumors circulated in the press that Givton was about to resign.[52] As their arguments revealed, much of the radio station personnel's fear over television centered not on Rothschild's project per se, but on the widespread belief that his was merely an interim step to general television: "Educational television—even as an experiment—is a short way away from general television. There is no self-respecting broadcasting professional that will agree to stay at Kol Israel when Israel would have a separate television service."[53]

In turn, Givton was reprimanded, as a spokesman told the press the government was "not alarmed by the threats" and, owing to a tight schedule, the hearing would go on as planned.[54] "Kol Israel personnel are dreaming a bad dream," Ben-Gurion's deputy told reporters, "and are arguing with the dream, instead of facts."[55]

The notion that Rothschild's television could offer the means of establishing a parallel broadcasting venue that, through its incidental origin, would sidestep legal accountability disturbed some Knesset members, as well as reporters and radio workers. "Maybe their demands are justified?" wondered one Knesset member. "We need to establish whether the pretext of an educational television justifies the creation of a powerful entity that parallels Kol Israel—with all that is good and bad in Kol Israel. Maybe we should establish, in accordance with the broadcasting law, a public service, not a government service." "[W]e must prepare," she warned, "that in the future we could handle the instrument's sting while enjoying its honey."[56]

As a counterstrike against the Rothschild educational-television plan, Nakdimon Rogel, production head of Kol Israel, submitted a report that enumerated the dangers and disadvantages of educational television. In it, he played up all the familiar fears of Arab broadcasts and reception that had plagued many government debates in the past:

> The educational service is proposed under the conditions of absence of a general Israeli reception service on the one hand, and the possibility of reasonable reception of programming across the border, on the other. The danger is clear: unless this service is a closed-circuit one . . . it would be impossible to limit the purchase of television receivers through import law or heavy taxes. But there's no reason to assume that owners of such cheap sets will be satisfied by viewing educational programs; in fact, this will be a subsidized possibility of increased viewership of broadcasts from Egypt and Lebanon.

In addition to drawing from the deep well of Arab-broadcast paranoia, Rogel raised the questions of relegating frequencies that would leave enough room for general television and of the location of transmitters. As he pointed out, Rothschild's plan called for an initial phase, beginning with broadcasting to urban centers like Tel Aviv, far from the schools identified as needing the service most—those located in the remote and least populated towns in Israel. Aside from pointing to the discrepancy between the service's aim and its initial target audience, Rogel's fundamental critique was of the "artificial limiting" of the television project as envisioned by Rothschild: "There is no country in the world that would dedicate all its broadcasting resources—in fact, all its broadcasting potential—for a limited purpose that is not fundamentally and basically a broadcasting purpose at all, but an educational goal that can be obtained by other means."[57] In this argument, Rogel outlined a view shared equally by many proponents and opponents of television: that educational television was inevitably a mere first step to a general service, and that this service characterized the "natural state" of the broadcast medium.[58]

For its part, the Kol Israel staff released a statement, delivered both to the press and the Knesset, that included an overview of the role of television in other nations and a demand that Kol Israel personnel (as the only segment of the population that actually worked in broadcasting) not be passed over and ignored: "The workers of Kol Israel see their professional future and their natural development in the television field. However, we should not ignore the fact that radio will continue to fulfill important assignments right beside television. The separation of these two media will surely cause radio to atrophy." The only way to assure the future of both media, concluded the statement, was to keep "both broadcast forms united together . . . without blocking [the] path of natural . . . development."[59]

Claims for "naturalness" quickly fell into common rhetorical use in press reports and commentary about the burgeoning turf war over the airwaves. One commentator called Kol Israel's planned exclusion "baffling, since television services all over the world always develop from within . . . radio" and argued that the only logical course of action was to keep both services under one management roof.[60] A long, impassioned article in *Ma'ariv* cast Kol Israel as a new mother fighting "for the return of the fruit of its womb." Television, as the author put it, was "taken from its natural progenitor, even before it entered the world, and given to suckle at the breast of a surrogate, a philanthropic stranger."[61]

Accounts like these, mostly offered in support of Kol Israel's fight for inclusion, often betrayed a series of assumptions about the fundamental nature of television, its structure, and its possible uses. Rothschild's intention to keep his television service free of current events or entertainment seemed, to many within and outside the Israeli radio service, a concept wholly foreign to television, and as realistic as windmill slaying—a schema that fundamentally misunderstood the very essence of its object. Yet such a narrow and targeted conception of television was precisely the one used by its early proponents, and a key part of a strategy that managed to convince so many Knesset members to lend it support. Such claims for the medium's "natural" development and its inherent connection to radio, then, paradoxically became the very line of reasoning that many within the protelevision camp found themselves vehemently denying.

Even under the Office of the Prime Minister's supervision, Kol Israel was often the target of government and Knesset complaints that focused not only on its political coverage but also on its popular radio programming. The service chafed critics with its lack of attention to religious issues and content, its failure to fully reflect "Israeli national values," and its perceived "lack of proper standards." In addition to decrying the "disrespectful" humor and sexual innuendo in entertainment programs, critics singled out the commercially supported Light Wave channel as a leader in a trend of substandard Israeli radio.

With the impending independence of Kol Israel from direct government control, the new medium of television appeared to offer a multitude of second chances: an opportunity to mold a service according to specific national needs; a chance for the government to maintain control over an extremely powerful broadcast medium; an occasion for creating a noncommercial service that focused on education, not entertainment; and a chance for various interest groups to mold a television service from scratch, with the benefit of long-range planning and careful design. For all these would-be broadcast architects, the view that television was merely a visual extension of Kol Israel was far from natural, or welcome.

"This may be uncomfortable for [television advocates] to admit, but this is the beginning of actual television in Israel, though the worst beginning possible, a start on the wrong foot," argued Lea Porat, a member of the Kol Israel managerial board. Calling educational programs a "boredom stew," Porat suggested that the very notion of a purely educational television was a dangerous oxymoron: "'Educational' television?!" she asked incredulously. "You can even call it 'Rabinovitch television' [but] television is still television. People will still buy receivers and watch Arab programs while an explicit national service, run with talent, may still offer us a chance to compete."[62]

Using the same argument highlighted by Rogel, Porat suggested that with the lack of general-appeal programming, educational television would encourage the purchase of sets without providing sufficiently interesting programs for the public, making Israelis even more dependent on Arab broadcasting services. "This dependency," she proposed, "will engender fear and apathy in the consciousness of the Israeli viewer, and would be difficult to extricate later."[63]

As we have seen, a debate on the nature of the medium pre-dated Rothschild's plan, as critics, educators, and commentators alike worried that, despite all good intentions, television would sooner or later "disintegrate" into its "true nature," a commercially supported medium that would cater to the lowest common denominator and saturate the airwaves with sex and violence. For its supporters, the only chance for television's introduction into Israel was via the argument that it could be a national tool to benefit Israel and provide a solution to its most pressing social problems. The protelevision argument, then, rested on the premise that television was inherently flexible and able to conform to any nationally and culturally beneficial purpose and structure. To put it plainly (as Rothschild's representative did), television was not necessarily an entertainment medium, an information tool, or even a mass technology.

To stake its claim for a role within the changing environment of the television debate, Kol Israel was reluctantly pressed into articulating a contrary argument, one that insisted on a particular, natural course for television, both in development and basic use—a use that could not be deliberately avoided. As if to further push the paradox, Kol Israel was forced to rely on a uniform international history of television and to portray itself as inseparable from that history. Such claims of international predetermined continuity, like other components of the "nature argument," ran in direct opposition to the established argument about the unique ability of Israel, *unlike* other nations, to harness television and bend its powers to its own needs and will.

Shmuel Shnizer, a prominent commentator and opponent of television, used this logic to ridicule those who would promise an Israeli television "that is not corrupted like those of other nations. Ours would be different: cultural, clean, educational. We would preserve high standards." For Shnizer, such plans for a "cultural, high-standard" television were foolishly unrealistic, but so were the claims that "the argument is lost [and] you can't stop the wave of progress." "Television is not an earthquake," insisted Shnizer. "It is a man-made disaster," and as such, it could be "rationally evaluated and stopped."[64]

Thus, Kol Israel's manager, Givton, who only three years earlier had argued to a reluctant Ben-Gurion about television's malleable nature and practical independence from a competitive entertainment system, was now aligned with an argument that regarded television through the lens of "natural" technological evolution, use, and competitive essence. In a related ironic twist, Kol Israel, as a general service used primarily for information and entertainment, had to present television in the image of radio, an image that, by definition, included all the political and entertainment elements—as well as the specter of possible commercial support—that so dogged television supporters.

RAISING THE GOLEM: TELEVISION AS SERVANT OR JUGGERNAUT

No one has yet died from lack of television![65]

Today we are only talking about television for a few dozen school houses, and already the whole country is whipped into a frenzy.[66]

Despite his grim resignation to television's arrival in Israel within a year, Ben-Gurion's prediction was wide of the mark. Rothschild's proposal ushered in a most violent and impassioned debate that reverberated well beyond the Knesset walls.[67] For the first time, television leaped into Israeli headlines and stayed there, as educators, film exhibitors, radio employees, public figures, Knesset members, and private citizens arduously deliberated Israel's video future.

Models and predictions proliferated, but one thread remained constant: Television would utterly transform the young state. One Knesset member turned directly to the Rothschild family, pleading with it to "pull its hand away from the endeavor, as large parts within the population see that its danger is great and its utility false."[68] The most vexing accusations, however, remained the charges that the baron planned to introduce television into Israel only to turn it into a commercial venture.

"Educational television will not be used for political propaganda or entertainment—it will educate," insisted the baron in an interview with *Ma'ariv*, sounding at once defensive and exasperated:

> I want to strictly deny that [the offer] to establish educational television in Israel includes some secret clause that would bring us commercial utility. We want to help in solving the most burning questions in Israel through concrete solutions. . . . We investigated and found that television can contribute something to the education of children and immigrants, to the dissemination of Hebrew, and the instruction of different topics in schools, . . . that's it. We will not press. If we continue to meet with such stiff resistance, we will give the program up.[69]

Yet Rothschild's television, seemingly at the center of the debate, was actually beside the point. The real debate was over an eventual general service and over what form it would assume. Few Israelis imagined the Rothschild project as anything but a "first step" toward general television or regarded his furious protestations as authentic or practical. For supporters of the strict "educational" model of television, this, precisely, was the problem.

If for the past five years the most public aspect of the television discourse was the prominent argument that television was unnecessary in Israel—an argument that led to the emergence of a "purpose" as the start of the television discussion—the current, second phase involved a reconsideration of television as a possible solution to the problems of education and cultural assimilation. Further, Rothschild's educational-television plan seemed to offer a convenient in-between path that avoided both the blatant dangers of commercial ownership and the politically suspect prospect of government television. Yet anxiety and suspicion persisted over the "true" nature of the medium and the degree of control well-meaning managerial forces would have over its development.

Categorical resistance was still prominent. To many staunch opponents, broadcasting was fundamentally incompatible with learning. "Television pushes away the book," asserted one Knesset member in a typical critique. It was, "by its very nature, anti-educational and an anti-learning element." "Television hurts the reading of serious books, prevents devotion to study, and is used as a substitute for refined culture and beautiful art," argued another.[70] In letters to the editor, readers warned that television would destroy the love of books and learning as the fundamental cultural heritage of the Jewish people.[71] A September 25, 1962, cartoon in *Yediot Ahronot* needled supporters with the same suggestion: The drawing portrayed a classroom of small children entranced by a television set in the front of the room. At the back of the class, one boy ignores the broadcast and sits reading a book with a pen in his hand. "Aha! I caught you," admonishes the teacher, standing over the disobedient student. "You are reading homework instead of watching television!"

Set ownership in itself proved a potent argument for some among the opposition, who saw it as a potential class marker and a troubling sea change toward a consumer-oriented society motivated by greed, material envy, and passive accumulation.[72] For others, the set, along with its offer of programming, would "encourage the public to excessive consumption and destruction of morals," or worse, prove a threat to humanity itself.[73] "Television," wrote one such commentator in December 1962, is "an invisible cord around your neck . . . [that] pulls you with its magnetic power and makes you a slave to your set. . . . The moment you let television into your home, you have ceased to be human, lost your independence and delivered yourself to a new God, in body and spirit."[74]

Despite this lingering "older" strain of television opposition, however, the crux of the argument had shifted irrevocably. By now, the major contention was between those who saw the technology as malleable, flexible, and ideologically neutral, and those who saw its emergence as a juggernaut that was not so much developed as unleashed.

The notion that television could be a tabula rasa, to imprint on as its planners pleased, was stressed by proponents such as Minister of Culture Abba Eban, who insisted: "This instrument has no character— you get what you put in it. That is why the question is not whether we have faith in television, but whether we have faith in ourselves."[75] However, most supporters were cautious in their endorsement of television, pointing out that it could be a superb teacher's aid but could not be "allowed to slip" into general, commercial entertainment.[76] Even its most ardent advocates were careful to point out that television would require a short leash for fear it could degenerate into a "low-brow" entertainment medium. In this, both sides shared the view that television—like the young and the immigrant populations it would serve—needed supervision and cultivation. What emerges from the various opinions is a sense that television could be a success only if its "true nature" were somehow kept at bay. The undertone of caution that characterized common expressions of support was itself a troubling cue for opponents, as one Knesset member observed:

> According to the news, they are about to institute, as an experiment, educational television. Yet it is clear that this is the beginning of [full] television with all its ingredients. [Note] only the fact that its supporters feel that this instrument called television is not so plain and simple—that it is not so straight and wholesome—that [they] need to diminish it and bring it in as if by the back door. This alone proves that they too were not at peace with their conscience regarding the introduction of television.[77]

Repeatedly, television was cast as a force of nature that must be conquered and harnessed—prevented from reverting to its natural state of mass appeal, worthless entertainment, and sexual titillation. Knesset Member Emma Telmi described television as just such a natural force, one "that we must subjugate as we did other natural forces."[78] Likening television to a coherent organism with its own evolutionary drive had a more basic and controversial dimension: This position held that, like a natural force or evolution, television's introduction to Israel was itself inevitable, part of an unstoppable wave of progress, simultaneously a symptom and its cause.

Notably, considerations of television's capability to deliver "proper" education, or to navigate between the polar dangers of tedium and sensationalism, rarely invoked particular programming. Rather, the discourse focused on the presumed essential quality of the technology in total—and the "slippery slope" of progress. Such a construction was already overworked—indeed, prior to the emergence of the "culture problem," the widespread dismissal of the medium depended on the perception that television, by its very presence, would uncontrollably alter Israeli society. Contemporary invocations of television as a "natural force," however, may well have been bolstered by the ongoing debate over radio's role as a "progenitor" and by the gathering popular sense that Rothschild's television was only a "first step" in the eventual maturation of the medium. These, in combination with incessant comparisons to U.S. programming, produced a new "evolutionary" discourse that posited television as having its own internal development trajectory, which, once set in motion, could not be led off course.

What is notable in such constructions (by no means original to the Israeli case) is that just as they limited discussion of programming and viewing practices by ascribing intrinsic characteristics to the medium, they assigned a strikingly similar set of attributes to television's popular audience.

In her work on evolutionary narratives of technology, Jody Berland points out how such paradigms permit commentators to privilege mythic metanarratives and slip easily between metaphor, historical hypothesis, and description.[79] Although Berland's focus is on ecstatic transformative claims for the Internet and computer technology, her observations also hold true for the various evolutionary claims for television in Israel. Here, the anxious formulations of cultural (and televisual) deterioration conformed to a metanarrative about the national utility of cultural practices and tastes, and the national project of assimilation and cultural cultivation. For both supporters and opponents, associations with television in the early 1960s were of the "shallow materiality" of U.S. entertainment, the "low" and hostile programming of enemy Arab countries, and the "impressionable" viewership of Arab and Eastern immigrants in Israel. For television's opponents, this connection made the technology particularly ineffective as an education and integration machine. Conversely, for proponents, this linkage produced television as a unique tool for instruction and the installment of "proper" culture by way of its popular appeal.

The suggestion that television was naturally "base" and therefore must be cultivated and controlled to be worthy of Jewish consumption resonated with the general framing of Israeli cultural existence within the Arab world and the integration of Eastern immigrants into a European-inflected national culture. Arab television was thus cast as appealing to low tastes—primarily the tastes of non-Western viewers—and the project of Israeli television, much like the project of cultural assimilation, was to educate and civilize.

What is particularly interesting in the rhetorical uses of nature and evolution in the Israeli television debate is that, unlike most technoevolution narratives that link human and technological progress, the Israeli example also saw television characterized as a deteriorating force having a particular regressive nature. The bind here is in the opponents' assumption that technological evolution would go on quite aside from human direction, but in step with the most base of human choices. In this case, then, broadcast technology emerges as paradoxically primitive.

Viewed from within the debate, the prospects for Israeli national culture faced two divergent but rhetorically united threats: From the East, Arab culture beckoned to immigrants with familiar images and traditional cultural expressions; from the West, U.S. popular culture lured the young with its offerings of passive pleasures, consumerism, and explicitly sexual and violent entertainment. Both threats involved cultural disunity and deterioration, and both were made available through television. These two "lower" forms of culture may have differed; nonetheless, they were both constructed as powerful specifically because of their inherent passivity, sensational appeal, and visceral character. Educational television, with its promise of active learning, intellectual stimulation, and cultural participation, was called on to mitigate this downward "slide" into popular culture—a curious task for a technology so closely identified with just such a "sliding" effect.

The tension between "low" and "proper" culture, then, paralleled that between "entertainment" and "educational" television throughout the debate. These rhetorical alignments thus continued to shape both the imaginings of an Israeli television system and a hierarchical view of national culture that located Eastern tastes alongside those of the young and immature.

The range of topics debated in the context of television can easily be viewed as a checklist of issues foremost on the nation's mind: solving the education gap; the immigration/integration problem; the cultural expressions that should be included in the developing notion of "Israeli culture"; the problem of Palestinian broadcasts within Israeli borders; the problem of Arab residents and their national allegiance within Israeli borders; the tension between Israel's wish to distinguish itself from other nations, but to be included in the roster of "normal" sovereign states; the proper place of religion in everyday life, culture, and government decisions; and the problem of shifting values from agricultural pioneer Zionism to urban and distinctly materialist aspirations. Still, with so many fundamental discourses intersecting at the (imagined) site of television, the technology itself cannot be said to have created these issues, nor, conversely, can it be said to have simply borne witness to them. Rather, television—or more generally, broadcasting—was the primary point at which all these discourses and points of contention met and intertwined. Seen through the television debate, the issue of the educational gap appeared intimately tied with Arab cultural influence; issues of public taste intermingled with security concerns; and the evolution of standards of living and consumer culture were suddenly relevant to immigrant integration.

To this extent, the debates I have traced so far were not so much about television itself; rather, the nascent conceptions of television provided an ideal arena for the expression of pressing issues, and a specific point of reference through which their meanings could be defined. Whereas concerns over immigration, education, Arab-Israeli relations, religion, and consumer culture pre-dated even the earliest debates about television's installation, the possibility of television allowed these discourses to come into focus as central preoccupations for the developing nation.

Television was not, however, a mere facilitator for such a national conversation and debate. Although its introduction to Israel—even as a possibility—came late in the technology's history, it did so extremely early in the nation's history and forced a period of social, political, and cultural introspection, as television's promise of a great leap forward remained speculative, risky, and, most important, irreversible. The accelerated deliberation about television in the new nation, and its theoretical recruitment in the service of cultural, educational, and political development, served to artificially join Israel's most immediate problems and place them together in a kind of ideological incubator. As a result, television not only focused the nation's attention on its cultural and political process of maturation, but also made that process visible and publicly contentious.

As 1962 drew to a close and the fate of Rothchild's offer remained fodder for editorials and noisy Knesset sessions, Amkor's summer vision of popular television all but faded from collective memory. All agreed that television, if introduced, must serve a national purpose. Still, with a few thousand television sets already flickering nightly in Jewish and Arab homes across Israel, the future shape of Israeli broadcasting was far from clear.

3 THE BELLY-DANCER STRATEGY
Israeli Educational Television and Its Alternatives

Whoever says that Jewish broadcasts will intercept those from Arab countries is also saying that Arab broadcasts will intercept Jewish ones. If we get to that, then viewers will watch more Arab programming since belly dancing is much more attractive than philosophy.

—Ygaal Allon, Minister of Education

It seems to me that precisely for security reasons, we must prevent the installation of television. . . . Educational television . . . will heighten the security threat that [viewers] will watch Arabic programming during the day.

—Menachem Parosh

Television is control of souls. That is why it can be a good educational instrument.

—Emma Telmi

On January 30, 1966, a small cartoon appeared among the letters to the editor of the Israeli newspaper *Davar* (see figure 1).[1] The drawing was one reader's modest contribution to the ongoing public debate over television in Israel—invigorated by Rothschild's educational-television proposal more than three years earlier. The cartoon depicted a television screen in the midst of a highly poetic signal crossing: The screen is bifurcated, with its top portion portraying a classroom lesson bearing the caption "Educational Television: Channel 8." In it, a severe-looking bespectacled teacher points to a blackboard; at her midriff, the image is interrupted by another—the scantily clad pelvis and legs of an undulating belly dancer. At the lower half of the screen, the caption identifies the trespassing signal as "Belly Dancer from Cairo: Channel 8."

The amateur drawing of the impossible figure constructed by a foreign signal aptly captures the complexity and ambivalence associated with the Rothschild plan. By literally picturing the hypothetical concern about signal overlap between the future Israeli television service and the existing Egyptian signal, the crude little drawing managed to encapsulate a decade's worth of anxiety. The jarring union of the two competing television broadcasts, so different in content and intent, spoke volumes of Israel's sense of identity and location within the Arab world and wryly commented on the lurking attraction of Arab programming. Yet the overwhelming question is posed not in the juxtapo-

FIGURE 1. Letter to the editor cartoon by S. Ben David, *Davar*, January 30, 1966.

sition of the two, but in the contrasting choices they offer: How, the cartoon seems to ask, can we compete with *that?*

This tension between "beneficial" Israeli programming and its rival, "cheap" and salacious Arab programming, was a central fixation in the debate that led to the eventual, hard-won approval of the Rothschild plan. As a typical argument expressed it: "Even if our content is of the right level, our sets will be open to broadcasts from Cairo and Lebanon, and tomorrow Syria; . . . the result: an increased demand for Arab broadcasts, the same movies and performances of lower moral and artistic level which we will be bringing to our public's eyes."[2]

In the public sphere, however, the cartoon was an emblematic entrant into the discourse of telespeculations that preoccupied Israelis throughout the 1960s. As the possibility of an Israeli television service became a subject of debate in the Knesset, it also emerged as an object of public fascination, anxiety, and conjecture.

These speculations often went on in direct contradiction to government assurances and directives. Where the government predicted an ideological dissemination system, these expectations imagined popular entertainment; where official discourse insisted on a state-supported agency, public discourse imagined a commercial system; and where official statements charged the future service with representing the nation's distinct cultural identity, these counter-versions anticipated

a broadcasting format heavy with Western-style programs and imported films. Most significantly, where government plans envisioned a
television service that would compete with and eliminate Israeli spectatorship of Arab broadcasts, public and commercial discourse regarded
Arab broadcasts as another (more alluring) programming option. These
counter-imaginings often found expression in the popular press through
editorials, reader letters, and cartoons, as well as through advertisements for television sets. Taken as a whole, these rhetorical and visual
predictions not only gave voice to competing expectations about
broadcasting per se, but also revealed a struggle over the place (and use)
of popular culture in Israel's national aspirations.

Only six years before the appearance of the belly-dancer cartoon,
the idea of an Israeli television service seemed nearly preposterous, dismissed within the government and by most public figures as the ultimate "idiot box" (see chapter 1). As we have seen, however, the
growing presence of television sets in Israeli households, and the emer-
gent popularity of Arab broadcasts in Jewish and Arab Israeli homes,
prompted calls for a service "of quality" that would capture this audience and wean it off enemy broadcasts. The 1962 Rothschild proposal
appeared to address one of the main items of concern: education (particularly that of immigrant children). Yet Rothschild's vision deliberately left adults (immigrant and otherwise) out of the signal's target
range. Just as it offered a potent solution to the problem of an "education gap," the Rothschild television plan plucked the idea of broadcasting out of its discursive moorings, leaving a host of television
anxieties—immigrant cultural absorption, Arab programming, and anti-
Israeli television propaganda—unaddressed.

Arab broadcasting remained a prominent point of contention.
Television, after all, came to public consciousness in light of the available Arab signal, and arguments about its cultural and security implications roused official interest in the service. As the *Davar* cartoon's open
question reiterated, How was instructional television a salve?

Since the debate began, apprehensive predictions abounded that,
with the growing availability of sets (and under the guise of instructional access), Israelis would soon be the targets—and consumers—of
anti-Israeli propaganda efforts. As an early column in *Al-Hamishmar*
warned: "Israel is situated within the air and television space of the Arab
states . . . and aside from Israeli programs, we would receive only the
broadcasts from Arab stations. We already receive these broadcasts and
if we install general television here, the budget for their propaganda will
grow two-fold. Arab stations will increase their propaganda, and even
accompany it with cultural programs or half-naked belly-dancers."[3]

Repeatedly, the belly dancer, the iconic stand-in figure for Arab popular culture, worked to focus apprehension on Arab television's twin dangers of propaganda wrapped in low-brow salaciousness. As we have seen in earlier chapters, such anxieties focused concern explicitly on Israel's Eastern immigrant population, and on the ability of television to seduce viewers away from "Israeli" cultural preferences and values. However, as educational television grew to dominate discussion, Arab television was increasingly viewed not only as a targeted threat, but also as mass competition. As one article on the subject explained, the dilemma was in the balance between "good" programming and audience preferences: "One thing is clear; . . . Israeli television will have to be of a high standard and, at the same time, more engaging than neighboring Arab broadcasts that suit the tastes of at least part of the Israeli viewing public."[4]

Another common debate pitted educational television—described alternately as "spiritually uplifting," "uniquely Israeli," and deadly dull—against entertainment television, characterized most consistently as "American sex and violence."[5] Few Israelis—especially journalists or public figures—expressed any interest in entertainment television; nevertheless, a view was commonly advanced that commercial television would naturally lead to such deterioration, while a noncommercial alternative would either collapse for lack of financial support or draw too small a viewership.

One satirical article suggested a solution by which educational television might both keep viewers captivated and avoid boring and dry programming like "another Shakespearean lecture by Abba Eban" (the British-educated minister of culture and education). In a series of sketches, the author suggested various plots—based on real-life scandals—in which teachers embezzle money, deal drugs, seduce students, and smuggle electric goods, all between commercial breaks and lessons in history, good citizenship, and the like. Although the article clearly meant to skewer inappropriate behavior and poke fun at several criminal incidents that involved teachers, it also offered a rather telling parody of television that portrayed many of the causes of anxiety among its opponents: commercial structure, morally questionable influence on young viewers, and even the lost battle over mass attraction between educational programs and entertainment.[6]

The perceived tension between beneficial but boring programs and exciting but "cheap" ones was often invoked by various articles that tried to anticipate just what Israeli television would look like. "Boredom Isn't Necessary in Our Television," proclaimed one newspaper headline, but the article it headed sounded a more hesitant note. Like many other articles on the subject, the piece compared plans for Israeli television with a "sex-and-violence" U.S. system: "Even sworn enemies of television believe that here we would try to keep some kind of standard. But in the end, programming will be made on a commercial basis and there will be no escaping cheap spectacles."[7]

COCA-COLA AND THE SECRET CLAUSE:
THE LAST ANTITELEVISION STAND

Newspapers may have snubbed Amkor's 1962 television debut that June, but Rothschild's proposal and the ensuing firestorm could scarcely be ignored. What is more, every mention of the television battle, developments in radio, or reports on prominent figures in the television debate triggered a cascade of reader mail, turning the Letters to the Editor pages of every major paper into a public arena where the television question was theorized, attacked, and defended daily. In addition to reportage and readers' views, newspaper editorials also weighed in on the debate. Most vociferously represented by the three major dailies, the newspaper establishment held fast to a fundamental opposition to television. Despite the arguments that raged on in the middle pages, the tone and selection of headlines and news articles left little doubt about the publications' institutional positions.

Notably, a print medium's chief anxiety, the decline of literacy, was rarely mentioned, as few publications deigned to address television as a possible competitor, although one lengthy article from the *Ha'aretz* correspondent in New York was headlined "Television Does Not Compete with Newspapers." The article included a glowing appraisal of the state of newspaper reading in New York and reassuringly reported that newspapers were safe from competition from television, which "only whets the appetite for a detailed report" provided by the paper. The author further suggested that, as far as the *New York Times* was concerned, the "intellectual public" who read newspapers did not resemble the masses who enjoyed television. Despite the fact that the bulk of the article was dedicated to the (healthy) state of journalism in the States, the report began with a quick trip to the television studio: "In the United States, television penetrates every apartment and the level of most programming is low, ridiculously so. . . . I sat in the three studios and watched the programs categorized as 'interesting' here and 'excellent' there, and prayed that this awful trouble does not penetrate Israel."[8]

Stories that dealt with television outside Israel were uniformly negative and often explicitly critical of its effects. *Yediot Ahronot* and *Ma'ariv*, the two largest Israeli dailies, were especially zealous. "A Child

Killed His Mother . . . Providing a Typical Example of the Bad Influence of Television and Corrupting Literature in the United States," cried a *Yediot Ahronot* headline on November 28, 1962. "Television Educates Towards Crime," stated another in the same paper on November 30, above an article that dealt with juvenile delinquency in Britain. "Educational Television? Education in Superficiality!" a *Ma'ariv* headline proclaimed about Italian television on November 11. "A Student of Television Warns: Don't Institute Television in Israel" read a heading to a November 30 commentary section in *Yediot Ahronot*. The papers' position against television had turned so explicit that this itself became the subject of debate.[9] "I am a loyal reader of *Ma'ariv* and have been following the stories. . . . For the past two months, the editors have become overt in their opposition to television," one reader complained, while a columnist for *Ma'ariv*, Arie Goldbloom, published an article that took his own paper to task for its "crusade against television in general and Israeli television in particular."[10]

The daily *Herut* launched a series of long features written by Dan Margalit on the status of television (ironically, by the late 1970s, Margalit would become one of Israel's most popular and enduring television personalities). The first installment in the series, "The Silver Screen: Reality and Illusions," featured a skeptical evaluation of Rothschild's offer and warned that commercial television would probably be established in Israel by 1968. The full-page story, entitled "Television: Classroom or Marketplace?" was illustrated with a drawing of a child seated in front of a giant trash can and watching a television screen installed in its side. Inside, and spilling over the sides of the container, are human figures engaged in various violent acts; on the television set, directly facing the child's mesmerized gaze, a hand clutches a knife.[11]

The article's catchy opening pictured a nightmare scenario in which a television teaches kids history as "action skits," advertises Coca-Cola, and informs students that there is no homework since there is a great crime thriller on television tonight. Such a scenario might be an exaggeration, the article argued, but nevertheless television was essentially related to commercial interests, and any educational effort would quickly become a commercial enterprise. This view represented the foreboding subtext of the "natural evolution" argument and combined the prevalent distrust in television's "true nature" with suspicions over Rothschild's true intentions.

Until now, the bulk of the television debate had relied on a formulation that saw proponents and opponents in agreement over the end result (better education and immigrant cultural integration) and over possible dangers (Arab broadcasting and commercial infiltration), clashing only on the fundamental question of whether television could be harnessed to meet these goals while avoiding hazards lurking along the way. The wave of suspicion around Rothschild's proposal and the treatment of Kol Israel, however, introduced a denser coiling in the discourse: The notion that television possessed a particular essential nature now commingled with suppositions about a deliberate institutional direction and a preconceived use. As one MK argued, the idea of television did not "grow from the soil of our reality nor [was it] fed by our needs or priorities. . . . The government's decision is about educational television, but everyone knows that it's nothing but a passageway to general television—political, entertaining, commercial, et cetera."[12]

Television itself was no longer the only suspect but was now joined by those who would intentionally channel its power to bring about undesired change under false pretenses. "We have two arguments here, one following the other; the plan to try this instrument in school, and the later plan to expand the service nationally. . . . When they speak of the first, they mean especially the second; and television to all the people, that presumably will be the end result."[13]

As Margalit had argued in several essays, Israel would not be able to maintain television without turning to commercial interests, and television supporters within the government knew this full well and had planned for it all along.[14] Such sentiments were repeatedly expressed in the press with a remarkable sense of self-assuredness. "We can assume that members of the committee understand that 'educational television' is nothing but a back door that will facilitate the entrance of regular television, with commercials," one *Ma'ariv* article asserted.[15] "Should we entrust the safekeeping of our cultural future and our children's education to the hands of advertisers?" demanded another.[16]

Echoing the position of several Knesset members, a few journalists questioned the intended purpose of the service. If, went this often repeated argument, the government and the baron truly had immigrant children in mind, television transmitters would be set up in development towns, and not in the highly populated—and economically thriving—cities of Tel Aviv or Ramat Gan. The repeated charges that the baron's motives included profit prompted an indignant response from the foundation: "The Rothschilds have enough sources of income—they want to help, not to profit. . . . We came with an offer. If you want to utilize it, you are welcome to it, if not, too bad. We cannot fight for it."[17]

Whereas Rothschild insisted that his television plan would service schools exclusively, the common foregone conclusion was that television would invade the home soon after its educational introduction. In "Television Will Enter Here by the Back Door," the weekend edition of *Yediot Ahronot* framed the decision over television in military metaphors:

> After Ben-Gurion admits that his war with the home screen is lost, the schoolhouse will be the main bridge, and from it a conquering journey will be launched on the nation as a whole. . . . According to television proponents there is the sense that things will progress as follows: First television will be installed in schools and will broadcast lessons. Later, the matter will broaden, and there will be broadcasts of news and other "public broadcasts"; it will be "television in the service of the public" just like network A of Kol Israel; this will be known as "educational television." In the end, there will be no escaping the notion of regular television, as is common in other nations, that will include entertainment and diversions, and even commercials.[18]

The "back door" metaphor—a phrase originally uttered by an MK who accused the government of planning to "sneak in" general television under the guise of education—had become commonplace in deliberations on the question. In its headline on November 2, 1962, the daily *Ha'aretz* predicted, under the headline "The End of a Fundamental Argument," the certain inauguration of television in Israel. Quoting a confident Teddy Kollek, the article announced that educational television would have its debut broadcast as early as September 1964. "Those who support general television see this as an opportunity to bring television into Israeli homes, under the respectable attire of educational programming. It is clear to all that following educational television there will be instructional television—that will broadcast programs of the sort heard on Kol Israel. There are those who go further and foresee that following instructional television there will be entertainment television, which many fear . . . and object to.[19]

Yet several potential viewers and commentators wrote to advocate a commercial service, especially after a series of articles made public the probable cost of television to Israelis. The cost of a set was estimated, after taxes, at close to 1,500 lira (about five hundred dollars), and many commentators warned that after the Rothschild experiment ended, educational television would surely have to be supported by more taxes. One letter to the editor argued that the idea of "quality educational programs" might be beneficial, but few viewers would tune in, especially if required to pay for the privilege through receiver and program taxes. For many letter writers, television was a mark of progress; moreover, as many noted, it commanded public interest well beyond the narrow confines of the classroom:

We cannot stop television from coming to our country, just as it was impossible . . . to stop the growing number of private cars. A person who wants to study and be educated has plenty of opportunities, and much cheaper ones than purchasing a set for 2,000 Lira. A person who can afford such a sum wants to be entertained, not educated. I am sure that there are many commercial interests that want to invest their money in television. . . . Let them. If the programs are no good, the audience will continue to tune in to Arab programming, or to better programming, at any rate. No public money will be lost.[20]

In an article about opposition to television among schoolteachers, a Tel Aviv principal stood out by endorsing both educational and entertainment programming, employing the same metaphor of modernity: "I am for educational television, instructional television, and entertainment television. . . . Am I for or against private cars? I am for cars and against reckless drivers. I am for television and against reckless television. To broadcast cowboy movies on television is, in my opinion, reckless television. We shouldn't dismiss television because in the United States they use it for ill."[21]

A similar proentertainment position was expressed in the weekly *Al-Hamishmar* by a commentator who insisted that entertainment television had its own advantages and could be used for Israel's benefit: "[F]or disseminating knowledge and culture, . . . entertainment is not necessarily anticultural. The face of Israeli general television could definitely be shaped to our needs and cultural and social mission. Films? Why not? But artistic, scientific, and documentary; . . . Westerns, sex films, and suspense we shall leave for the movie theaters."[22]

Another writer observed that Israelis who already owned television sets, or those who listened to the popular and commercially supported Light Wave on Kol Israel, had grown to regard the occasional commercial as the price of entertainment. Such a price, he argued, would be much cheaper than the taxes the government would have to levy to support a general service. This letter is unique in its complete disregard for "proper standards" and its wholehearted endorsement of both public taste and Arab television.

It is clear to me that a station broadcasting two hours of educational programs, and remaining silent the rest of the day does not cover its expenses. Therefore, it is my opinion that we should establish a general television service, from which educational programming to schools will be broadcast, among other programs. For almost a year, I've been following Arab broadcasts, especially two commercial channels from Beirut that have no support from the government. About 30% of programs are educational and the commercials are much fewer than on "Light wave" of Kol Israel. . . . Most people . . . are not bothered by the commercials, as long as the programs are good; . . . more commercials, less taxes, this is also a good rule for Israeli television.

The author went on to suggest that television should be turned over to commercial investors. Further, a public committee "that will really represent all segments of the public" should be appointed to supervise general programming and keep it "representative of the public's will." Public institutions, he observed, and not the public itself, often decided on programming on Israeli radio. "As long as programming does not satisfy the will of the people, Israelis will keep watching Arab programming."[23]

Such a letter may well have struck fear in the hearts of legislators since it focused so precisely on the very aspects of television so many had worked so hard to expunge from the discussion. In direct opposition to the narrowcasting and "uplifting" function of the envisioned service, the letter highlighted the broadcasting quality of the medium, backed up by the threatening specter of Arab programming as an alternative choice. Similarly, a *Yediot Ahronot* commentator opined that educational television would surely be a failure; instead, Israelis should embrace television's true purpose, entertainment, and accept it as another aspect of technological progress.[24]

"There's no ignoring the developments taking place in this field all over the world," a film distributor reluctantly admitted in an interview; "it is impossible that they will pass over Israel."[25]

Yet acquiescence was far from an endorsement. "Should we bring this trouble on ourselves, or should we avoid, delay, and save ourselves?" asked one Knesset member, while an influential columnist pointed out that introducing popular television into Israel might hurt the Jewish nation's image and fundraising efforts: "How can we turn to Jewish and non-Jewish sources all over the world, and ask that they help sustain the State of Israel, when the State of Israel is busy providing amusements and entertainment . . . for its citizenry?"[26]

Slow, repetitive, and hesitant, the debate dragged on, as Knesset members examined the question of television (educational and other) through the lenses of integration, cultural unity, education, ideological deterioration, and Arab-Israeli relations, pondering a broadcasting system that would be equal to but no greater than Israel's most pressing problems.

A MOST SUITABLE TECHNOLOGY:
THE FINAL DEBATE ON EDUCATIONAL TELEVISION

What is worthy in this instrument is the ability to create bridges and acquaint different groups, different societies and areas. . . . To exchange opinions and contact one another, to be seen truthfully by them and form a connection—across walls, be they of stone or rhetoric . . . or propaganda—between human beings that are open and searching, with all their human ability, for the better and for enlightenment.[27]

Don't tell me that after three years of experiments, if it doesn't work, they'll come and remove all the antennae and receivers.[28]

Despite television's gathering momentum, resistance within the Knesset remained more solid than anticipated: A late-November motion that sought to stop the Knesset-wide discussion and establish a special television committee failed, and in a close twenty-nine to thirty-five result, a Knesset majority voted against the implementation of the Rothschild plan. Although some newspapers celebrated the "anti-television majority in the Knesset," the vote did not actually signal the defeat of the television offer, but it did prolong the initial deliberation phase by keeping the offer on the Knesset floor.[29] But on December 30, 1962, in a swift maneuver that circumvented a Knesset-wide discussion, the government cabinet sidestepped the earlier vote by approving a different version of the Rothschild proposal. As the decision spelled out: "The license granted to the Rothschild project is non-renewable. After a period of experimental, educational operation, if it is decided to continue with television broadcasts, television will turn into a municipal body, part of the Broadcasting Authority—for radio and television."[30] This statement, geared to mollify the swelling hostilities between Kol Israel and Rothschild supporters, incensed television opponents, who saw the government's unilateral skirting of procedures as proof of sinister intent, and left Rothschild representatives fuming over the change. In effect, the decision had artificially shifted the terms of the debate, forcing the Knesset to reexamine the issue as a proposal for a mere "test."

In its three-year passage through the mill of political and public debate, television had gone from an inconceivable luxury to a national necessity, from an object of government dismissal and public derision to a politically volatile possibility that bitterly divided the Knesset. As 1962 drew to close, television proponents readied for the final debate that would cement the future of educational television in Israel, but one central point of contention was now settled. Television would be part of the Israeli Broadcasting Authority, and that budding agency would be independent of direct government control. Thus, a surreptitious, messy, and contentious government decision spelled out the birth of Israeli public broadcasting.

On January 1, 1963, in a period characterized by complex and often contradictory notions about television, when the debate thickened with rumors of governmental backroom dealings, Abba Eban took the

Knesset floor to deliver the longest and most impassioned protelevision speech in Israeli history. Despite its ultimate failure to win enough converts, the speech is important not only for its timing, but also for its attempt to weave together the dispersed and multiplying discourses around the television question. In its endeavor to meld what was ultimately irreconcilable within the television debate, Eban's speech provides a telling encapsulation of the kinds of contradictions and assumptions that nevertheless propelled the television discourse forward, oscillating between Amkor's early global cornucopia and Rothschild's narrowcast educational model.

Eban began by addressing the prevailing fear that a vote for Rothschild's proposal was in actuality a vote for general television. "The Knesset is not asked to decide or make up its mind about introducing general television in our country. . . . The only question up for discussion now is: Is there any chance that this technology can advance us towards improving and raising our instruction standards; . . . does the condition of education allow us to miss this opportunity and not put this thing to the test?"[31]

Here Eban did his best to both distance the project from general television and make the experimental phase of Rothschild's plan seem paradoxically less significant, insisting that no one is "less interested than Rothschild in television and more interested in education." To disassociate the proposal at hand from general television, Eban's opening argument positioned Rothschild's plan as an educational technology, *not* a media system, and sought to isolate most of the objections and fears that swirled over television's "social and cultural" effects.

Maintaining that "there is argument over the spiritual and moral influence of *entertainment* television, not television in total" (664, emphasis mine), Eban attempted to reposition television and distinguish it from mass entertainment or even from a necessarily public medium. In stressing the magnitude of such distinctions, the minister suggested that his opponents harbored the misguided logic of technological determinism, and he admonished Knesset members for displacing their anxiety over general entertainment television onto the education plan—mistaking the technological qualities these systems happened to share for a predetermined path of maturation.

However, much of the infectious enthusiasm in the minister's speech stemmed exactly from this "displacement," as Eban proceeded to locate television technology firmly within a grand singular history of technological developments, beginning with the industrial revolution and on a par with innovations such as the steam engine, the car, and the airplane. Emphasizing the transformative power of such developments

and their ability to "unite humanity and advance equality," Eban compared television's opponents to Luddites and doomsday prophets. He
continued in a rousing call that characterized television technology simultaneously as inevitable progress and utopian opportunity: "Awesome
historic forces are at work today whose final achievement could be the
unity of all mankind, granting equality of access to all reserves of spirit
and matter. . . . The brilliant research that made possible this visual communication across distances, it too is part of the revolution of technological development in our time, and we would sin against the truth if we
reduce this revolution to petty details about the poverty of a given unsuccessful film or questionable entertainment" (660).

Eban stressed caution against technological determinism in the
early part of his speech, yet he slipped easily into just such a model of
transformation only moments later, pressing his audience to recognize
that television has rapidly become a central technology to human development. Similarly, in his attempt to frame television positively,
Eban struggled with the same discursive contradiction that plagued Kol
Israel's argument about the "origins" of television. Both positions appeared caught in a proverbial nature/culture debate as television was
described both as an "open" technology that easily facilitates choices
and control over its operation, and as a "predetermined" technology
that naturally evolves to ends that can be only delayed, not avoided.
Thus television was the product both of inevitable movements of time
and history—"awesome historical forces"—and of individual discovery
and mastery of "brilliant research," combining to produce a "truth"
whose denial was tantamount to "sin."

The "open" technology premise allowed Eban to frame television
as a classroom aid and ask: "Because someone in America shows stories
of murder, should we not show physics or literature lessons?" Simultaneously, the "natural-evolution" model conjured up a global gateway
that would "open the gates of the world" (663) and enabled the minister to accuse the Knesset of irresponsible stewardship: "At some point,
the Knesset will have to decide . . . if we have the authority to impose a
level of isolation on the Israeli from the world, its sites and its experiences" (660–663).

The "nature" of television was not the only area to produce such
rhetorical contortions. Eban's argument stressed Israel's unique educational situation, a particularity of circumstances that would benefit
from (and indeed required) the special solution of Rothschild's classroom television. Yet along with a national focus that highlighted Israel's special needs was an appeal for modernity and Western parity.
Here, television would bring Israel closer to the "developed" industrial

nations it aspired to resemble. "At [this] rate of development . . . there will be no country, among those where education is advanced, where there will not be systematic and widespread use of educational television. . . . Then Israel will have to decide whether it wants to be the only state that turned its back to the educational possibilities of this technology. . . . Why should only a child in California, Paris or London get to see a biological experiment performed by experts along with a good . . . explanation? . . . Why not a child in Israel?" (660–663).

Despite his initial attempt to preempt any mention of general television, the minister's most stirring comments imagined television in a global and all-inclusive incarnation. Eban invoked small and distant towns in America, Europe, and Asia who all watched the first U.S. trip to outer space, painting television as an instrument of equality, global unity, and national identity, and endowing it with the contradictory power to integrate and differentiate its viewers. This television utopia left the student and the classroom far behind as the transformative force of broadcasting moved outward to the community, the nation, and the world:

> Destroying the difference that accumulated for generations, between the experience of the city- and country-dweller . . . citizens can see the goings-on in the wide world, the views and scenery of other countries, the great men that shape their generation, and through this, the very essence of the term citizenship. In this process, we turn our gaze today to the possibilities of this technology for education and culture. . . . Elements that were, until now, concentrated in the hands of a small, urban elite in every country, can now penetrate every village and small town. This is the great social significance of this communication technology. After all these generations, there is for the first time human dialogue beyond national partitions, a worldwide dialogue. (661)

Eban's vision of global fraternity within national specificity again points to the kind of embedded, productive contradiction that structured much of the protelevision rhetoric of the period, just as it echoed the ecstatic visions of global contact that accompanied technological developments from wireless radio to the Internet. Television was both unstoppable and controllable, its deployment targeted and general, its benefits global and particularly suited to Israel; its impact would advance citizenship and national distinction while promoting universal harmony and equality.

Of course, such a flexible, world-spanning informational service bore little resemblance to the limited, classroom-based educational programming proposed by Rothschild. Yet Eban's speech seemed designed to infect his listless audience with the exhilaration of the technology's global promise, to extol its national potential, and to attach the label of "backward, antidemocratic isolationist" to television's opposition.

Even through Eban's speech, television could not, apparently, be enclosed within classroom walls. And despite his early assurances that discussions of "social and cultural problems" or "general television" were beyond the scope of the offer on hand, Eban's eager slippage toward television's global dimensions and wide appeal spoke to the very difficulty of containing what such utopian telespeculations forecasted. Earlier attempts to eschew a broad discussion of culture notwithstanding, the minister's last argument targeted Israeli cultural enhancement—an issue of particular resonance for both proponents and opponents of television. His argument here again placed cultural uplift in the context of television's global reach and innate egalitarian nature. Speaking of television's ability to widely disseminate cultural products that were once the province of a cultural elite, Eban proclaimed that "for the first time . . . culture is becoming a democratic, mass possession" (661).

However, it was precisely this "mass" quality of television that so alarmed its opponents. Using Eban's own example of a Molière play— seen on French television by more people than had ever read it—Knesset member Emma Telmi interrupted to ask, "If a great work of Jewish literature can be shown on television in two hours, who would devote six days to the book?"[32]

Whereas after Eban's speech, newspapers in January proclaimed the sure coming of television as an easy victory for the administration, by February, speculations were not as surefooted. "Television Is Thrown into Doubt," reported *Ha'aretz* in a front-page story. Covering the Knesset debate and the strong opposition to the educational TV proposal, the article concluded that "the scrapping of the agreement with Rothschild is possible" and cited tensions over control and unyielding opposition within the Knesset's religious bloc.[33]

When Eban commanded the Knesset floor again in March, he took new pains to restrict his description of television to its educational parameters and classroom application (avoiding news, leisure, and domestic use and assuring the religious bloc of strict government control over content), to stress the alarm over Arab programming (and their growing popularity in Israeli households), and to avoid the florid appeals to the global imagination that had characterized his previous effort.[34] This succinct approach may not have won over the most resolute opponents, but it moved just enough among the undecided and the capricious to score a firm victory for the Rothschild plan. With a majority of fifty-five to forty-four, educational television was finally approved.

This strategy succeeded in gaining approval for the service, yet, in the process, much of the original reasoning for instituting television was gradually effaced from the proposal. Whereas the Rothschild-financed service would target children (particularly immigrant and poor children) with basic courses of schoolroom instruction, the original arguments that galvanized the protelevision movement were concerned less with children per se than with a specific "other"—Eastern immigrants and Arabs. Although these two groups were finally absent from educational television's address, the two issues—cultural integration and a proper response to consumption of Arab programs—persisted to dominate discussions over television throughout the early and mid-1960s. In a country where no Israeli-born child had yet reached adulthood and adults were all potential soldiers, internal unity and external differentiation were still at the core of Israeli identity.

As it entered the age of television, Israel's Ben-Gurion era was coming to an end. The Old Man, Israel's most revered leader and its only prime minister to date, was now embittered and besieged by controversy in the fallout of the Lavon affair. By the summer of 1963, Israeli politics had experienced a momentous upheaval, suspending all other developments: Ben-Gurion's leadership of the Mapai Party, already weakened by the scandal and the disappointing election results, was faltering, even as internal tensions left the party in turmoil.[35] Amid lingering accusations and a widening rift between Ben-Gurion's "New Guard" and Labor veterans, the Old Man stepped down as prime minister in June 1963, formally resigning from the party he had formed; he retired (temporarily) to his desert home in Kibbutz Sde-Boker.[36] With Ben-Gurion's departure, and the rise of his successor—former minister of the treasury Levi Eshkol—Israel had gone through an important transition; the "pioneer" era was over. For television history, the Old Man's departure meant television had lost a most formidable opponent.

Following the passage of the educational-television plan and the political shakeup that followed, the television question temporarily receded from headlines and public discussion.[37] The problem-solution model, used so efficiently in the conjoined discourses of education and culture, may have produced Rothschild's educational television, yet the troublesome reality of home receivers and Arab programming remained unaddressed and vexing to officials. The repressed notion of a "general service" returned—just as its opponents had predicted—but this time, the nudge came from the prime minister himself.

The first indication of Eshkol's interest in television appeared in a 1964 letter from Kol Israel director Hannoch Givton to Nahum Shamir, the Israeli consulate in New York. In it, Givton referred to the prime minister's intent to propose in the Knesset the creation of general Israeli television. He requested that Shamir keep an eye out for venues that would enable the education of personnel in television matters, and for local Jewry who might be willing to fund the project. A series of meetings with CBS soon followed.[38] Already involved with television in Latin America, CBS saw this as a way to win favor among the U.S. Jewish population and a chance to rival ABC and NBC, who competed in the development of television in the Arab world. Sketchy news reports that Israeli representatives and CBS president William Paley were discussing a CBS donation to a newly planned television center in Jerusalem led to a brief flare-up of press speculation over the government's actual agenda regarding television. A general-television frenzy fed conspiracy theorists of all stripes. Some accused the administration of secretly selling the Israeli airwaves to a commercial U.S. network, and an internal Knesset rumor had Israel's military establishing its own television station in tandem with its radio service.[39]

"Little by little, Kol Israel personnel made their way, some to Europe and some to America, to observe this medium called television, to study its problems and its operation," wrote one *Ma'ariv* reporter. "They traveled secretly, even before the prime minister made his definitive hint."[40]

The "hint" came in early 1965, when Eshkol wrote a letter to several Knesset members, urging the resumption of a serious discussion on the question: "Each passing hour proves our reluctance to deal with the issue of television. We ignore what is going on around us, we ignore the power of this instrument in internal and external matters."[41]

For Eshkol, television's potential to address Israel's "internal and external" problems appeared a paramount benefit.[42] "We cannot ignore television and the necessity of instituting it," he wrote, suggesting that the service would primarily feature news and documentary programs, and assuring anxious members that he did not intend to use television as a political tool in the upcoming election.[43] "It is my intention," concluded the prime minister, "to shortly raise the question of a general television service in front of the government."[44] Eshkol's letter was further significant due to its precise timing; it arrived only three days before the Knesset ratified the IBA law making Kol Israel a municipal agency and removing it from the supervision of the prime minister's office.

THE IBA LAW AND ITS TELEVISION FOUNDATION

> The Israeli tendency to disperse the vote among several parties un-
> derlies an inherent distrust of power and suspicion of authority. The
> shadow of nineteenth-century Eastern Europe still colors the Israeli
> political culture. This government of consensus is attained only at the
> cost of decisiveness.[45]

The initial IBA proposal came on the heels of the Lavon affair but was
the culmination of more than a decade of criticism about government
control of Kol Israel. The proposal was meant to create a public agency
with full responsibility over broadcasting content, and while the mention of television was expunged from the law shortly before its passage,
television's possible introduction remained an issue in the subsequent
Knesset discussions and surely guided the drafting of the law. Running
in parallel, the Knesset debates over radio's independence and over
television's introduction informed each other, as Knesset members repeatedly struggled with issues of control and ownership.

When the IBA law finally emerged in March 1965, it was a serpen-
tine document that described a complex and cumbersome structure
that seemed intent on evading a single clear hierarchy. The authority
consisted of a thirty-one-member plenum led by a chair and a deputy
chair; a five-member executive board selected from within the plenum;
and a managing committee made up of the chair, deputy chair, and the
executive board. Aside from the plenum, a general director would be
appointed to implement the decisions of the managing committee and
the board—yet would not directly preside over either.

Throughout the debates over the status of Kol Israel, the BBC
model of public broadcasting was held up as an example for Israel. Particularly, it was depicted as a "third way" between the antidemocratic
model of direct government supervision and the irresponsible and dangerous U.S.-style model of commercial ownership. A BBC-like structure,
it was argued, would allow the radio service to maintain proper cultural
standards as it achieved editorial independence.

In the presentation of the draft to the press, government officials
were quick to compare the proposal to the BBC and to point out that
the Israeli model provided more freedom and less direct government
control.[46] However, the Israeli plan endowed the government with the
authority to appoint the committee chair and deputy and gave it significant influence in the selection of the plenum, the appointment of
the director general, the allocation of funds, and the resolution of internal disputes. Further, whereas the primary purpose of the law—and

indeed the impetus for its drafting—was the prevention of direct government interference in broadcasting matters, special "emergency provisions" stipulated: "The government was permitted, whenever it sees
the need due to military necessity or under the force of other emergency conditions, to suspend the agency's authority by this law or limit
it, for a period under the government's discretion."[47]

Eddie Soffer has argued that the top-heavy, committee-laden structure was typical of the Israeli political style—drawn from the socialist
tradition of consensus building and developed through the age-old political structure of autonomous shtetles in eastern Europe.[48] Soffer's
analysis certainly explains the broader Israeli political structure of
strategic coalitions and negotiation, but the IBA structure also produced a system whose independence depended on absolute agreement
among its thirty-one members. According to the law, and due to the
absence of a decisive internal authority, a disagreement among the
members empowered the government—even, in some cases, the prime
minister—to directly intervene to resolve disputes. Further, the government's active involvement in the selection process of plenum members
ensured that the agency would always include a significant number of
members sympathetic to the administration's interests. Remarkably,
the IBA quickly emerged as a controversial agency that often criticized
government actions and repeatedly came under its fire—as we shall see
in the final two chapters. Yet such clashes occurred not due to the IBA
structure, but despite it.

Following the initial implication of broadcasting in the cultural-
integration process (a rhetorical link that, as I've argued in previous
chapters, gave life to the problem-solution model of broadcasting),
much of the ideological role for the IBA was depicted in terms of its capacity to educate immigrants and to promote a unified national culture. In defining the service as a cultural link to Jewish identity,
architects of the IBA law echoed the conceptual understandings of
"uniquely Jewish" broadcasting that characterized contemporary discussions of television. Moshe Oneh, chair of the legal committee in
charge of writing the broadcast law, expressed these objectives: "What
we need the broadcast service to do is to help deepen our roots. What
we are missing is a continuum of Jewish culture. This danger exists because we've been torn from our origins. . . . What we need is that our
culture not be detached, not be without roots and without ties to the
Jewish People's rich past. This must be emphasized."[49]

Whereas the IBA's embattled formation from its radio origins is not
a central narrative in my account (in fact, its intricate history has been
much truncated here), it is nonetheless important to note the degree to

which earlier imaginings of television have left their markings on current articulations of the service. The very parameters within which the public service was now drawn and the goals inscribed into its establishment bear a striking resemblance to the categorical definitions that brought the possibilities of television into the light. In tandem with these goals—the ideological linkage between cultural unity, immigrant integration, and the discourse of education (and likely spurred by Rothschild's reimagining of television as a classroom technology)—the committee turned to the law of state education as the guiding blueprint for the IBA's mission. The 1953 state education law defined the goals of national education as: "To establish basic education in the state based on the values of Israeli culture, scientific achievement, love of the homeland, and loyalty to the state and people of Israel, on faith in the work of the land and labor, on pioneer training, and on the aspiration for a society built upon freedom, equality, tolerance, mutual help and love of all creatures."[50]

Similarly, the IBA law specified that the IBA would "further the aims of the State Education Law" as it fulfilled its function to "broadcast educational, entertainment and informational programs in the fields of politics, social life, economics, culture, science and art."[51] These programs, according to section 3 of the IBA law, were geared toward a specific set of national goals: "(1) Reflecting the life, struggle, creative effort and achievement of the state; (2) fostering good citizenship; (3) strengthening the ties with, and deepening knowledge of, the Jewish heritage and its values; (4) reflecting the life and cultural assets of all sections of peoples from different countries; (5) broadening education and dissemination of knowledge; and (6) reflecting the life of Diaspora Jewry."[52]

In addition to targeting an Israeli population and promoting Hebrew and original Israeli work, the law stipulated broadcasts to the Jewish Diaspora and to foreign countries, and made specific provisions for an "Arabic-speaking population and broadcasts for the promotion of understanding and peace with the neighboring states in accordance with the basic tenets of the State."[53]

As such stipulations of content and address made clear, the radio service was envisioned to perform a vital role in Israeli national life, as its capacity to entertain, inform, educate, and self-represent was directed toward specific national objectives. In the IBA law, specific functions defined the broadcasting agency's purpose: Reflecting and representing state life, Jewish heritage, and Israeli cultural assets; promoting good citizenship; disseminating knowledge and education; and addressing the Jewish Diaspora. The collective priorities these

principles embodied were conceived not just as positive effects of a national broadcasting system, but as the service's sole reason for operation. The principles that anchored such a goal-driven national service
would play a pivotal role in defining, in even narrower terms, the function of a so-called general television.

In a government announcement on March 17, Hannoch Givton
was officially named head of the Israeli Broadcasting Authority. As if to
reinforce a certain government ambivalence, however, the IBA law stipulated that Givton's appointment would be reevaluated upon the introduction of television. Nonetheless, television quickly became a
priority for the newly created national broadcasting agency, as Givton
moved to solidify the IBA's role in an eventual television service. Kol Israel technicians were sent, with Eshkol's encouragement, to the United
States, France, and Britain to train in television broadcasting, and, as if
auditioning for its future role, the IBA coproduced a television film
with Italy about Masada. Ironically, the mythic tale of Jewish sacrifice
and perseverance in the face of Roman military might was screened
only in Italy—the Israelis would wait five more years for television.

THE "BIG HINT"

In early 1965, reports of Prime Minister Eshkol's interest in general television appeared side by side with news that the U.S. *Ranger* spacecraft
would attempt a live television broadcast from the moon. Just as the
1962 news of Israeli television experiments shared the newspaper page
with accounts of U.S. satellite broadcasts to Europe, the question of local broadcasting—anchored as it was in national unification and insular concerns of external contamination—once again rubbed up against
a global television universe, a worldwide technology that cheerfully de-
fied the limits of time and distance. Television, Eshkol told the Knesset
a few months later, "has ceased to be an innovation in the big world;
. . . we are not free to ignore this important instrument of national,
public communication."[54]

For Eshkol, educational television had done little to address primary national concerns of "integration and forging a nation." Remarkably, Rothschild's intervention, the prolonged argument that followed,
and the final introduction of the cautious classroom service had neither transformed nor redirected the logic that structured the preexisting general-television debate. "We are facing the task of immigrant
integration," Eshkol continued; "for our country, television means
bringing cultural life to all areas. From this aspect, it would be instrumental in unifying the population" (1936).

For the first time, a prominent government official had explicitly called for the institution of general television in Israel, a call that all but ignored the educational goals prescribed for the Rothschild plan in favor of a national service, motivated by a practical reality and the problem of control. And it was all so familiar: "The existence of many television receivers in the land set to receive programming from neighboring countries instructs us on the severity of the problem, and, it seems to me, pre-empts an argument. Television already exists in Israel, only it does not operate from our center and with our broadcasts" (1936).

With this highest-level endorsement, a foreign committee was invited again to investigate, this time from the European Union of Broadcasters, of which the IBA was a member. In June 1965, the union's three representatives—from France, Italy, and Sweden—submitted their findings to the government, reaching practically identical conclusions to those in the Cassirer Report nearly four years earlier. Again, immigrant integration and hostile neighbors gave shape and rationale to the Israeli television project.

On July 17, 1965, the governing coalition, led by Levi Eshkol and his deputy, Abba Eban, announced that it "sees in a favorable light the creation of a general TV service as a municipal service, part of the Broadcasting Authority."[55] The declaration certainly appeared dramatic and decisive, but it lacked any practical authority (or commitment, as the IBA well knew) since, according to the original Rothschild proposal agreement, the question of general television had to be put to a Knesset vote. Moreover, the appearance of unity among coalition members on the subject of general television was itself illusory; even within Eshkol's cabinet, the television debate raged on, as religious MKs and Labor Minister Ygaal Alon led the offensive against Eshkol, Eban, and other television proponents.

However, the coalition government's outwardly favorable view of general television triggered widespread sentiment in the press and the communications industry that general television was almost a fait accompli. By the summer of 1965, a general domestic television service appeared certain and close, enjoying the support of many government officials and a begrudging acceptance on the part of the press. For the newly formed IBA and journalists observing the progress toward educational television, preparations for a general service had all but begun. Describing the construction of the educational-television studios in Ramat Aviv, one reporter was quick to note how easily convertible the facilities were to general domestic broadcasting: "Educational or general television . . . are the same thing. The studios being built at Ramat Aviv could [also] be used to broadcast general television programs; . . . it is possible to build two additional studios here and turn the facility to a broadcasting center on a broader scale."[56]

However, pervasive incongruity between a persistent opposition to general television and an undercurrent of expectation for its imminent institution had come to characterize reporting on the issue. Commenting on this disparity, one journalist observed: "The argument in the government on the advisability . . . of instituting television in Israel and the practical preparation for its introduction continue on two completely different planes. Words are disconnected from actions."[57]

Following the European Union of Broadcasters report, the projections about television had changed somewhat to include a heavy emphasis on journalism and news gathering. Yet, the accent remained on education and on cultural standards of quality—partly in accordance with the problem-solution model and partly due to the prevailing assumption that general television would grow directly from educational television after the initial two-year contract with Rothschild expired.

The detailed Union of Broadcasters report gave substance to the abstract idea of an Israeli national television service, which for the first time would be designed with the average Israeli viewer in mind. "Practically, the [European] experts presented us with television on paper, drawn in plain lines," reported *Ma'ariv*. According to the plan, Israelis could already anticipate "with minimum changes" what general television would look like:

> Television would not be commercial but instituted on a municipal basis, and would not broadcast in color, but in black and white. When it is established, we would be able to view a variety of programs, for two hours each evening, and an additional 25 minutes in the late afternoon devoted to Hebrew lessons and programs for children. Programming will not consist of the broadcasting of movie-features, as is the practice of Arab stations, but of educational and musical programs. A news broadcast, that would bring images and updates of daily events in the nation and the world, will run for 20 minutes. Television will program many documentaries and would occasionally broadcast theater shows directly from the playhouses of Tel Aviv or Jerusalem, as well as sport events of national and international importance. . . . There will be no shortage of programs such as "around the world" and "journalists on the events of the day," as well as agricultural programs and, of course, entertainment.

The mention of entertainment, albeit at the bottom of the programming list, was directly followed by careful qualification. Such entertainment programs, the article went on to say, would be entirely based on acclaimed local talent and "the strengths that currently exist in Israel." As in past mentions of culture or popular entertainment, the notion of standards compulsively and predictably followed: "'The challenge,' explained . . . Hannoch Givton, 'would be not in the hours of broadcasts but in its quality. We must achieve high quality from the first broadcast.'"[58]

For one *Ma'ariv* columnist, the fight against television, an instrument which was "worse, much worse than radio" in its potentially corrupting influence, was practically over, yet the question of quality now united all participants in the argument: "Even if the public debate over television continues, . . . we must change the basis of that debate. The question that must occupy the public, and especially the educators, writers, artists, and journalists is: what kind of television will we have? If the institution of a general television can, it seems, no longer be prevented, the institution of bad, boring, cheap, and anti-educational television is still preventable."[59]

Along with the emphasis on quality, the issue of Arab-language programming was also widely discussed, with some speculation that Arab production facilities would be made available along with the dominant Hebrew ones. By contrast, the European experts' report viewed such "specialty" programming as too costly and recommended instead dual-language alternatives such as subtitles or even multiple audio tracks to accompany all programming.[60] In the summer of 1965, the idea that Israeli broadcasts would be available with an Arab soundtrack seemed a sensible solution to many commentators. This approach appeared to fulfill two needs at once: to provide programming for Israel's Arabic-speaking residents (both Jewish and Arab) and to communicate—however tacitly—with Israel's neighbors.

The vote in favor of educational television and Eshkol's open endorsement of a general service no doubt softened the somewhat harsh notion of television as a counter-propaganda machine. It did so primarily by explicitly making mention of entertainment and information in its projected content, and by actually including the mass Israeli public among its prospective viewers. This roomier, popular model of television captured the public imagination but left many officials cold.[61] For the time being, reported the daily *Yediot Ahronot,* whether through specialty service or through the dual-language track recommendation, the government was resolute that Israeli television broadcasts be received in Arab countries.[62]

Following a protelevision decision in a contentious coalition meeting, Eshkol attempted to hasten a general vote on the subject yet met with Knesset-wide protests and delays. Rothschild's plan, with its wholesome promise of education and government supervision, was far enough removed from "empty" entertainment to allow some Knesset members to grudgingly let it pass—despite apprehension that educational programming would increase television sales, expose more Israelis to Arab programming, and pave the way for entertainment television. Earlier warnings of the "slippery slope" of television had proven more relevant than ever as anger and suspicion at the coalition's motives mixed with indecision about television itself and its possible impact on Israel. Whereas integration and Arab broadcasts still motivated the debate—fortified by the European committee's recent conclusions—many were unconvinced by the conclusion that general television was the ready-made solution.

For Abba Eban, however, general television was better equipped to address just those cultural and political problems. Reinvigorated by high-level support, the former education and culture minister resumed his role as television's fiery advocate, arguing that general television could unify Israeli society and bring culture to remote areas. As for Arab programming, Eban added, "instead of Arab penetration into Israel through television, we would penetrate the eyes and hearts of the Arab world."[63]

The use of such loaded war metaphors to portray Arab infiltration into Israel through television was carefully one-sided, in contrast to Israel's honorable attempts at explanation, communication, and, most important, representation. Whereas Arab broadcasts into Israel were most often characterized as politically aggressive and culturally ruinous, Israeli cross-border broadcasts would focus on self-representation (a kind of electronic calling card) rather than propaganda (known by the euphemistic term "explanation"). On its face, such a rhetorical strategy seemed to belie the narrowcasting model of television in favor of a mass broadcasting system that communicated openly to all. However, this approach understood television content as open to international—and hostile—scrutiny, and television as a broadcasting medium that, in every frame, transmitted an image of the nation as a whole. Such a construction, in turn, helped to bolster the original vision of television as a vehicle for delivering a proper sense of Israeli nationhood to those who did not share it—not to mainstream Israelis, for whom such a "correction" was unnecessary.

A handful of distinct and opposing versions of television now presented themselves as possible viable contenders for the Israeli airwaves. First was the educational classroom service already in the implementation stages. However, it was becoming increasingly clear that domestic television was bound to follow, embodying several disparate visions of home broadcasting along with diverse visions of its audience. Still latent was the early "national utility" model, born of integration pressures and anxieties over Arab programming and aimed at specific "problem" populations as viewing subjects. Television's subsequent incarnation expanded to include a news service and claimed a closer kinship with radio, yet (as the continuing tensions with Kol Israel illustrated) still contained the basic tension between television as a mass broadcasting service and television as a government tool of official information. The notion of television's public service was further expanded by Abba Eban, whose vision of television included educational programming for both adults and children in the home setting, cultural programming to integrate immigrant groups, and the creation of strong international links facilitated through shared programming between Israel and the world at large. With Eshkol's support, an imagined Israeli municipal service moved even closer to a mass broadcasting medium by specifically including entertainment and news programming for all Israelis, albeit with stringent supervision regarding "proper standards" and quality.

All the while, U.S. involvement—and reported pressures—in the Israeli television debate easily facilitated an unsettling vision of "American" television: supported by commercials, replete with violent and sexually explicit programming, and appealing only to the lowest, "least cultured" elements of the Israeli populace. These divergent visions of an imagined service, proposed and argued in such a short period of time, did not so much follow each other in rapid succession as coexist, sometimes confluent, sometimes divergent, commingled in a confusing, unsettled grab bag of possibilities.

AT HOME WITH THE RECEIVER

> All over the country, the city and the village are already fed through [television receivers] with rubbish and refuse from our neighboring countries; . . . television as something that represents a status symbol, a show-piece, a fashion, something that everybody wants and is willing to get into debt for, is already here.[64]
>
> "Tens of thousands of antennae . . . all over Israel . . . no longer ask *if* television will come but *when*; . . .and they are right."[65]

The uncertainty and official proclamations about a "purely educational" service did nothing to slow the brisk pace of set acquisition among Israelis. According to *Ma'ariv*, the rate of increase of television homes in Israel was overtaking that of car acquisitions and appeared unrelated to economic status. Set imports had grown dramatically: In

1963 only 2,000 sets were imported into Israel, but in 1964, the number grew to 14,000. In 1965, *Ma'ariv* estimated that between 30,000 and 40,000 sets lurked in Israeli homes and "receive primarily entertainment and propaganda broadcasts from our neighboring states."[66]

The summer of 1965 also saw the first full marketing campaigns for television receivers, as importers forged manufacturing agreements for sets from Europe, the United States, and Japan. Capitalizing on the new excitement about television, the ads also betrayed the uncertainty over future broadcasts, as anticipation of educational television mingled with expectations of an eventual domestic and commercial service.

In one of the earliest ads by the television manufacturer Olympic (see figure 2), a drawing depicts an operating television and its projected audience: A man with his arm around a young boy, presumably a father and son, watching an educational program. Notably, the pair watches in total darkness, the outline of their bodies drawn in white against a dark background and contrasting with the set—the only bright spot in the room. "Educational Television in Your Home!" reads the caption above the Olympic logo.

FIGURE 2. Olympic television advertisement, *Davar*, July 21, 1965. "Educational Television in Your Home!"

FIGURE 3. Olympic television advertisement, *Davar*,
August 18, 1965. The caption reads: "Children's
Films in Your Home!"

As an early entrant into the receiver market, Olympic stayed close to
the official vision of educational television familiar to the Israeli public.
Authority and supervision reassuringly encircle the boy in the advertisement, from the directed exactitude of the tele-teacher's pointer to the approving weight of the paternal arm that hugs him in place. In this first,
cautious ad, the image of television was sober, prescribed, and thoroughly permeated by a "public-good" rendition of domestic instruction.

Olympic's next effort, published in the same paper a mere month
later (see figure 3), had already moved to refine its message from reas-
surance of wholesomeness to enticement of carefree pleasure. This ad
also pictured children as the set's primary audience, yet it softened the
image of stiff attention and educational benefits: This time, the two
viewers are both young boys and the bespectacled teacher and his map
are replaced by a cartoon. In further contrast, the room is no longer
dark and the children exhibit none of the rapt attention implied in the
earlier ad—in fact, they appear animated, in midconversation, dividing
their attention equally between the screen and each other.

Olympic's campaign, while keeping up with quickly evolving perceptions of television's role in the home, remained focused on children
as a primary audience. At the same time, other television companies attempted to attract buyers by using alternative aspects of television's
promise—and by suggesting a different programming emphasis, as well
as a different audience, for their products.

FIGURE 4. Amkor advertisement, *Davar*, July–September 1965.

The Israeli Amkor Company—which pioneered television in Israel in its Easter Fair exhibit in 1962—crafted its campaign for the Nord-Mende receiver by using the image of a classical ballerina to give its focus on cultural and technical quality a double resonance. In the company's ads, which ran in the summer and fall of 1965, the image of the ballerina appeared both as content on the television screen and as a design element on the logo (see figure 4). The caption, exalting the quality of the image and sound, made the culture connection explicit by identifying Amkor as the "prima ballerina" of television receivers.

By contrast, ads for receivers from Ranvit Importers took a minimalist approach that simply accentuated pleasurable, leisurely content: "To See, To Hear, To Enjoy" read the slogan accompanied by a photograph of a receiver—in no particular setting—transmitting a soccer match in midplay.[67] Ranvit's ads eschewed emphasis on the receiver, the technology, or a particular domestic situation. Their ads downplayed all else in favor of programming itself, positioning the (presumably male) reader as a television viewer and providing a vision of would-be popular television that resembled nothing if not Amkor's 1962 popular cornucopia.

The Grundig receiver (advertised through its Israeli importer) took a different tack, emphasizing not programming but the set's sophisticated technology. A series of ads featured close-ups of the receiver's advanced tuner knobs, sketches of its various parts, and photographs of the set (notably with a blank screen). The copy emphasized superior technology, cutting-edge developments, worldwide popularity, and the Grundig set's particular strength in clearly receiving faint and distant signals. Contrasted with Ranvit's promise of easy masculine leisure, Amkor's cultured, feminine quality, or Olympic's child-centered vision of television content, this technology-centered campaign focused on the inner workings of the machine and thus its compatibility with existing viewing conditions—namely, the sole availability of Arab programs. In their appreciative attention to equipment and know-how, Grundig's ads also recalled television's early start by appealing to hobbyists and local "television buffs."

Later ads engaged in literal projection: The Telefunken brand advertised sets that pictured dancing women in twirling skirts—constructing the television screen as a domestic extension of a performance space. The Pilot Company went even further, picturing Israeli entertainers framed within a television set in a simulated future broadcast. By contrast, American Westinghouse receivers suggested a direct link to U.S. programming in their futuristic hail: Under a brief caption advising the reader to "Buy the Best," a television set projected a close-up image of the Statue of Liberty.[68]

It is important to emphasize that all these campaigns appeared before *any* Israeli television service existed and when the only television system in (early) development was educational—designed to supplement instruction in a targeted classroom setting. In this context, each advertisement can be read as its own projection, a selected slice from the wide array of possible forms television could assume (or, more precisely, the one its projected future user would find most appealing). Taken together, the advertisements illustrate the range of options imagined for not only the nature of the content, but also its origin (Israeli, European, Arab, American), its various (although decidedly male) viewing audiences, and the general role of television within the home. At a time when only about thirty-five thousand sets operated in Arab and

Jewish households across Israel, and despite the government's repeated rejection of general programs, television's role as leisure-time, domestic entertainment was acquiring a sense of fait accompli.

Such fantasies of general entertainment television were still the province of the hopeful and the anxious; nonetheless, actual progress was taking place at the educational-television service. As a special committee worked on programming content and technological actualization, it reported that, as a first phase, educational broadcasts would be received in thirty schools spread out across development areas: eighteen elementary municipal schools, two Arab elementary schools, and ten high schools. Early programs would be in the instruction of math, biology, and English (to be followed eventually by lessons in Hebrew and literature) and targeted toward upper-level classes.[69] According to a Kol Israel spokesperson, Israeli radio was cutting back on its educational service in preparation for the introduction of educational television.[70]

Rothschild funds helped build the new Education Television Building, erected on a hill in Ramat Aviv, north of Tel Aviv. The two-story structure—described as "modest" by its architect to "keep proportions appropriate to our small country"—contained two studios, a control room, rehearsal spaces, a makeup and costume room, and an observation bay for visitors.[71] Equipment imported from England was installed with the assistance of BBC advisors, who also helped train the Israeli personnel. In July, auditions were held to select "TV teachers" from a group of 103 candidates ("all required to have academic education, several years of teaching experience, skill, a pleasant outward appearance, and a radiophonic voice").[72] The nine teachers selected were teamed with a scriptwriter, director, and producer to form a "program unit." By late summer, all program teams were undergoing training and anticipating their debut in early 1966.

On January 3, 1966, the Ministry of the Post began the first in a week-long series of experimental broadcasts to test television's technical range.[73] At eleven o'clock in the morning, Israelis whose sets were tuned to channel 8, one of four frequencies allotted to Israel, could make out the postal service's familiar logo, a galloping deer, and hear the "first" (Amkor's experiment all but erased here) Hebrew-language voice ever to emanate from an Israeli television receiver. The official voice-over identified the experimental broadcast and, as the deer image dissolved to a mailing address in Jerusalem, requested that viewers report in writing about the quality of the image and sound.

For the next twenty minutes, viewers watched the first (state-sponsored) images to be broadcast from within Israel: still images of the television relay station, photographs of local wildlife, landscapes, and various scenes of urban and rural life (immigrants arriving at an airport, workers at a factory, and a military parade), accompanied by symphonic music and Israeli folk songs.

Familiar, quotidian, and affable—after all, they were there merely to "test the pipes"—these images nevertheless appeared deliberate and meaningful by their sheer transmission through the airwaves. Israel's connection to the pristine land, its agricultural achievements, its industrial development, its growing immigrant population, and its capable army all were made manifest through the generic images, imbued with restored narrative power. The attention paid to these, in tandem with the preoccupation over the range of broadcasts across Israel's border, only reinforced their implicit role as the state's electronic calling cards. For some, it also substantiated the enemy's gaze: "And so owners of television sets in the old city and Ramallah in Jordan could see broadcasting [from] Israel, view pictures from our land and even discover a 'military secret': One of the photographs from this year's march showed the famous 'Hawk' missile."[74]

For the next few days, postcards and letters streamed in with detailed descriptions of the signal and sound, along with compliments, observations, and queries. Although the address on the screen included no title or office (just a P.O. box in Jerusalem), many Israelis addressed their correspondence to nonexistent titles in an imaginary "Israeli Television Office." Personal comments often accompanied the reception reports. Some wrote about crowds gathering in their apartment to watch the test broadcasts, others commented on the music or the images, and a few wrote in with alternative content suggestions. One viewer even provided such content himself: "We were so happy to see the pictures and music. Two months ago, I threw a Bar Mitzvah party for my two sons and I am sending you some of their pictures. The boys are really asking that you broadcast these; . . . I look forward to seeing them on the television screen."[75]

The test images, especially the photograph of the Jerusalem relay station, quickly became a symbolic promise of a burgeoning television service. Within days of the first test, ads for television receivers that featured a photograph of a set tuned in to the experimental broadcast appeared in national dailies. The English Pilot receiver ads proclaimed: "Television broadcasts have begun in Israel! Buy a receiver now."[76] Other ads featured various receiver models tuned in to staged "entertainment broadcasts," suggesting that such Israeli-produced programs were at hand.

The television set was rapidly shedding its status as a novelty item and fanciful technology and assuming that of an everyday appliance.

Television centers and electronic specialty stores were opening across Israel, and advertising supplements profiled sets in detail and dispensed purchasing advice for the high-profile device. Although the emphasis on future Israeli broadcasts remained in some television ads in early 1966, commercial copy grew more explicit in its acknowledgment that, for the time being, Israelis were watching and enjoying Arab programming. Most purchasing guides reminded the potential buyer to shop for a set in the evening—when most Arab stations took to the air—and to examine the antenna to ensure good reception in all directions: "If placed to the north, for example, the set should receive Beirut, to the south, Cairo, and so on. To fully utilize your antenna, it is advisable to purchase one that allows easy turning to all desired directions."[77]

Israeli set owners were also instructed on proper treatment of the receiver and warned against the Israeli "do-it-yourself" spirit and other maltreatments:

> The television receiver is a complex and fragile instrument that should not be treated as a regular radio receiver. "Home repairs" by various family members are not useful here. More than that, they will only worsen the malfunction and that would mean a higher charge by the technician. Another tip: Avoid excessive handling of the tuning buttons, dials, and the instrument itself. When you turn it on, find the station best suited to you, adjust the brightness, picture and sound, and leave the machine alone. The less you work the dials, the longer the instrument will last.[78]

In the process of cautioning consumers against buying too hastily, one advertiser described a commonly held view about the near future of Israeli television: "After a long period of hesitation, argument, preparation and uncertainty, Israel has finally entered the age of television. The steps are still slow and careful—in the guise of educational television—but it is clear to all that the road leads to regular, commercial television, as is the convention in the world, and already there's talk of color television."[79]

The growing presence of receivers as desirable ordinary objects for everyday use was also suggested by an ad campaign for Perma-Sharp razors. In a published quiz (in which contestants were asked to identify a series of famous bearded personalities—Marx, Lincoln, Zola, and Rodin—whose images were drawn clean shaven), the company offered an RCA Victor television as the first prize along with other everyday items like watches, cameras, and flashlights.[80]

Whereas advertising copy can hardly be taken as a straightforward barometer of public sentiment, such campaigns do suggest a certain entrenchment of television viewing—especially of Arab television—as an acceptable and commonplace leisure activity. In the fantasy universe drawn by advertisers and the future as articulated through public tele-speculation, television offered an array of choices, both Israeli and Arab, Western and Eastern, educational and entertaining. Clearly, commercial Israeli television represented a windfall advertisers and manufacturers eagerly awaited. Yet projections of imminent entertainment programming—and the specific reference to educational television as nothing but a "hesitant step," and finally, a temporary "guise"—undoubtedly resonated with a consuming public, whose sudden increased interest in and purchase of receivers did not stem merely from putative offerings of morning arithmetic lessons.

As the first airing date neared, protelevision commentators continued to press their case: Although a step forward, educational television was distinct from a national television service, and the latter was still lacking. Anticipating the first broadcast, Haim Mass, writing in *Ma'ariv*'s weekend magazine, described the scene of "thousands of people" who, along with students and government officials, would tune in to the "historic broadcast" of the debut of educational television. These domestic viewers, he mused wistfully, "will follow the images . . . with a curiosity mixed with disappointment since this broadcast, and those that would follow it, were not meant for them."[81]

Whether educational television would be the "first step" toward other broadcasts meant for a mass Israeli public, "problem" populations, secular, Jewish, or Arab viewership remained the site of persistent conflict within the government. One paper expressed these known tensions by parodying the recent experimental broadcasts. A large drawing depicted a television set bearing the now familiar message "You are watching an experimental broadcast," yet underneath, the cartoon pictured Abba Eban and a member of the religious party exchanging furious blows in the center of the television screen.[82]

At midday on March 24, 1966, about two hundred distinguished invitees gathered at the Ramat Aviv studio to watch Prime Minister Eshkol and Lord Rothschild usher Israel into the television age with "the push of a button." In sixty designated classrooms across Israel, students and teachers sat transfixed—by a blank screen. The program was due to begin at noon. At 12:15, the sounds of bodies shifting in chairs, book bags opening, and impatient whispers were abruptly silenced as the screen suddenly flickered to life with the single message: "Educational Television Trust—Channel 8." A disembodied voice emerged from the cheerful accompanying music to identify the broadcast as the first for educational television. The message was replaced first by a photograph of the Ramat Aviv studio and then by the beaming face of MK Zalman Aren, minister of education and culture.

"You are privileged to be among the first to enjoy this experimental broadcast," pronounced Aren in a prefilmed statement. "Much labor and great loving care were invested in each lesson and program." In at least one classroom, students impatient with the ceremony began noting the curious effect of the talking head's virtual presence in the classroom. "He's reading from notes," whispered one student. "But looking right at us!" remarked another.[83] Rothschild's brief greeting followed Aren's message, and in sixty predesignated classrooms and a collection of Israeli homes, the first lesson in mathematics—calculating distance—was soon underway.

That television could traverse both geographical and ideological distances to communicate with Israel's Arab neighbors would find new currency shortly. For the time being, most ongoing arguments about general television focused on the availability of Arab programs within Israel, and on their possible preponderance. Eshkol's attempt to expedite general television's introduction, commentators suggested, was motivated by such concerns and some one-upmanship. As *Davar* reported, delaying the process would impede "the race to complete television service between Israel and Jordan."[84]

Quite separate from questions of content, the political implications for Arab-Israeli relations of instituting television crystallized after the European committee had made its recommendations regarding frequencies. One reporter mused that the frequency problem was also a "political problem" and, as such, presented a certain political potential: "It turns out that Israel and the Arab states occupy the same broadcasting frequencies. In order not to maltreat Israeli viewers and Arab viewers at the same time, the sides would need to arrive at a 'ceasefire.' . . . Experts are currently working on preventing the signals' crossing in the future. . . . But in light of our relations with these states, can this be seen as a merely technical question?"[85]

Six months later, as the split-screen belly-dancer cartoon appeared in the pages of *Davar*, this sentiment would seem touchingly naïve. Far from a cease-fire, Israeli broadcasting would once again be drafted into national service—and this time, it was war.

PART TWO

IMAGE AND NATION

Broadcasting in Conflict

CLENCHED FIST AND OPEN PALM

4

The Six Day War, the Combat Radio Formula, and the Launch of General Television

Jerusalem, the only city in the world where even the dead are given voting rights.
—Yehuda Amichai, "Jerusalem" 1967

A place changes in quality according to the facility with which it can be crossed.
—Paul Virilio, *Bunker Archaeology*

As the chapters in part 1 have shown, much of the discussion over television centered not on its address to a common Israeli public but on its targeted application to specific populations deemed potential threats to Israeli unity and security.[1] This preoccupation with security and cross-border communication fueled political interest in television and kept the question of "general" television alive even after the founding of educational television in 1965. In accordance with this targeted imaginary, a favorable official view toward a "general service" would emerge in the context of yet another military conflict. More than any other single event, the Six Day War, fought between June 5 and June 10, 1967, would transform Israel and alter its standing in the region and its image in the eyes of the world, reconfiguring Israeli nationalism as it reshaped its borders.

In the tense period before and during the war, Israel made extensive use of mass media, employing wartime broadcasting strategies that precisely epitomized (and indeed, justified) the three-pronged model of broadcasting it had been nourishing for over a decade. As I show in this chapter, Israel used broadcasting for three distinct audiences in three discrete but now familiar ways: in shaping world public opinion, in presenting a carefully managed internal image, and in communicating with Arab listeners. The war experience and its aftermath solidified official plans for broadcasting and shored up the evolving image of television in the

Israeli political imaginations as a consummate national technology with special allegiances to the state and its supreme concerns.

Security, as Anthony Giddens points out, is at the core of the nation-state and is the structuring substance in the relationship between the state and the individual.[2] No example better illustrates this principle than the Israeli case, where the "security ethos" has so clearly dominated in the very self-definition of the state and its citizenry from its establishment in 1948 to the present tug-of-war between safety and rectitude.

As I will argue in what follows, security concerns—and the media's ability to act on these concerns at a pivotal time in Israeli history—made the establishment of a general television service particularly desirable for official forces. That this preoccupation should prove a galvanizing force in the establishment of television is, in itself, unsurprising, yet what emerges in the process is the degree to which broadcasting discourse helped define and direct particular approaches to national problems while precluding others.

Israeli media attitudes toward the "security ethos," as Yoram Peri recently observed, manifested collective conceptions of citizenship throughout the nation's history.[3] Whereas the contemporary relationship between the military and the Israeli media has been characterized by repeated confrontations and antagonism, broadcasting's early history in fact depended on a bond of sympathetic cooperation.[4] The symbiotic relationship between Israeli radio (the Kol Israel service) and the military during the 1967 Six Day War not only roused the efforts to establish television by giving it a rationale but also blueprinted its use. That this blueprint would prove wholly impracticable laid bare the limits of ideological consensus in the workaday realities of public media.

THE COUNTER-SIGNAL: ISRAEL GALILI
AND HASBARAH-STYLE TELEVISION

> There is no doubt that, in the given reality and present conditions, we must use the same tools as our enemy uses.[5]

> The main reason . . . for Israeli television . . . has nothing to do with either peace or war; . . . television is a measurement of a developed society. A modern society without television cannot be imagined. I think that it is time to get over that complex.[6]

Much of the antitelevision anxiety continued to focus on the Jewish and Arab Israeli families who could watch neighboring enemy broadcasts. These broadcasts, it was feared, would dull Zionist beliefs and extend viewers' affinities beyond the Israeli border. With the educational service fueling record set purchases, anxieties over the penetration of Arab broadcasts into Israeli homes seemed only to grow:

> The age of television began . . . when scores of citizens began watching television from Arab countries—of Alexandria, Cairo and Beirut. . . . The age of television began then but our government's eyes were shielded from seeing where this was leading. . . . We know the number of receivers in Israel. . . . Not only [Arab] minorities who speak Arabic but also sons of this nation, that speak Hebrew, buy receivers. Each night they gather around the instrument and watch the sights from Egypt and other places. Those who don't understand Arabic, they too, watch television.[7]

A number of commentators suggested that the popularity of receivers was merely an indication that Israelis *wanted* television and turned to Arab broadcasts in lieu of domestic programs. "I have no doubt that the owners of these sets, their families, their children, . . . friends and neighbors, all watch, for lack of choice, broadcasts from neighboring countries" a deputy minister reflected, but "this has a very damaging influence, from an educational and cultural standpoint, and also from a national and morale standpoint."[8]

Just as before, opposing poles in the television debate enlisted such fears of Arab telepropaganda and posed them as deterrents (discourage sets to avoid exposure) and incentives (provide counter-programming) respectively. However, emerging converse hopes for television envisioned Israeli messages that transcended those same borders. The result was a parallel discussion of two sets of cross-border viewerships: Israelis watching Arabs, and the reverse, Arab viewers watching Israel. In a new wave of Knesset debates, television's potential was now considered through the prism of self-representation as communication. By the summer of 1966, the argument had gained new purchase: If Arab nations used broadcasting as a propaganda tool, Knesset members argued in a pivotal meeting in June, an Israeli television service would constitute the perfect countermeasure: "The time has come . . . to implement a plan for the founding of television. This must be done at full speed so that the state of Israel will have the most modern instrument in the field of communication and counter influence with the Arab countries."[9] Until now, television was largely perceived as a "national" technology that communicated collectively, yet some Knesset members considered it an especially effective tool for cross-national communication precisely because of its ability to enter domestic, intimate space and address individual viewers directly. For MK Uri Avneri, television was first and foremost a humanizing technology—for both sides:

> I do not agree . . . that it is a great disaster that we see Arab television. I think it's very good . . . that the children of Israel will get used to seeing in every Arab not an enemy and murderer, but flesh and blood—that there are Arab children, Arab women, an Arab society, that they have an inkling of what is going on across the border. . . . But we need an Israeli television as soon as possible, so that Arabs would see us too, so that across the border they see us not only through slogans, articles and speeches, but . . . see Israel with their own eyes, without mediators, the good that is in it, and a little of the bad; let them see women and children, let them get a real sense of the state instead of abstract concepts that are far from reality that exist today across the border: This is an important reason for the creation of Israeli television.[10]

In these new discussions, television functioned as an electronic national calling card that would represent the "real" Israel to its Arab neighbors—both its achievements and its peaceful intentions. Yet the vision of direct—and equal—communication mingled easily with considerations of counter-propaganda and cross-border influence that explicitly posed Israeli programming as culturally superior and naturally more compelling:

> If we had an Israeli broadcast, we could be broadcasting to Arab countries. I read in one of the papers that heads of Arab nations have had a consultation in regards to the question: what would happen if the state of Israel founded a television apparatus that will be pointed towards its neighbors? They spoke of a means to prevent this, to block Israel from broadcasting to these countries. Why would they? Because of the fear that the Israeli service will be of a high standard, it would have something to broadcast about the acts and achievements of the state. It could also conduct effective propaganda in Arab countries towards the peace we want. This apparatus could serve as a propaganda machine of the first order, like it happened all over the world. . . . This is also the most precise answer to the broadcasts that go on non-stop, at a growing rate, in the Arab states.[11]

As this discussion illustrates, the idea that television would serve to extend both national goals and state power emerged as the primary and practically sole role the technology was projected to play. Electronic broadcasting was thus drafted in infancy to embody the ideal of Israeli national identity: Like its people, went the rationale, television would be a peace-loving soldier. Despite disagreements about the precise nature and efficacy of such programming, there seemed to be no fundamental quarrel with a basic and curiously unexamined premise that constructed a foreign, enemy people as the audience for national broadcasting.

Considering the intense interest in Arab public opinion, Israeli self-representation, and instruction through television, it was no coincidence that Israel Galili, the government's would-be "television czar," emerged from the Hasbarah Office (literally "explanation," the official name of the Israeli information and government communication office), where he oversaw matters of immigration information. More than any other government official of his time, Galili would work to reshape the original vision of Israeli television, aiming to direct its creation as a nationalist utility and a propaganda arm. That this midlevel government bureaucrat would quickly establish himself as the television authority in Prime Minister Eshkol's cabinet is significant not because of Galili's political adroitness but because of his unqualified investment in the image of television as a cross-national technology. Similarly, Galili's domineering presence at this stage of television history (and in what follows) is more a symptom of his absolute embodiment of the television model embraced by most government officials than evidence of his single-handed influence on that model. Galili's appointment conformed to the presumption that television, as an apparatus of national address, was a natural extension of Hasbarah (and thus, of propaganda), while his recent experience in targeting new immigrants kept alive the initial preoccupation that set television discussions in motion.

Skilled in the art of public influence, Galili embarked on a campaign to link television with national security as the highest priority for the fledgling state, and to discredit those who would threaten broadcasting's potential by removing television from the sober business of national politics.[12]

Although the government had voted to delay the establishment of television early in 1966, negotiations continued with a clear understanding that TV broadcasting had shifted from a possibility to an eventuality (see chapter 3). Later that year, Israel signed a consulting agreement with the American CBS network to receive much-needed assistance in the preparations for general broadcasting. As was commonplace by the late 1960s, the U.S. company anticipated a reciprocal relationship. In return for programming and technical guidance, foreign television protégées were expected to purchase electronic equipment from the network's parent company (as in the case of NBC and RCA) or, as was CBS's practice in Latin America, neophyte television services would sign a multiyear contract to buy various programming from the networks and their production affiliates. The agreement was particularly ironic since initial opposition to Israeli television— expressed with general vehemence—fixated on the lurid excess and passive materialism of U.S.-style television (see chapter 2) and the pervasive dangers of its influence and reach. Although no records suggest that Israel intended to enter into a long-term agreement with the Americans, it was, for the time being, in sore need of help.

In hastily improvised facilities, Israeli crews were put through the paces of rudimentary production training with little or no suitable equipment. In one such session, would-be camera operators were outfitted with empty cardboard orange crates with lens-shaped holes as practice cameras. Despite the temporary halt to general-television implementation plans and the low-tech conditions production trainees contended with, TV proponents remained optimistic, fortified by the recently signed CBS agreement, the newly operational educational television, and the brisk sales of sets. All augured well for an imminent general service. Politicians publicly speculated about the coming boom for the electronics industry in Israel pending approval of a television service, and newspaper editorials once again alternatively buzzed with excitement and hummed with disdain.

For Galili and fellow proponents of a Hasbarah-style television service, there was still some stage setting left to do before television's grand entrance. Galili began by demoting Hannoch Givton, the outspoken director of the newly established Israeli Broadcast Authority, ensuring that the seasoned journalist would never head the IBA in the television age. As his replacement, Galili appointed an army man, Major General Elad Peled, who at the time headed a military training institute. Peled was now charged with the task of establishing a television service and then assuming leadership of the semi-independent Israeli Broadcasting Authority. The maneuver alarmed many commentators and Knesset members, who charged that Galili meant to reintegrate the public broadcasting agency under government control. Some speculated that he was laying a foundation for a military broadcast system. "What would this army man do that the IBA cannot do itself?" one MK asked on the Knesset floor; others quipped that the exemplary soldier's best broadcasting-related qualification was absolute obedience.[13]

The concern was due not only to Peled's appointment, but also to the cabinet's silence as to why he was chosen. Further, as Peled had not stepped down from his army duties, the entire television project appeared to be falling under military supervision. "The appointment of Major General Peled to take care of television creates grave suspicions about the government's intentions towards the Broadcasting Authority," charged one Knesset member in an impromptu protest during a budget hearing. "Is this appointment an attempt to 'purify the authority' of those workers loyal to its state-public mission? Is [it] a government hint of a new direction for the Broadcasting Authority, turning it . . . to a government agency?"[14]

Yet Galili's appointment of Peled was both politically shrewd and richly symbolic. The decorated army man represented the best of the state; assigning such a distinguished soldier to the television post signaled the serious regard with which the government viewed the new technology. Despite all previous discussions of culture and artistic standards (see chapters 2 and 3), Peled's appointment indicated that broadcasting was foremost an issue of national security, worthy of the practical attention of Israel's finest. To the public, the army was beyond politics, beyond the petty bickering over power, and beyond reproach. Thus, Peled's embodiment of army ethics enabled Galili to cast doubt on the loyalty of those who questioned the selection; he characterized such critiques as "strange" and as betraying "negative attitudes." Challenging opponents to point to a better institution than the army for the development of qualities such as "devotion to the people, the country, national independence, or the state," Galili charged his critics with "diminishing the characters of [Israel's] finest . . . heroes" and warned that "miserable generalization" will lead critics on a "dangerous road." Galili offered no specifics for why he selected Peled, reminding the Knesset that such staffing decisions were "still" within the government's purview. He did, however, reassure his uneasy audience that he intended "to suggest that the government, with the Prime-Minister's approval, include television within the Broadcasting Authority, and we have no intention to expropriate television from its public responsibility and place it in the hands of a government office."[15]

With Givton weakened at the IBA and a military man at its helm, little apprehension remained in Eshkol's cabinet about launching general television; two weeks after Peled's official appointment, the inner cabinet voted eight to five in its favor.[16]

For Galili, there were pressing reasons to institute television, reasons that he saw as its unique calling. In his initial 1966 protelevision address to the Knesset, Galili collected several arguments from earlier reports, presenting a rather standard case for television as the instrument that would "unite the people, [serve] the integration of immigrant groups, improve language knowledge, . . . general knowledge, education and the enrichment of social life."[17] Yet, as relations between Israel and its Arab neighbors worsened in the next few months, Galili moved to propose an "emergency television service" to address these tensions and to raise morale for Arab and Jewish viewers.

A CAREFULLY PLANNED EMERGENCY: GOVERNMENT
TELEVISION AND THE PROBLEM OF PUBLIC MORALE

We hear from our leaders every day, every month, and every year—from the birth of the state until today—that we are in a state of emergency.[18]

The main reason . . . for Israeli television . . . has nothing to do with either peace or war; . . . television is a measurement of a developed society. A modern society without television cannot be imagined. I think that it is time to get over the complex of . . . the head of the government in the previous era.[19]

In retrospect, Givton's replacement with a military professional patently communicated Galili's vision and illustrated the decade-old conflict that characterized so much of the medium's Israeli history. Far from the educational and cultural goals emphasized only a few years earlier, television was now directly associated with national security and Arab-Israeli communication as an official agency of the state. Yet, as I have argued in previous chapters, the current approach was not a radical departure from the first television model proposed in the late 1950s. Galili's areas of influence—immigration and official state information—precisely dovetailed with the concerns of integration and cross-border communication that marked the originating point of the television debate. Galili, however, had taken a more direct route to the heart of the problem, bypassing the concept of culture as a medium through which such changes could be effected and envisioning television as a direct mouthpiece of national priorities. Whereas the realm of culture was posited by Givton and Eban, among others, as a convenient mediating arena where issues of national and ethnic difference would be resolved by representational means, cultural education, and "taste adjustment," Galili required no such refinement or euphemizing; his television model would tackle the growing tensions between Israel and surrounding Arab nations head-on. It seemed only appropriate that such a project would fall under the symbolic leadership of a military figurehead.

Several events had made the period between late 1966 and early 1967 particularly volatile for Israel's relationship with its Arab neighbors. The Palestinian Liberation Organization, formed in 1964, began a series of incursions into Israel from the Gaza Strip and the Sinai. More damaging was the radical Syrian-based Fatah, which inflicted numerous casualties in repeated infiltrations into Israel from the Golan Heights and Jordan. Israeli retaliations, coupled with a continuous conflict with Syria over land and water rights, worsened the tensions, resulting in repeated exchanges of gunfire along Israel's northern border.

In Egypt, the stresses of overwhelming unemployment and financial strain (caused in part by a cutoff of monitary support from the West and the IMF) were pressing on Nasser's regime, already bristling from Saudi Arabia's criticism of Nasser for allowing UN forces on Egyptian soil and provoked by taunts of Nasser's perceived tolerance of Israel. In response to Soviet reports of Israeli-planned belligerence, Nasser, in a show of strength, dispatched troops to Israel's southern border, assembling them near Eilat.[20] The Soviet Union's increasing support of Syria and other Arab states and Israel's alignment with the West provided the regional conflict a broader narrative frame of international and ideological proportions.

Within Israel, the IDF (Israeli Defense Force) had grown bolder and more powerful under the leadership of Yitzhak Rabin and, as military historian Martin Van Creveld argues, was "spoiling for a fight" by 1967. Finally, Israel's attempt at nuclear developments at its Dimona plant prompted Nasser to warn that Egypt would not accept the existence of an Israeli bomb and would embark on "a preventive war" to avoid it.[21] In a noteworthy parallel, Israeli papers in the mid-1960s repeatedly referred to an impending threat of Arab attack, while Arab papers referenced the Jewish nuclear threat. By April 1967, a short month after the Israeli cabinet had voted for a general-television service, a chain of events that led to the Six Day War had been set in motion.[22]

On May 15, Israel's Independence Day, word came of large numbers of Egyptian forces mobilizing to cross the Suez Canal into the Sinai. The war that erupted three weeks later was either, as Benny Morris notes, a product of mutual miscalculation and plain error or, as Martin Van Creveld maintains, a welcome set of coincidences for Israel. Either way, Nasser's deployment of troops was probably meant to deter Israel from engaging Syria, and to signal Egypt's key role in a pan-Arab show of strength. By late May, however, the Rabin-led army was in full readiness and in favor of a war, and Arab leaders like King Feisal of Saudi Arabia, Iraq's president Aref, and Nasser were calling for a united Arab "jihad" against Israel to avenge the outcome of 1948. For both Jews and Arabs, the coming war would determine Israel's survival in the Middle East; if the Arab campaign prevailed, it would "exterminate the state of Israel for all time."[23] For the Israeli public, news of a joint Arab force advancing on Israel caused widespread panic about "a second Holocaust just around the corner."[24] As the army mobilized for a strike, the public prepared for calamity: Israelis painted car headlights blue, taped windowpanes, and readied bomb shelters; hospitals prepared an unprecedented number of beds; and public parks were hurriedly sanctified as emergency burial grounds. The nation turned to grim collection, amassing death certificates, coffins, and shrouds along with food and medical supplies. Early tax payments, savings, and other donations, even jewelry, poured into government offices from a fearful public.[25]

Galili's plans for Hasbarah-style television did not materialize in time to be tested in the war. Radio was called on to do the work of public outreach that Galili originally envisioned for the "emergency broadcasting" television service—boosting Israeli morale and representing the nation abroad. Together, Kol Israel and the military Hasbarah Office perfected the art of wartime radio, using both domestic and foreign resources.

As Sachar notes, the evocative Arab threats to destroy and drive all Jews into the sea only worked to marshal Western sympathy for the fledgling Jewish democracy, as did the Soviet and Chinese backing of the Arab states. These sympathies, and Israel's eager courting of Western interests, contributed to the unprecedented number of foreign print and television reporters—eight hundred—that would cover the Six Days War from inside Israel. Seizing the opportunity, Israel made every effort to maintain its sympathetic position in Western eyes, orchestrating an impressive media-access campaign for international radio, television, and print sources that proved the high point in the coordinated operations of Kol Israel, military radio, and the IDF's information office.[26]

The effort to expand the army's capacity to create a favorable image for world public opinion began well before the war and involved much more than the mere briefing of journalists after the fact. The developing practice of Hasbarah and access stood in sharp contrast to the Arabs' complete refusal to allow foreign coverage and their notoriously unreliable reports.[27] In Israel, foreign news organizations were provided with constant material, special communications liaisons, and information officers; briefings were held at 6:30 P.M. so that correspondents could make the following morning's deadlines; and journalists were taken to the sites of border incidents, admitted on military planes, and allowed to interview soldiers who participated in military actions.

The attention lavished on foreign reporters and the seemingly casual attitude toward access quickly established Israel as the hands-down winner in international public opinion, ensuring further interest and sympathetic coverage once the war began. As a Hasbarah project, foreign media access was carefully orchestrated, as one IDF journalist recalled at the end of the war: "A particular problem that bothered the foreign division [of the information service] was how to organize the foreign journalists' tours so that they would always be at the right place at the right time . . . without thinking that they were led together like sheep . . . and [how to] separate the reporters, who are able to work in teams, from the television people, who love 'solitude.'"[28]

The effort followed and built upon laudatory representations in Hollywood films, such as the widely successful *Exodus* (1960), *Judith* (1965), and *Cast a Giant Shadow* (1966). As Ella Shohat argues in her reading of *Exodus*, the film—and Paul Newman's casting as the Jewish lead—suggests that "the Israeli experience has normalized the Jew." The state of Israel, presented as an ideological project of moral aspiration, simultaneously became a "normal" and primarily Western-style nation—a "solution" to the problem of Jewish difference.[29] In this sense, Israel had "cured the Jewish problem" of persistent alien presence within the Western world. In these narratives—as in many Israeli national aspirations—the Jew had been integrated into the Western mindset by leaving the West.

In the popular media imagination, particularly in the United States, Israel not only deracialized the Jew but also served as a breeding ground for moral champions. The heroic images of the Israeli soldier—bolstered by widespread orientalist narratives and poised against the murderous Arab zealot or backward primitive—emerged as an injection of Western modernity into the intractable East, order into chaos, democratic progress into despotism, and reasoned humanism into religious fanaticism.[30] Thus, the Jew had been rehabilitated through a remarkable cultural transformation from a sinister other within to an agent of Western sensibility in a hostile, savage elsewhere. On the eve of the 1967 war, this cultural shift and narrative trajectory made a tidy fit with the work of the Hasbarah Office. The explanation project took up considerable effort and stretched IDF resources to their limits, yet by the time the war broke out, foreign journalists already had their story.

WARTIME DOMESTIC RADIO

The media, too, was both a weapon and a shield in the war.[31]

On the morning of June 5, sirens were heard all over Israel as the radio reported that the war had begun. Fighting broke out at approximately 8:30, and by 9:30, the first report of the air force's success was already filed with the radio news editors.[32] At 10:30, Defense Minister Moshe Dayan addressed the nation on Kol Israel in a speech designed for international, as much as local, consumption: "We are a small people, but a brave one. [We] seek peace but are ready to fight for our land and our life."[33]

Above all else, Israeli radio was determined to maintain a constant presence on the air. As the central radio broadcast station in Jerusalem

was located less than half a mile from the border, Kol Israel erected a series of relay stations—with battery-operated equipment—scattered all
over Tel Aviv and Jerusalem to function as alternatives in case the main
Jerusalem or Tel Aviv studios were bombed.[34]

Days before the first military engagement, Kol Israel had already
prepared a careful plan of wartime broadcasts. Once fighting broke out,
all regular programming would be suspended and Kol Israel would
instantly assume a twenty-four/seven war format consisting of three
program types: an hourly news briefing, battlefield reports, and prerecorded music. The last was planned as both a backup—programming
that could run for hours without live supervision or interruption—and
an emergency decoy, allowing the radio crew to move and set up an alternative broadcast location.[35]

In the early hours of that June 5 morning, broadcasting began as
on every other day, with a morning prayer and the morning news—
with no mention of the impending war—followed by cheerful music
and the daily exercise program. At 8:00, the music stopped for the reading of a special news bulletin about the first battle, marking the beginning of Kol Israel's "war mode." All commercials ceased, all Hebrew
channels (classical music, popular affairs, pop music, and the army
channel) were unified, and the presenters instantly replaced the standard identifier, "From Jerusalem, this is Kol Israel," with the nonspe-
cific "This is Kol Israel on the network of Hebrew broadcasting."

Changes in radio format extended beyond the elimination of commercials and the suggestive dislocation of the service from an embattled soil. Wartime radio positioned the public as both an extension of
the military effort and its sheltered subjects. Carefully managed and far
from transparent, the broadcasts sought to soothe public fears and to
nourish patriotic sentiment while obscuring the actual progress of the
war. The challenge of maintaining "positive inscrutability" with a live
presence highlighted the unique properties of wartime, cross-border
broadcasting, as always doubly addressed to friend and foe, Israeli and
Arab, here and there.

Although concerned with public morale, Kol Israel and its military
censors were acutely aware of radio's effect on the fighting itself, even
as they remained attentive to Israel's internationally perceived image.
During the six-day combat period, the service would air thirty-one
news magazines, hourly reports, and 109 separate stories from the bat-
tlefields, yet the broadcasts' reassuring directness and their immediate
sense of presence were largely illusory. As one correspondent later observed, to the public, glued to radio reports from the battleground, it
was impossible to discern that the fighting had shifted away from the
Israeli border and was actually taking place on Egyptian territory.[36]

Other wartime editorial adjustments included the elimination of any foreign-language songs—a practice continued to this day in times of military emergency and periods of mourning—and instructions to editors to dispense with any content that was "too sad or too happy." Satires, erotic songs, and current pop hits were replaced with national choral songs, army and navy choirs, and "songs of the homeland." Military songs were played only until the late afternoon, giving way to "calming music" toward the evening hours. The official programming directive was to "not get on the public's nerves."[37] One genre conspicuously eliminated in the war format was the popular greet-and-request program, which often featured prerecorded messages from soldiers at their stations. The risk of exacerbating civilian anxiety was compounded by the chilling prospect that unaware loved ones would be greeted by the cheerful voices of now-dead sons, husbands, and fathers.[38]

Due to the continuous presence of radio recordings from the battlefield and the army's complete involvement in the radio broadcasts (soldiers and commanders of all ranks routinely delivered tape to radio personnel), Kol Israel amassed an unprecedented sixty hours of battlefield recordings. The tapes included sounds of reporters caught in fire exchanges with Egyptian soldiers, battlefront interviews with wounded soldiers awaiting rescue, and other moments from the thick of the fighting. Many of these, however, were cut by the censors, who carefully reviewed each tape and information bulletin before its airing. By the third day of fighting, Israeli listeners knew they were winning, but the speed and dimension of Israel's victory would become apparent only after the war.[39]

Despite the initial obfuscation of combat information, musical selections assumed a kind of reporting quality. By the third day, as military gains were made public, a musical pattern paralleled the Israeli advance. On Wednesday, as reports arrived that IDF soldiers had reached the Old City of Jerusalem, Kol Israel supplemented news with several hours of Jerusalem-related songs. As Israeli forces overwhelmed the Jordanian troops and programmers exhausted the Jerusalem theme and returned to more general fare, the studios received many angry calls demanding it resume the Jerusalem motif and suggesting song titles that might have been overlooked.[40] By the fifth and sixth days, as Israeli units pushed through to the Golan Heights, the war ended with songs that celebrated the Sea of Galili and the plains of the Golan Mountains.

In marked contrast to Arab radio reports, Israeli broadcasts deliberately downplayed military gains, instead emphasizing all bombings and attacks on its territory, whether successful or not.[41] The tactic had initially taken a toll on the morale of civilian Israelis, who spent much of the war in bomb shelters, yet proved immensely successful once the victory reports finally aired—enhancing the heroic stature of the IDF in the eyes of the public and adding a mythic dimension to the war. The strategy further functioned to discredit Arab sources and helped create the narratives of "siege and reluctant response" and the "few against the many" that would serve as the blueprint for Israeli war narratives for years to come.

Nurit Gertz identifies the narrative of "the few against the many," or "David and Golliath," as a central mythic narrative in Israeli culture (illustrating the degree to which military metaphors have structured the Israeli popular imagination): "The story of the few against the many reveals, in its political incarnation, the Israeli public's conformity to collective values and its confidence in its own righteousness and virtue in victory. . . . This confidence does not stem from historical or rational claims but from the actual connection, with its origin in past myths, between the suffering of the Jews and their righteousness."[42] Offering a modern rejoinder to the ordeal of Jewish history, this mythic narrative distinguished Israeli action from diasporic passivity while bearing out the final victory of the suffering and the righteous. It also achieved its pinnacle in the Six Day War, as Israeli broadcast coverage strategy lent a nearly supernatural quality to the Jews' swift and seemingly impossible victory over the larger Arab armies.

This narrative also enjoyed common international circulation, particularly in the United States and western Europe, where Israel's victory was celebrated as a Cold War triumph over a Communist-supported Goliath, a ringing blow to the Soviet Union and its ambitions in the Middle East. Although the United States, France, and Britain had refused to uphold the 1957 Strait of Tiran agreement only weeks before, they now hailed Israel's victory as a Western one—an alliance Israel was quick to embrace and encourage. As Van Creveld argues, this jubilation at Israel's victory ("They Did It" was the headline in the British *Economist*) was also motivated by the West's own recent failure to maintain control over former colonies and over insurgence by "little brown men . . . in black pajamas."[43] The outcome of the war, and the subsequent erosion in diplomatic relations between Israel and the Eastern bloc, brought Israel yet deeper into the Western fold and won it the favor (primarily in weapons support) of the United States.

As the so-called new reality sank in, the expanded borders afforded Israel a fresh sense of security and insulation from both real and perceived dangers. With its borders more secure, its Western ties stronger than ever, its military admired internationally, and its public morale at an all-time high, Israel quickly settled into its new role as a Middle Eastern powerhouse. The original plans and arguments for Palestinian autonomy and statehood faded along with the moral and practical arguments against a long-term occupation.[44] With the occupation of the Gaza Strip and the West Bank, Israel would see its claims to moral righteousness severely eroded and engage in an escalating cycle of violence and retribution that remains ongoing.

The Six Day War would also provide the most compelling arguments for the creation of a general-television service. These arguments would not only rely on Israel's new reality, but also draw strength from its recent experience with "emergency broadcasting." Since the military stressed constant communication and interpretation of the war proceedings to the Israeli public and the world at large, broadcast media emerged as the perfect medium for instantaneous information and cross-border communication—and, in what would later prove to be an anomaly, fostered close and warm relations among Kol Israel, army officials, and the government. Radio had won the public's trust and its attentive ear throughout the anxious period. As reports suggest, local newspapers frequently complained of being left out in the cold, yet this was not a print medium's event. As MK Gabriel Cohen observed: "I have no doubt that any examination of the eve of war period . . . and the battles themselves . . . cannot be understood without observing the role of radio, and of television—in deeds or omissions."[45]

The outpouring of public appreciation for radio, and Kol Israel's wartime performance and manageability, had a redemptive effect, rehabilitating the agency's image in the eyes of its critics and easing the tensions that had built up in the pretelevision period. Whereas general television already had the tentative support of a cabinet majority, Israel's broadcasting experience in wartime mollified the qualms of television opponents and imparted fresh momentum to the Israeli television project. In arguing that television should have been deployed during wartime, one MK presented this new vision of television communication: "Television was missing in order to prove, again and decisively, to our friends, the Arabs, who seeks war and who wants peace; who avoids spilling blood, and who thirsts for it. There is no doubt that this would have changed the picture and strengthened our position in the eyes of the United Nations."[46]

In its speed of transmission, its unifying capacity, its international address, and its political utility, radio proved a natural technology for an isolated nation at war; television would amplify these capabilities with newly acquired poise.

The extreme fear and apprehension in the days before the war led to what Van Creveld has termed an "iron consensus." The effect of the war on Israeli national culture depended in large measure on that fear, and then on the surprise and elation that followed the unexpectedly successful outcome. As Creveld puts it, this was "one of those rare instances when the political objectives of the state all but coincide with the feelings of its people."[47] As Ori Ram notes, the territorial conquests of the Six Day War breathed new life into the idea of 'a united [whole] land of Israel.'[48] With the euphoria of victory and with a newfound national and military confidence, the postwar atmosphere provided a prime opportunity for latent religious and ideological currents to resurface. Practically overnight, the nation grew larger, stronger, and internationally celebrated.

Paradoxically, these new developments gave rise to two seemingly contradictory currents in the collective Israeli psyche: a heightened promilitary nationalist consensus coupled with economic prosperity, an abatement of anxiety, and a widespread embrace of capitalism and consumer culture.[49] This atmosphere provided the ideal climate for the introduction of television. Arguments for its impractical extravagance and recreational nature—which had dominated discussions in the early 1960s—lost their purchase, and its purported abilities to instill national ideology and cultural standards appeared more relevant than ever.

TO TIP THE SCALES: KOL ISRAEL BROADCASTS TO THE ARAB WORLD

We need to have more Hasbarah among the Arabs. This is a very complicated element in the population, problematic in many aspects; . . . we must conquer it, and this demands Hasbarah.[50]

We must not pass up any possible chance to be understood, and any medium that could assist in explaining our enterprise, in representing the good, the beautiful and the useful in our mission, is wanted.[51]

The idea that we must begin television broadcasts to the Arab population in Israel began in the days of tension that preceded the Six Day War. [W]hen the battles ended, it was clear that the issue had changed; while before we wanted to focus on the Arab citizens of Israel, the need presented itself to also focus on the large population that resides in the territories.[52]

The entire history of the television debate in Israel, it now appeared, had led to this moment. In the wake of the war, Israel emerged to find itself not only a powerful military presence in a region still stunned by defeat, but also holding a realm that had doubled in size within a week. In addition to the new territories and a "united" Jerusalem, the nation suddenly counted over a million Palestinian

Arabs, mostly from the West Bank and the Gaza Strip, as new, reluctant, and overwhelmed subjects.

Recalling the Knesset debate over the introduction of educational television, MK Benjamin Shachor found the current situation a study in contrasts. His comments make plain the degree to which the television debate would shift in direct response to the problem of the so-called "held" territories:

> Those who objected to television at the time had good and convincing reasons. But today's discussion has an entirely different character. Those who objected then cannot persist today in the negative position they took then. Today, when we inherit large territories with a mass population that consume all the different negative influences of programs broadcasted over neighboring television, there is no possibility to take the same approach that many did . . . a few years ago. This foreign television targets the areas most vulnerable. The way to fight this negative and harmful influence . . . is to provide other attractive programs with a positive influence.[53]

As Galili argued, "emergency broadcasts" would be able to present the Israeli government's position to the Palestinian population in the territories and simultaneously block enemy broadcasts into the area.[54] By this time, Israel remained one of the few countries in the Middle East without television. Lebanon and Egypt were on a full twenty-four-hour broadcasting schedule, Iraq was programming fourteen hours a day, and Syria was on the air for five hours daily. Jordan, too, reportedly was only months away from launching its television service. "The anti-Israeli element in television broadcasting in the Arab countries has been strong for some years," warned Galili, "and more so after the Six Day War."[55]

For those who wished to reach out to the new Arab populace, television, like Kol Israel radio before it, was a "natural" technology for communication through both information and cultural exchange. Television, as one politician argued, would "present the Arab population on the borders . . . with everything that is good, beautiful, and noble in the state of Israel."[56] For another Knesset member, television could appeal to the "democratic aspirations" of an Arab/Palestinian viewership as it worked to bring the populations closer: "The Arabs in the held territories need to learn from Israeli television that they are held in respect as equals and are offered concrete ways . . . to build a bridge of understanding between Jews and Arabs.[57]

This stated desire to promote understanding through self-representation—against the backdrop of Palestinian experience—smacks of a certain disingenuous naïveté, presuming, as it did, that anti-Israeli hostility and aggression must have arisen through some fundamental misunderstanding, whose clarification would lead to normalized relations. Thus, television's persuasive capacity, as it emerged from Knesset debates and public discourse, appeared to operate both within the political realm and well beyond politics, having the ability to circumvent both Arab national propaganda and the state apparatus as a whole (notably on the Arab side only) to appeal directly to the Arab people through the presentation of the "true Israel": "Why should we not use this all-powerful and influential instrument to appeal to the Arab people over their leaders' heads, and call for understanding and peace with us?"[58]

Galili himself presented a similar vision of understanding through self-representation when he suggested that television would "show the life and values of Israel, . . . simple, human things, . . . how things are progressing here. We'll show the country as it is, explain our desire for peace and the need for direct negotiations."[59] In Knesset arguments over broadcasts to the Arab world, the representation of Israelis as peace-loving people who wished only to raise their children in their own land was thoroughly entangled with representations of superior progress and cultural refinement. Television here assumed a kind of ambassadorial role, displaying Israeli industriousness, agricultural achievement, and cultural and political advances. Once introduced to these, went the rationale, Arab viewers would cast away animosity and come to accept, and even admire, Israel's accomplishments.

Not all politicians saw wisdom in that approach: "What means something to the Israeli public says something different, maybe opposite, to the Arab public. We will show a kibbutz on Arab television [but] the Arab will see not a flourishing kibbutz, but the land where an Arab farmer sat yesterday. We will show him a growing Israeli city, Ramlah or Jaffa, and he will think of refugees in camps."[60]

Yet, the self-representation approach held obvious appeal to the Israeli political establishment, reinforcing the David and Goliath myth, the siege mentality, and other narrative constructions that dominated popular fictional representations of Israeli life. Two major tropes of this literary tradition were the desert-to-bloom rhetoric so central to Israeli pioneer ideology of the pre- and early statehood era, and the trope of the good Arab who becomes an ally and sympathetic supporter of the Zionist cause. As Ella Shohat has argued, this variation on the familiar colonial trope—a tradition she terms "Israel's Prospero Complex"—was pervasive in Israeli cinematic and literary narratives.[61] One such example is worth quoting here since it so precisely echoes the hoped-for effect of Israeli television upon the Arab population. In Eliezer Smoli's novel *The Sons of the First Rain*, an Arab teacher marvels at Israeli achievements:

We have very much to learn from you, the Jews. This place was abandoned and desolate—and then you came along with all your energy and transformed it into a veritable Garden of Eden. . . . Every day I read diatribes in the newspapers against the Jews, and there are a lot of agitators who stir up trouble between us and you! But as I walk through your streets and as I see the tremendous labor you have invested in these desolate, abandoned sand-dunes, which you've turned into such flourishing land, I have to say to myself that it was God who sent you here to serve an example to us, so that we could look at what you do and do likewise ourselves.[62]

Television was no longer foreign to Israel's sense of collective identity; the war had articulated broadcasting into the central mythic narrative of Israeli culture. In the new reality of postwar Israel, television could do more than offer a helping hand—it finally found its lifeblood at the heart of Israeli priorities.

WARTIME ARAB-LANGUAGE RADIO

Those who doubt emergency broadcasting should remember that the struggle of influence over the ether is the sign of the times . . . we cannot expose ourselves or give up on the great potential Israel has in this area. We need to learn to speak to the Arab nations by every means of persuasive speech.[63]

Galili's proposal for Arab-targeted television met with initial approval, particularly since it so closely followed Kol Israel's highly celebrated wartime formula. This format included not only the Hebrew broadcasting marathon but also a collaboration between the Arab-language wing of Kol Israel and the Hasbarah Office. Israel had been broadcasting daily Arabic programs since 1962; most such broadcasts—to resident or neighboring Arab populations—consisted of news, music, and light fare that assumed a communicative, self-representational quality.[64] On the eve of the war that June 5, however, all regular programming ceased in favor of targeted broadcasts to Arab listeners, especially outside Israel, to "create insecurity among the enemy population and undermine their confidence in their military leadership."[65] These goals were articulated explicitly through news broadcasts, but also implicitly through fiction and information programs designed to strike fear in the listener's heart. Science programs discussed the terrifying ordeal of surviving in the Sinai Desert among snakes and unclean water, and drama programs featured skits with titles such as "Dead without Burial" about the horrors of war.

At the start of the war, Arab-language broadcasts had turned to heavy-handed propaganda, inundating the airwaves with relentless messages of Arab surrender and defeat. Along with the temporary scrapping of its regular format came a change from Kol Israel's usual literary, high-brow language to a colloquial style in various dialects—Egyptian, Palestinian, Syrian, and Iraqi—for an added effect of immediacy and direct address. Kol Israel even warned listeners that a house would be bombed if shots were fired from it and provided instructions on how to surrender ("Get in your homes and wave a white flag from the window or roof").[66] According to a Lebanese source, Israeli radio worked not only to sow suspicions about the futility of the war itself but also to raise doubts about Arab military leadership. Broadcasts sought to escalate ethnic tensions among the Arab troops and to inspire anxiety in the men by suggesting that their wives might stray while they were away at battle.[67]

Another psychological weapon of Israeli Arab-language radio was the routine broadcast of interviews with Egyptian prisoners of war. It is not known how effective these broadcasts were, or whether they had a wide listenership in the Arab world. However, various Arab radio stations in Cairo, Damascus, Baghdad, and Rabat-Amon repeatedly warned their listeners to pay no mind to the Israeli broadcasts—certainly a heartening sign to Hasbarah officials. Syrian president Noor A-dyn Al-Atasi, speaking on Damascus radio only days after the initial cease-fire, also accused Israel of waging a cruel psychological battle, and, as reported in the Israeli press, a July 1967 article in a Lebanese military publication called Kol Israel's broadcasts "Israel's most destructive weapon."[68] Whatever the actual effect of the Arab broadcasts, the reaction assured Israelis that the broadcast medium—whether aimed at the world at large or at its Arab neighbors in particular—was an extremely potent technology when properly targeted.

Thus, with two modes of address that both had proven successful, Galili's subsequent proposal for an Arab-language television—still defined as an "emergency service" designed to address drastic postwar changes—was a plan acceptable to both doves and hawks among Knesset members. Television would be useful for those anxious about ongoing Arab hostilities from within the territories, and for those hopeful for a new era in Arab-Israeli relations.

CONQUERING VISION: THE EVOLUTION OF THE EMERGENCY SERVICE

> I have no doubt that the new circumstances which we find ourselves in following the Six Days War have moved television significantly ahead in the priorities ladder.[69]

We are in the midst of a struggle for the soul of the Palestinian people.[70]

You may agree with me that the emergency has not passed with the end of the fighting. Moreover, it can be said that at a time when the cannons went still, bombardments by the Arab media go on. In this sense, we can say that on the ether waves, there was an emergency before the war, during the war, and is still on. And, unfortunately, it could go on for a long time, as long as our enemies still have hope to destroy Israel and no peace treaty is signed between us and our neighbors.[71]

In the midst of the postwar euphoria, as Galili's "emergency service" began to take shape, General Peled was having second thoughts. Still an army man, Peled had played a key role in the Six Day War as a commander of the northern units. His recent success and the much-praised performance of the IDF may have made him regret his decision to leave it for the tangled politics of the nascent broadcasting service. But more than anything else, Peled had begun to sense that he and Galili were destined to clash over television's future within the IBA. "I see the independence of the Broadcasting Authority as a cornerstone to a democratic way of life in Israel," wrote Peled in an early draft of a letter to Galili. "It is my impression that we do not have a full agreement on the meaning, in practice, of this independence principle." Informing Galili of his decision to step down from his appointed post, Peled wrote of his "great anxiety" when imagining "days of bitter internal struggle" over the role of television within Israeli politics: "I have no doubt that TV and radio will be forced to play a part in this political struggle, in one way or another. . . . I do not believe that the Israeli political lifestyle and democracy will make it possible for radio and television to stay above and away from these future struggles. I am not sure we share a common assessment of the coming developments, and so I doubt my ability to manage the broadcasting service by the principles of non-dependence."[72]

Peled's retreat left Galili angry, pressed for time, and determined to appoint a trouble-free and popular successor, an authority who would appear above political motivation and would bring unquestioned expertise to the post.[73] Significantly, he turned from the military to the academy: to Professor Elihu Katz, chair of the Communications Department at Hebrew University and a prominent communications researcher. The U.S.-born Katz, who would become one of the foremost communications scholars in the world, was already well known for a 1955 study with Paul Lazarfeld that proposed the diffusion model of persuasive communication in mass media. As Katz recalled a few years

later, he immediately accepted but made his own disagreements with
Galili plain: "In choosing me, the government could not have found a
more skeptical person as far as belief in short-term mass media effects
are concerned. I did not think that television could by itself cause the
Arabs to like Israelis. . . . I thought that, used properly, television could
broaden the image of Israel beyond the highly political, highly military
image that was current, and extend it into areas of mutual concern—
agriculture, medicine, the family, entertainment and so forth—where
Arab and Jew might find common interest."[74]

Katz's moderate views on the use of Arab-targeted broadcasting
were not an obstacle to Galili, for whom the appointment of the professor was an ideal way to broaden his emergency broadcasting plan
while fortifying it with academic credentials. Further, as a respected
scholar and an authority on media, Katz would face none of the criticism that followed Peled's nomination. Yet significantly, according to
Tzvi Gil, the minister did not offer Katz stewardship of the broadcasting service—as he did to Peled. Instead, the minister limited Katz's duties to getting television off the ground as head of the Television
Operation Team.

Shortly after Katz's appointment, Galili proposed that the emergency television service also include some Hebrew programming,
defining the division as a 75 percent to 25 percent split, with the lion's
share of programming targeting the Palestinian population in the
"held" territories. To promote his Hasbarah television model, Galili
suggested that the government install television receivers in coffeehouses, social clubs, and schools to "reach different publics, and influence previously conceived, anti-Israeli opinions."[75]

As Galili recalled years later, he saw the service as a perfect mixture
of entertainment and information, a broadcasting medium that could
easily adjust to shifts in the political climate: "I saw the exposure to
television as awakening meditation and encouraging action; . . . I saw
for television a role of making leisure time more pleasant, bringing cultural matter to people. . . . Also, I saw in television a vehicle for providing knowledge to those who need it and also messages in times of
emergency, when the moment requires a call for the people. Although
here we get into the problem of what is knowledge and what is propaganda; there is a very fragile line here."[76]

The idea of government-installed receivers in Arab communities
was met with nothing but embarrassment and was quickly scrapped.
Yet, a government committee did approve a budget for the implementation of an emergency service for the Arab territories, and by November, emergency broadcasting was taking legislative shape. The service, it

was decided, would include four broadcasting hours per day—three hours in Arabic and one hour in Hebrew. In its report to the Knesset, the committee further projected that, with the establishment of general television, daily Hebrew programming could be expanded to as much as two and a half hours—yet the bulk of broadcasting would remain in Arabic.[77]

Among the goals outlined in the report were "explaining the institutional and elementary positions of Israel to the residents in the territories, disseminating the Israeli version of current events, and presenting to the territories' residents the history of Israel, its achievements and problems." The report also addressed the still-prevalent problem of Arab-speaking Israeli viewers and the popularity of Arab programming, suggesting that the service would also "shift the attentions of Arabic-speaking Jewish viewers away from foreign, hostile broadcasts." Despite its emphasis on self-representation and propaganda, the same document did envision television's specific utility to Palestinians. The service could be employed by Palestinians to "serve as an authorized source for opinions, views, positions and difficulties in the territories; and provide an arena for public figures and talents within the Arab population."[78] By winter, as equilibrium returned and Israel settled into postwar life after the turbulent summer and fall months of 1967, "emergency broadcasting" gradually lost its high-pitched urgency, and the television discourse progressively turned to a "normalized" service that was equally mindful of the Israeli viewer.

Practical considerations gnawed away at the "emergency plan" as well. First, it became clear that regular television broadcasts would necessitate a regulated programming schedule and a better-prepared and better-organized television production crew. Moreover, Knesset members doubted that Israel could reasonably provide three hours a day of Arabic programming within six months without turning mainly to imported films. Perhaps, some suggested, the first Israeli experiment in television should be in Hebrew and not in Arabic, since the stakes for Arabic programming were so much higher.[79]

Another concern was inviting and integrating Palestinian participation in the service: "How do we gain cooperation from the residents of the new territories? Without it, this will be television of Arabic-speaking Jews who speak to Arabs."[80] Whereas this was doubtless the original plan—following the wartime Kol Israel model—promoting regular and friendly communication required establishing credibility. To earn the viewers' trust, one MK argued, Arabic television must use local talent and not just Israeli Arabs. This necessity presented two delicate problems. First, what if Palestinian performers refused to show their faces on Israeli television? Second, what if they did agree but included anti-Israeli rhetoric? Censorship would immediately erode any credibility, while anti-Israeli programming was unthinkable.

The ideological association between the problem of credibility and the dubious delegation of Hebrew programming to a mere half-hour was addressed by Arab Knesset member Emil Habibi, who denounced a television service "for the almost sole needs of foreign propaganda and not the needs of the internal population of the nation." This, he argued, "creates suspicions in the population towards whom the programs are targeted and therefore misses the declared purpose of bringing hearts closer." Kol Israel's wartime format, Habibi added, significantly diminished trust in the service. "I'm an Arab and I listen to Hebrew also. I listen regularly to Kol Israel programs in Hebrew and do not rely at all on the Arab broadcasts on Kol Israel." For Habibi, the entire enterprise of an "emergency service" was tainted from the start; the only Israeli television that could earn the trust of all its viewers was a general Israeli service, in Hebrew and Arabic, that would serve the "cultural needs of the residents of Israel and advance the interests of understanding and fraternity, . . . serving the interest of Israeli-Arab peace."[81]

Further, a broadcast intended for a Palestinian audience invited uneasy political questions for Israel and forced Knesset members to tackle an issue many wished to delay or to avoid altogether. "In the current situation," noted MK Navon, "there's one problem that consumes the Arabs to whom we address this television: What do you want from them? What is their future? Arabs that will watch television . . . will demand to know your thoughts concerning them."[82] Another MK, Uri Avneri, made the point in blunter terms, pointing out the heretofore disregarded link between political communication and action: "We want to speak to a million and a half residents who live in the held territories, and to Israeli Arabs . . . but what should we say? We are in the midst of a struggle for the soul of the Palestinian people. . . . The conditions for any successful propaganda is that the propagandist knows what he wants . . . a clear plan. What plan does the Israeli government have? What do we want with the held territories? . . . What should we say to these people? Will we speak of annexing the territories to Israel or their return to Jordan or Egypt; on the founding of a Palestinian state or the creation of a federation?"[83]

Minister Avneri's comments captured the ideological power surge that the promise of technology bestowed on the uninitiated, directing the Knesset once again to the much-neglected question of actual content: "Here comes Minister Galili and advises us to erect a large cannon. That is good but . . . he doesn't offer a map or artillery. What should we fire with this cannon? Should we use this large cannon to fire a cork?"[84]

With all the emphasis on the collective, immediate, and direct access of domestic broadcasting technology to a "problem" audience, the communication process itself—and the meanings its target audience would make of such messages—was initially perceived as singular, manifest, and unproblematic. Such naïve perceptions about the inherent power of television as a national tool were, of course, commonplace and all but defined the early stages of television in nearly every national context, yet the Israeli case presents a unique instance in which such formidable technology of national address was to be directed outside national borders. This intent required a more complex model of representation: Instead of aiming to present a collective national identity for the viewer to partake in, it planned to present such an image to a viewer who was, by definition, opposed to and excluded from that identity.

As theoretical debates gave way to more practical considerations about television's actual implementation, Galili's original vision for Hasbarah-style service grew murky and finally unworkable. With this, Israeli television's architects had learned a lesson about the complexities of representation and about the often unanticipated subtleties that distinguish cannonball from cork before a single image was transmitted.

The swing back to internal audiences and the singular articulation of national identity was relevant once again: "It is enough for us that two things would be the foundations to the creation and operation of television: Peace and the education of the entire populace towards the cohesion of the people, the shaping of national character, and the integration of all groups and classes into a joint Israeli power united in its opinion, its ideas, its purity of heart, and its thought towards survival and well-being."[85]

By early 1968, talk of "emergency television" gave way to "experimental broadcasts," a term that both anticipated a normalized general service and carefully eschewed the explosive questions brought on by the suggestive "emergency plan." With no fanfare or explicit acknowledgment, without the typical Knesset debates of past transitions, with no demarcation at all, it had all but disappeared. Public excitement at the news of a coming service mounted, television receiver sales soared, and foreign television volunteers began arriving in Israel to assist the skeleton crew of Professor Katz's television team, now preparing for general television. The rush was on.

"FINALLY, SOMETHING TO WATCH!"

Whether we want it or not, we are clearly a militaristic society, and this militarism is also the central organizing principle around which Israeli society moves, operates, determines its limits, its identity, and its own rules of the game.[86]

> The broadcasts of Israeli television will add a new dimension to the concretization of the existence of the Jewish nation in the Middle East and will help frustrate the efforts of all those who seek us harm. (Israel Galili)[87]

Television's ideological and policy implications had been scrutinized from every angle over almost a decade. Logistics and technological readiness, however, had been left practically unexamined, aside from a few training sessions abroad and sketchy exercises for a novice crew. Suddenly, as news came in early February 1968 that Jordan was preparing to debut its own television service, the idea of going on the air in May with Israel's Independence Day parade had caught fire among Katz's team and government officials alike, and quickly spread to ignite public enthusiasm. The parade, an IDF showcase march in "united" Jerusalem, was to be the most significant symbolic event in the nation's life, rivaled only by Ben-Gurion's historic radio announcement, twenty years earlier, declaring Israeli statehood. A ritual culmination of the Zionist dream, the parade was planned as a proud display of Israel's powerful army marching in its newly conquered capital—the cherished center of Jewish religious identity. Marking the first anniversary of Israel's triumph, as well as the decision to institute television, Independence Day emerged as the perfect occasion for unveiling the national service—and the parade as a perfect event to do so with flair.

The final decision to embark on the project came in late February, only nine weeks before the parade. The feverish preparations by Katz's staff seemed to grow in complexity with every passing day. Aside from a small inexperienced staff, a meager government budget, and a CBS consultant, there was little they could rely on. In addition to a lack of skill, language barriers among crew members, culture clashes, equipment shortages, and numerous bureaucratic misunderstandings lent the production facilities a "Tower of Babel" air.[88]

Other problems threatened the project's completion by the May deadline and underscored the sheer bravura of the undertaking. The television equipment contract signed with RCA had specified that Israel would not receive broadcasting equipment until the late summer of 1968. In the midst of preparations, Katz's crew realized they had committed to be on the air months before a mobile unit and other equipment would arrive. A frenzied hunt ensued, commencing in mid-March in London, where Katz's deputy secured the needed equipment, barely outbidding a Jordanian television representative who intended to purchase the same mobile unit. The remote van arrived with only three weeks to spare. In the same month, the Israelis hastily assembled a transmitter tower in spite of the protests of its German engineering team, who futilely insisted on a three-month installation and testing schedule.

In retrospect, the idea of charging an inexperienced multinational crew with such an undertaking, without offices, studios, or equipment, seemed a sure recipe for a grand-scale public fiasco. Katz and other unit members later confided to reporters that much of their bravado and confidence came from a thorough ignorance of the realities of television production.[89] Yet excitement prevailed.

From February to the end of April, as news of the planned telecast circulated, more than forty-two thousand new television receivers were purchased.[90] New electronics shops mushroomed all over Israeli shopping centers, and by April, store owners were hiring extra staff for the sole purpose of explaining how a receiver worked to potential customers and curious bystanders gathering by the display windows. In the weeks before the first broadcast, a reporter counted more than sixty different television models for sale in electronics shops, as television advertisements and rates of purchase reached a furious pace.[91] Banners displaying countdowns to the "big day" appeared in storefronts, and Westinghouse, the leading television manufacturer, launched a print campaign that featured uniformed Israeli soldiers who marched out from the television screen and into the viewer's living room. Across the country, coffeehouses were suddenly taking reservations for May 2, with a cover charge for those who requested seats close to the television.[92] Meanwhile, awaiting the Israeli debut, thousands of viewers relaxed in front of their brand-new sets, watching *Perry Mason* and *Peyton Place* on their Lebanese-tuned receivers.

Early on the morning of May 2, Uzi Peled (no relation to General Elad Peled), the number-two man at Katz's television unit, was bypassing the security blockade on a last-minute check. The night before, Peled had placed large plastic signs identifying the location of "Israeli television" along the parade route, where, in a couple of hours, television cameras would be broadcasting live. Surveying the five cameras—the first erected high above the main stage, the second perched atop a dilapidated monastery roof above the main path, and three others spread out on the grounds—Peled urged his troops to "go for broke." As he reminded his crew, there was no second unit, no studio to retreat to, not even a "Sorry, technical difficulties" slide to slip on the screen in case of trouble.

By 8:30, the five cameras were in position along the parade route. As the temperature rose outside, the newly painted control van felt like a portable noisy oven. Inside, Louis Lentin, the wiry Irish director, and Haim Yavin, the young Kol Israel journalist and Katz's assistant, tried to keep cool as they performed a last check, nervously switching between monitors and issuing last-minute instructions—in multiple languages. Narrator Yoram Ronen was settling into the broadcasting booth, along with two IDF lieutenants brought in to stand by and assist Ronen— with hand gestures—to distinguish between the Skyhawks and Mirage planes and various tank models on parade.

At 9:00, the signal came. As the broadcast began with an elaborate air show, camera 1 trained skyward and its operator, balancing on a firefighters' hydraulic lift, strained to keep the fighting planes in frame as they whooshed by. In the announcer booth, Ronen welcomed the audience to the parade and the first Israeli experimental broadcast, then briskly moved on to describe the scene. The cameras swept over the cheering crowd and lingered as politicians and dignitaries took their places on the ceremonial stage.

Lentin sat stiffly, scrutinizing the monitors and awaiting his own cue from Yavin. Understanding not a word of Ronen's account, the Irish director watched for a hand signal from his Israeli assistant that would indicate an appropriate moment to cut away to the central stage. Unfamiliar with any of the ministers and public figures by name or rank, Lentin consulted a seating chart as Yavin quickly advised him on who should be highlighted.

On cue, camera 3, positioned at a sharp angle to the stage, attempted an ill-fated close-up of Moshe Dayan, who was seated too far for a clean reach; the image shook—a move that would be interpreted as a political critique in the following day's paper—and Lentin quickly cut away to a long view. On the official stage, in the Knesset bleachers, Foreign Affairs Minister Abba Eban held a small super-eight camera, filming the passing ground troops and the television camera above. Seated next to him was the information minister, Israel Galili, his head thrust downward, his gaze intent on the small portable television he gripped discreetly between his knees.[93]

As the tanks and uniformed men and women filed past the camera, Ronen's narration came in uneven bursts, as if he were suddenly aware of the redundancy of description. "Here they come," he would repeat with every fresh wave of marching soldiers, zooming planes, and rolling tanks. "Here they come . . ."

At 11:30, Israel's Independence Day parade was over, as was its first television broadcast. Both had gone without a hitch. The crew gathered for a quick celebration and readied the van for that night's assignment: the filming of the second experimental broadcast, Leonard Bernstein's festive concert with the Israeli Philharmonic, featuring the famed violinist Itzhak Perlman.

The following day, press reports confirmed the success. Nearly 60 percent of the population watched Israel's television debut, and among those questioned, 81 percent praised the broadcast as "highly success-ful."[94] Most reported watching the event with family, neighbors, and friends who assembled in groups as large as thirty and more to share an available receiver. In at least one case, a Tel Aviv resident set up a neigh-borhood viewing area by emptying his local synagogue of seats and ar-ranging them on the street below his balcony, where he positioned his television set.[95]

Television had entered Israeli culture with undeniable force and with all the pomp and circumstance the Independence Day military cel-ebration could muster. It is, of course, difficult to determine in retro-spect how much of the excitement centered on television in general and how much was the result of patriotic fervor. Yet that the two would be linked in such an explicit manner was itself significant, as one journalist ominously predicted: "The IDF's Independence Day parade flowed through the streets of united Jerusalem, through channel eight on the coast and channel ten in the Gulf, and continued to march, without in-terference, on glass screens in Jewish and Arab homes alike. Thus an-other fact was established, and it too has a meaning more political than technical: Israeli television has gained sound and light and the new medium will, from now on, be a regular weapon of propaganda."[96]

The "experimental" broadcasts that inaugurated the television era in Israel encompass, with startling clarity, the function television was expected to assume. In one sense, the first two television events—a mil-itary march on recently conquered territory and a classical music con-cert featuring two internationally known Jewish musicians—were meant to be celebrated as much as watched. Together, they worked to define what Israeli national identity so strove to embody and project: a highly cultured European tradition wrapped in new strength and re-gional dominance. The Arabic-language broadcasts inaugurated that summer—a much-curtailed version of the emergency service, consist-ing mainly of a news program, variety shows, imported films, and a children's hour—aimed to expand Israel's self-representational technol-ogy beyond Jewish households to Palestinian homes in Israel, the occu-pied territories, and the Arab world at large. These broadcasts, however, bore little resemblance to the Palestinian-centered programs envi-sioned by Galili. Rather, their focus on entertainment and local public affairs acknowledged Arab viewership as primarily a matter of internal cultural diversity.

Galili's initial plan for a government-controlled "emergency ser-vice" did not come to fruition. However, in promoting the emergency service first and keeping the initial experimental broadcasts under the Prime Minister's Office, Galili did ensure that television, like radio before it, would have its roots in governmental ideology. Despite its integration with Kol Israel under the public Israeli Broadcasting Authority, television's legacy remained entangled in its political beginnings. Conceived from anxiety and born through government machinations over nationalist priorities, Israeli television would repeatedly clash with the very forces that gave it life as it sought to move away from the problem-solution model of broadcasting and its initial role as a national utility.

For the next few decades, the "iron consensus" between government actions and public opinion would fray. Television's allegiance to political power and a unified national cause would repeatedly be questioned, often under the claim of national security and unity. To this extent, the story of the creation of an Israeli television service parallels the evolving narrative of Israeli nationalism, as it so faithfully reflected the priorities, fissures, and conflicts that structured it as a discursive formation. Thus it was hardly a coincidence that the pinnacle of this nationalist discourse, the May 1968 Independence Day parade in Jerusalem, marked not only the moment where the discourse of national unity, military strength, secure borders, and Western admiration reached an all-time high, but also the moment when Israeli television made its debut appearance. Yet such a moment of perfect containment was rare indeed; in postwar Israel, internal ethnic divisions would resurface, Israeli military superiority would be shaken in the early 1970s, Arab-Israeli relations would worsen still further, and the effects of a long-term Palestinian occupation would begin taking a toll on internal ideological cohesion—and on world public opinion. For television in the postexperimental phase, its struggle for independence, and its role in public and official discourse would continually encounter the same ideological obstacles, as the Zionist dream of national and cultural unity slowly dissolved into the reality of a splintering nation, embattled without and within.

JEWISH TELEVISION OR MICKEY MOUSE CULTURE? 5

The 1969 Election and the Sabbath Debate

Television is only a box, and we get out of it what we put into it.

—Golda Meir, May 18, 1969

It was obvious that Israelis fell in love with television from first sight . . . [like] a Bedouin on a plane trip for the first time in his life.

—Eddie L. Sofer, *In the Image of the BBC*

In the previous chapters, the story of Israeli television unfolded as a series of arguments, imaginings, missed opportunities, and miscalculations.[1] For more than a decade of discussion and throughout the formation of the service in the late 1960s, much of the rhetoric about television had focused on its nature and its service to the state, its targeted application to specific "problem populations," and, most prominently, its relevance to the Arab-Israeli conflict and the "Palestinian problem." Then, just as it was emerging from its pilot phase and expanding programming to a weekly nighttime schedule, television again found itself at the center of a political maelstrom.

More a catalyst than a cause, the first television debate in the post-experimental stage was again centered on a problematic shift in Israeli society. Once more, television was the arena for a political debate that stirred public passions, yet this time the battle prompted a Supreme Court challenge, threatened to topple a government, and involved combatants that few of TV's early stakeholders had foreseen.

This controversy addressed not an imaginary audience and targeted broadcasts but the "real" of popular sentiments; it was the last time a debate over television took place quite outside the question of particular content. The so-called Sabbath debate of 1969 was the bridging incident that demarcated the end of the "imaginary period" of television's government-directed origins and a transition into the television age and the first struggle for the mass medium's independence.

Inasmuch as the "Sabbath debate" was over definitions both of television and of national identity, it fits the pattern of ideological discourse formation that so typified the history of Israeli television thus far. Yet most remarkable in what follows is the extent of public involvement in the weeklong controversy. Public opinion played an unprecedented role in shaping this debate, as Israeli television finally came face-to-face with an actual community of viewers.

As an illustration of the argument developed in the previous chapters, the incident epitomizes a moment when a central national preoccupation—this time, the place of religion in civilian life—was defined and debated *through* a public argument about television. As the purported object of struggle, television provided a rallying point for public protest, an ideological problem for policy makers, and a political thorn in the side of government. And, like other examples explored here, the debate did not concern a particular programming choice or specific material; rather, it focused on the nature of television and on its ability to communicate a collective sense of nationhood.

In the week of November 5, 1969, Israeli television made a noisy, highly public transition from an imagined national technology to a popular cultural institution. In the process, it ignited a firestorm of protest and internal national division over the very meaning of Jewish and Israeli identity, a division that remains central to Israeli public life today.

"THIS IS JEWISH TELEVISION?"

If 10% vote for the religious, why should 90% surrender to their will?[2]

As head of the experimental television unit, Elihu Katz firmly believed that television should not turn to a casual, everyday schedule of programming modeled after radio, but should remain a "special events" medium. "I sometimes dream," he wrote in 1971, "of the television station that would go off the air after a special broadcast, announcing: *We have nothing more for you until our next special broadcast three days from now.*"[3] However, with the demise of the emergency-broadcast paradigm, the future of Israeli "general" television appeared to shift toward a more familiar, ordinary format. No longer a comfortable "absence," it was a highly public presence that demanded to be filled.

The final stage in the transition to general broadcasting (and away from a Palestinian-targeted "emergency" model) occurred in August 1968, when newly unveiled survey figures indicated that televisions were a scarce commodity in the occupied territories. Only a small number of Palestinians owned television sets, and an average of 15 percent of residents reported having access to it—a figure, according to Galili, "much smaller than previously thought."[4] Moreover, a utility survey revealed that a majority of Palestinians had never had electricity in their homes, and many villages had no electricity supply at all. As MK Yitzhak Navon observed: "It is obvious that these facts must dictate a new policy; . . . all the preparations made to create an emergency service with an emphasis on Arabic now require changes as conclusions are drawn from these data."[5] As the pressing threat of Arab television propaganda to Palestinian villages diminished, so did the rush and finally the plan to target Palestinians as the primary audience for Israeli television.

Early newspaper predictions about a shrinking Arabic schedule and an expanding Hebrew program had now been confirmed. By early 1969, as Israeli television was finally included in the IBA law, the programming schedule was officially reversed, with Arabic programming curtailed to a mere hour and Hebrew programming expanded to three. A more regulated schedule of broadcasts followed, with the full expectation that television, like radio, would soon operate on a regular, seven-day schedule.

Religious opposition to such a weekly schedule was not unanticipated; in fact, it was taken as a matter of course. After all, religious leaders and Orthodox politicians had fought a largely losing battle with the overwhelmingly secular radio service from the first. Their early calls to eliminate radio broadcasting on the Sabbath had garnered little attention in the Knesset during the Ben-Gurion era due to Kol Israel's affiliation with the Prime Minister's Office, radio's perceived role in national security, and the relatively moderate influence the religious party exercised in this area. Similarly, Orthodox members had consistently opposed the introduction of television, fearing its secular influence on Israeli youth and the possibility of programming on the Sabbath. However, significant debate over television's religious implications was originally sidestepped when its approval had projected an emergency-broadcast format that was an Arab-targeted wartime necessity.[6] By 1969, as Israeli television was emerging as a routine broadcasting service and the IBA was preparing for the transition to a full weekly schedule, the Orthodox faction in the Knesset was steeling to mount a renewed and formidable resistance.

Early indications that a seven-night broadcasting schedule could be controversial came as early as that January. On numerous occasions, Knesset members went on record asking Galili to confirm reports that such a transition was in the works, and religious MKs expressed concern that television staff would be made to work on the Sabbath.[7] Galili was less than direct about IBA plans but did not hide his own or the cabinet's support for Saturday broadcasting.

As Tzvi Gil argues, the pressures to instill a daily programming schedule came from several sources; public support appeared overwhelming just as politicians argued that more programs would wean Israelis from alternative viewing of Arab offerings.[8] A commissioned survey from the Israeli Center for Social Research in early 1969 suggested that 72 percent of Israelis strongly supported television broadcasts on the Sabbath and only 21 percent opposed them.[9] Television sets now occupied a full third of all Israeli living rooms, fortifying the perceived need for more programming to an eager and growing Israeli audience.[10] Galili and others in the Knesset further insisted that a seven-day schedule was important for political reasons in Israel's fast-moving and volatile news climate, both to keep the public informed and to establish a culture of constant readiness at the television headquarters. Prime Minister Golda Meir also expressed support for a daily schedule, encouraging IBA personnel to proceed with the expansion.[11]

Within the IBA, officials acknowledged the difficult demands of the task—and the lack of programming material—yet saw a seven-day broadcast as a logical move toward the integration of radio and television broadcasting under one authority. This integration was proving more difficult than anticipated. Relationships between the television crew and the IBA's government-appointed management board were strained and often hostile. The television crew complained of interference in editorial decisions, foreign experts grumbled about missed salaries and equipment shortage, and the Arab-language division protested a pattern of discrimination in pay, facilities, and reporting privileges.[12] By the spring of 1969, both Elihu Katz and his deputy had announced their decision to leave the broadcasting agency, and many in the television crew were threatening to strike.[13] Reports in the newspapers and many in the political opposition sounded a common critique that identified the root of the problem with the agency's lack of independence, yet for many others, the discontent—like the schedule expansion—was a sign of growing pains in the IBA's accelerated process of maturation.

At this time, Israeli television was on the air four evenings a week, with as high as a three-to-two ratio of local programming.[14] The nightly offerings included news, public affairs, sports, variety, and children's programs in Hebrew and Arabic, with some European and mostly U.S. imports such as *Mission Impossible, The Wonderful World of Disney*, and *I Spy*. The typical broadcast evening began at 6:00 PM with a half hour each of Hebrew and Arabic children's programs. Arab-language programming aired until 7:30, followed by youth-oriented Hebrew or imported shows, a brief news roundup, a general interest program, and, at 9:30, the nightly news—by far the most watched program on television. A short selection from the Bible concluded each nightly broadcast at 10:00.

Foreseeing that an incremental expansion of programming would lead to a bitter and protracted struggle with the religious bloc over the final addition of a seventh day, Galili advocated an immediate transition that enjoyed both the Knesset's and the public's approval. Despite bitter protests from its minority Orthodox members, the Knesset voted on May 12—a short year after television's debut experimental broadcast—to approve a seven-day broadcast plan, scheduled to begin in November of that year. In accordance with the broadcasting law, all decisions about the service expansion were granted to the IBA.

However, the October 1969 elections presented an opportunity for the religious party: In a climate of growing party splintering and ideological divisions, the religious party emerged as a small but significant player in Israeli coalition politics.[15] In order to form a Labor-controlled coalition and avoid a national unity government with the right-wing Gachal (led by Menachem Begin), Meir depended on the participation of the religious party (known as Maphdal); the latter had decided to make the television matter its major demand for concession. In a November 2 meeting with Meir, a religious-party representative informed the prime minister-elect that if the IBA went ahead with its plans for Sabbath broadcasts, Maphdal would refuse to join the Labor-led coalition, effectively dismantling Meir's government. On the floor of the Knesset and in private meetings, religious representatives and rabbis argued that television on the Sabbath would pose an unprecedented danger to a Jewish way of life and create deep fractures within the Israeli family—between those who wanted to observe the holy day and their children, who could not resist the temptation of television. A few commentators expressed dismay that Maphdal should place such priority on the relatively inconsequential matter of a few hours of television, yet others pointed out that the television issue was far from trivial to the religious bloc: "In conquering television, Maphdal sees a serious political goal, perhaps the most serious goal since the decision to form a State-run religious education track. . . . In the first round, they fought hard against the creation of television and lost. In the second round they threaten to forsake the government over the Saturday television decision. . . . And who knows, . . . if successful, they might turn their influence in this subject to a regular issue in coalition negotiations."[16]

On November 3, Meir summoned Shmuel Almog, the recently appointed director general of the IBA, and informally suggested that a seven-day schedule be delayed. Almog doubted the seriousness of Maphdal's threat and bristled at the prime minister's request, citing the IBA's charter of political independence. By the following day, Almog and other members of the IBA committee found themselves on the receiving end of mounting government pressure to delay the Saturday broadcasts, prompting the director general to announce that if the IBA conceded to the government, he would resign from his leadership post.

On Tuesday, with only three days to go before the debut of Sabbath programming (Friday evening, the start of the Jewish Sabbath), the government issued a formal request to the IBA to "suspend broadcasts on the Sabbath evening, allowing a discussion of the issue once a new government is formed."[17] Formidable pressure continued on various Knesset members to compel the IBA to follow the recommendation, in spite of a provision the Knesset itself had passed only a few months earlier making external interference in the matter illegal. Already commanding significant attention in both the secular and religious press, the conflict was becoming a major scandal, with revelations that a number of senior IBA personnel, including the director, now threatened to resign.[18]

The prominent journalist and commentator (and future minister of communications) Amnon Rubenstein published an open letter to the committee on the day of the decision, urging its members not to surrender to political pressure and "religious coercion."

> The upper echelons of Labor have acted as if there is no Israeli Broadcasting Authority, there is no law, there is no committee, ... calling upon you at the last minute to automatically rubber stamp their will. . . . But you must remember . . . to respect the will of the citizens who finance television from their own pockets. There is meaning to a decision and a promise; there is law. [Remember] that public officials like you are not play puppets in the hands of this or another party. Remember that there are also Arabs in this country and they too are human beings with rights. . . . You are now called upon to decide in a matter of the first order of importance pertaining to individual rights and the type of democratic governance in our nation.[19]

In a manner reminiscent of the 1962 television skirmish between Prime Minister Ben-Gurion's office and the IBA (see chapter 3), the national dailies largely took up the IBA cause, led by the liberal *Ha'aretz*, whose first story about the controversy, on November 4, 1969, was headlined "Our Nation Is Not for Sale!"

"The IBA board must uphold its responsibility to the public, and by the law, and ignore these threats," insisted an editorial the following day. "Enough lawlessness; ours is a nation of law and not the private property of Labor and its government cronies."[20]

Unlike the 1962 conflict, however, the issue of Saturday broadcasting seemed to strike a chord with the public at large. Heated reader responses began to pour in as newspapers devoted full pages to public venting on the television issue. Many readers questioned the distinction between television and radio, asking why television should be banned while radio operated on the Sabbath. Others asked how watching television was worse than other common Friday-night activities like card playing. By way of compromise, some offered that Saturday programming could include a religious theme (like candle lighting and prayer). But mostly, letters were angry, with the majority (in all but the religious press) united against the religious minority and Labor's attempts to appease it.

Most letters appealed to the tenets of democracy and Labor's responsibility to its voters. "Labor, as the party of the people, must implement the will of the people!" a typical letter argued. "It would be a grave mistake for Labor to belittle the general public who will not forget this shameful episode of 'selling' television to the religious," warned another. Other letters couched the right to watch television in terms that proved a sentimental favorite: "Think about the thousands of citizens who spend their Saturday at home, after the weekly stress, or since their loved ones are on duty, serving at the border. Soldiers who come home for Saturday to spend time with their parents, would prefer sitting with them to watch our programming, and not Arab stations. Why must television be a sacrificial lamb to ease government negotiations?"[21]

News editorials, too, centered on an apparent violation of democratic principles and a popular vote, and challenged the right of a small religious minority to impose its will on a secular majority. On the front page of *Yediot Ahronot*, along with the latest development in the television saga, the paper devoted a lengthy section to opinions from ministers and IBA committee members. Running the gamut from ardent television supporters to those arguing it posed "a danger to a Jewish state," the impromptu survey nevertheless reflected a clear protelevision majority.[22] The religious paper *Hatzofe* published its own public survey that featured more than twenty extensive quotes from academics, public and religious figures, and ordinary citizens expressing anger at the prospect of Friday-evening broadcasts. "The operation of television on the Sabbath damages the founding values of Judaism," argued the summarizing headline.[23]

Ha'aretz, the newspaper most vocal on the controversy, dedicated several days' ink to airing public opinions. Dispatching interviewers to six major areas in Israel, the paper published the comments of one hundred people—identified by name, occupation, and location—and concluded, in a front-page headline: "A Majority Is for Saturday Television!" In this survey, seventy-seven of the responses argued for television, sixteen against, and seven were undecided. A *Davar* editorial condemning "religious coercion" warned that television was only the beginning of a potential erosion of secular rights and political control, made possible by the current coalition system: "Maphdal . . . representatives could say, for example: 'We agree to join the government under the conditions that television programs are not shown on Saturdays and holidays, that public transportation in Jerusalem will cease from Friday morning to Sunday afternoon, and that, on the beach in Tel Aviv, bathing suits would be forbidden. And we still need to discuss a number of ministry posts.' "[24]

This editorial was typical in its approach to the controversy, not as a television matter per se (as some letter writers had done), but as a gateway issue. Yet in so doing, editorials linked television viewing to freedom, diversity, and self-expression in a remarkable departure from the discourses of national address and cohesion that had typified earlier discussions of the medium—as well as the rationale of those opposed to Sabbath programming.

On Thursday, with one day left before the launch of the controversial broadcast, the IBA committee met to vote on the matter. Outside, a group of demonstrators collected signatures and urged the committee to uphold the seven-day decision. Behind them, police officers on horseback stood poised to intervene, fearing a public disturbance.[25] Under this palpable pressure, the committee members began a stormy discussion punctuated by last-minute phone calls from Meir and other Knesset members and hurriedly passed notes to various members, pleading with them to consider the government's predicament.[26] The discussion lasted more than six hours and concluded with a secret vote: A majority of thirteen to nine resolved to let the original decision stand and to go on the air the following day.[27]

Most evening newspapers were jubilant, with *Ha'aretz* calling the decision "a victory for thought, courage and law" in its front-page editorial. Accompanying the story was a large cartoon of an IBA hand puppet punching the yarmulke-wearing Meir (see figure 5).[28] The message was clear: Puppet no more!

"The IBA committee decision . . . is an achievement for individual freedom and a victory for democracy," read a typical response letter to the editor.[29] As it emerged in the press immediately following the vote, the Sabbath debate represented for both sides an essential test case of

FIGURE 5. Editorial cartoon by *Ha'aretz* staff cartoonist Ze'ev, November 7, 1969.

the true independence and public nature of the service. For the religious minority, IBA's independent-minded defiance of the government's request, and its decision to uphold Saturday broadcasting, were incongruent with the agency's national responsibility, its state-supported structure, and its public charge. For the secular majority, the contest was between institutional politics and popular democracy. The narrative gloss of a small group of public servants defying the will of a powerful government lent the vote a touch of heroic flair that further enhanced its appeal. In the secular press's view, the independence of television was the point of the entire debate, yet the religious press repeatedly questioned such claims for independence. In religious papers, the IBA decision was termed "shameful" and blamed on internal political dealings by Begin's Gachal Party. Writing of the IBA committee, one editorial argued: "A body created by the government and supported by government funds cannot be allowed to mutiny; . . . the government should put these workers in their place."[30] In both secular and religious papers, observant readers voiced their frustration with the outpouring of support for Sabbath television and the IBA. For many, the issue was the collective image of the state, as expressed by the national service in general: "I have no television, but as a citizen of this nation, I'd like to make sure there is no broadcasting on the Sabbath. This, after all, is a public, not a private agency." Yet others expressed their understanding of the controversy using the same rationale of rights and discrimination employed in the secular argument: "Operating television on the day [a religious Jew] cannot watch it means the suspension of equality rights between religious and secular Jews. It is like a special prize to those who are not observant and a clear discrimination against the observant Jew."[31]

In an interview, Minister of Religion Zerach Verheftig disputed the notion that television was not a state institution and thus could be independent of government authority. When asked why television viewing should not be regarded as a private activity and an individual choice, Verheftig replied that, since television was financed with taxpayer money and IBA workers were paid from a government budget, operating television on the Sabbath was, in fact, an Israeli government activity: "Television is not private property; it is operated and paid for by the state."[32] Similarly, an editorial in a religious paper insisted that "this idea of autonomy that hovers in the IBA has no basis since the Broadcast Authority represents a national service."[33]

In an argument that mirrored the earlier definitions of television as a technology for Israeli self-representation, many religious commentators argued that television on the Sabbath was tantamount to state-supported sacrilege and represented a serious assault on Jewish national identity. *Hatzofe*, the largest religious paper, linked the decision to potential immigration as commentators asked how Israelis could, in good conscience, allow a state-sanctioned desecration of the Sabbath while in Communist countries Jews were being persecuted for attempting to observe it.[34] A *Hatzofe* editorial dubbed the decision the "Victory of Mickey Mouse over the Israeli Nation," charging that secular activist groups were using the television issue to eliminate any differences between Israel and other nations and working to disassociate "Jewishness" from Israeli identity.[35]

This rhetorical positioning of television as akin to foreign (and specifically U.S.) culture dovetailed with earlier debates about the commercial potential of the medium (see chapter 2) and the pernicious effects of U.S.-style popular culture on Israeli youth. Such constructions were also common in viewer letters: "The people of Zion saw a shameful picture; through anger at the 'religious,' our last cultural legacy, left for us amidst an ugly sea of Americanism, was trampled underfoot."[36]

The argument invoked fears of Israeli cultural transformation, but, most important, it tapped into a familiar discomfort with the medium as fundamentally un-Jewish in its accessible attractions and passive leisure. Jewish practice and tradition were posed here as vital to Israeli identity, and television, essentially a "foreign" medium, as a direct threat to that identity. By extension, religious leaders cast their anti-television stance as a preventative measure and a desperate bid for the preservation of Israeli culture and identity—an ironic rhetorical strategy in light of the Orthodox population's then relatively marginal place in Israeli society. A typical editorial in the religious *Hatzofe* argued that "this current battle over television . . . is a battle for the image and the future of our country." Writing for the secular paper *Yediot Ahronot*, a reader appealed for the importance of keeping Sabbath as essential to the very character of the Jewish state: "More than we have formed the nature of the Sabbath, the Sabbath has formed our nature," he argued. "Must we be dragged after the *Goyim* and allow its desecration . . . for the comfort and entertainment of the public?" A sterner position was articulated by the Chief-Rabbi of Israel, who called the decision to broadcast on the Sabbath a "destructive deed that deeply harms the Jewish soul, the honor of the nation, and its people."[37]

Aside from the specifics of the debate, then, the religious and secular positions on television reflected a more general disagreement about the nature of "public" media service. From the secular point of view, "public" constituted a service free of both political interference (in the form of government supervision) and private interruption (in the form of commercial interests), yet supported by—in fact, dependent on—a democratic process. From the religious perspective, the broadcasting service, by nature of its public standing, was a national service and, as such, couldn't represent simply the aggregate preferences of the people but rather the total will (and character) of the state. Several religious commentators linked the controversy to what they saw as a persistent antireligious sentiment in the nation's broadcast media, whose staff and crew were overwhelmingly secular. "Those with a religious outlook," argued one lengthy commentary, "have no one to fight their battles in Israeli media; . . . this is a social and national problem of the first order . . . since [media] shape public opinion in the country."[38]

The disagreement over the proper state of television as a national medium stemmed in part from a more fundamental issue: the unresolved place of religious practice in Israeli collective identity—especially when applied to matters of policy. Whereas most Zionist activists envisioned the state of Israel as a socialist, secular democracy, religious political parties had always been part of the Israeli governing structure. To prevent a social rift between the majority secular citizenry (defined in Israel to include the observant but not Orthodox) and the religious minority, no separation between religion and the state was stipulated, and the Ministry of Religion was afforded significant legislative power in family law, funerals, religious education, dietary restrictions, and

Sabbath-related matters (such as transportation and public services).[39] These broad powers were often controversial in Israel and were regarded by Ben-Gurion and other leaders as concessions designed to maintain a status quo.[40] As Limor and Nossek observe, the Israeli Declaration of Independence defined the new state as both Jewish and democratic; to the extent the Jewish identity was expressed (in practice) as religion, the two concepts would be in constant tension. Thus, the "struggle over the identity of the state of Israel moves between two poles: the Democratic pole on one side and the theocratic pole on the other."[41]

Such tensions between the secular and religious factions within the government and the Israeli public at large had been common, and they ran particularly high in the cultural sphere. However, the aftermath of the 1967 war saw the opening of an ideological gulf within the Israeli population and the emergence of a "hawk" coalition that joined religious longing for the biblical dimensions of the "promised land" with a "whole-Israel" ideology embedded in a rhetoric of national security. This shift granted Orthodox representatives more Knesset seats and the ability to yield new powers as an indispensable partner in the coalition-building process. Whereas the full impact of this ideological redistribution would not register until the late Seventies (see chapter 6), the television debate marked another step in the integration of religious discourse into mainstream politics and cultural life.

THE "WEEKEND MIRACLE"

> A democracy is the will of the majority, the opposite is tyranny. In our country, 90 percent of citizens are secular; . . . that is why there must be television on Saturday. The majority has never forced the minority, by law or by force, to drive or listen to the radio on the Sabbath.[42]
>
> With the outbreak of the television matter, an impression was created that this is the central problem facing us. . . . Not a stable government, not problems of security or economics, but the problem of turning the television off or on.[43]

As the dispute over television grew increasingly strident, the Israeli public seemed concerned with little else. Morning and evening papers featured the issue prominently on their front pages—with some adding special television sections to accommodate the swell of readers' letters. In an early example of media self-coverage, *Ha'aretz* even dedicated a special "readers' corner" to discuss the paper's own coverage of the matter. One reader wrote simply to protest the sheer amount of coverage: "I cannot recall another item that got so much attention in

Ha'aretz like the story of Sabbath television." Yet the inflamed passions over television also drew critiques from political pundits who argued that the firestorm had obscured the much more important issue of the structure and process of Israeli parliamentary elections: "There is no doubt that we have taken hold of this minor issue as a release for these tense times. . . . We should not avoid a simple hard truth by escaping to the polemic over television."[44]

Some apprehensive commentators observed that the Israeli public seemed to care more for their televisions than they did for politics. Pleading for priorities, one *Davar* editorial argued that no television on Saturday was a relatively small price to pay to avoid a culture war and, more importantly, to prevent the right-wing Gachal from gaining influence it did not earn in public elections.[45] However, much of the public's response bespoke a different view of the controversy's broader significance: "I was amazed to hear from Golda Meir . . . trying to convince us that Maphdal is right about stopping Saturday television. This is an ugly surrender of leadership! 2.5 million Israeli citizens do not want to dance to the tune of the 100,000 who voted for Maphdal. We must not surrender." "We should officially decriminalize blackmail in this country. If Knesset members and religious ministers are exempt, so should everybody else be." As it emerged from the majority of readers' letters, television itself was not the issue, but rather stood as a symbol for individual freedom and choice. As one writer succinctly put it: "I hope a coalition does stand . . . but not at the price of my individual rights."[46]

The unexpected public outcry regarding the government's television reversal had caught Golda Meir and Labor by surprise. Particularly stinging were accusations that the ruling party willingly succumbed to religious demands, disregarding the majority's sentiment. In an unprecedented move, the Labor Party took out a full-page ad in the largest national dailies to answer the charges and to blame the current situation on the lack of a clear majority. In effect, the ad accused the public of failing to heed the party's warning and of not voting solidly for a decisive Labor majority, thus enabling smaller parties to wield greater power over the government. "What has been done, cannot be reversed," concluded the ad, "but we had better remember this lesson."[47]

Concessions to the religious party were not new in Israeli electoral politics. In the recent past, these had included the elimination of bus services, the closing of shops and various entertainment outlets in many major cities, and other more general kosher-law restrictions on merchants, entertainment, education, and the like. Further, government involvement in the operation of television and other IBA matters was also a common enough past occurrence. What the intense interest and passion over the current dispute seemed to signify was the final and decisive passing of television—for better or for worse—into the public realm.

In the Sabbath-broadcasting controversy, television appeared yet again to occupy the intersecting point of several important discourses that, in combination, propelled it to the highest national priority. As the object in contention, television stood to signify the cost of Israeli coalition politics, the growing tension between religious and secular definitions of Jewish identity, the role of the state in the development of Israeli media, and an evolving relational complexity among the domestic, public, and political spheres that, in the postwar reality of Israeli life, no longer possessed the same lucid correspondence. Yet the current debate was also steeped in the discourses that informed television's recent creation. As selections from the nation's three largest dailies illustrate, anxieties over Arab viewership and the harmful influence of enemy broadcasts still circulated. "Canceling television on Saturday will achieve one . . . purpose: to enable Israeli residents—especially Arabs—to comfortably watch poisonous propaganda flowing from Arab stations." "If television does not serve the will of the people, we should not be paying a television tax. Instead, I will send my money to Cypress or Beirut." "The government should consider the Arab population. . . . With no Israeli-made programming, they'll be exposed to broadcast[s] from hostile countries."[48]

The argument that banning Saturday television would both expose more Israelis to Arab programs and discriminate against Arab taxpayers was a common line of reasoning in the liberal press, in readers' letters, and in interviews with the IBA leadership. Yet religious readers and journalists complained that the overwhelming press support for the IBA disparaged Orthodox beliefs and placed greater value on Israeli Arabs' interests than on religious (Jewish) concerns. "[The IBA] shows great consideration for the non-Jewish minority in Israel. I'm so appreciative of . . . all those who think like that . . . but I have one question: Why does the non-Jewish minority deserve . . . more consideration than the Jewish one?"[49]

Through this and similar responses, the television debate had extended to the edges of yet another political issue that, like television itself, was a product of the Six Day War; as once extreme positions increasingly resonated with a growing faction of the Israeli public, the problematic presence of an Arab "other" within the self-described "Jewish State" had never been greater—as an undertone of frustration with the left-wing leadership had begun to swell in the late 1960s. Whereas

the television debate did not produce these emerging ideological fissures, it brought them to the surface and gave them concrete shape.
Like every television dispute before it, the Sabbath debate had managed
to substantiate a national ideological problem. Unlike previous debates, however, this one was both public and popular, affording increased visibility and circulation to public definitions of the conflict.

Beginning largely as an argument about IBA's independence and
political pressure, the debate quickly evolved into a pitched, bitter battle between two distinct Jewish populations. The secular activist group
Can'anim hung posters and placed large ads in national dailies entitled
"The Standoff over Television: A Definitive Culture War!" One ad proclaimed: "Television is the straw that broke the public's back." Asserting that the religious bloc had launched "a war against the public, law,
and individual rights," the ad concluded with the cry, "War for Separation of Religion and State!"[50] The Can'anim's call may have been particularly incendiary, but religious activists employed the notion of a
culture war to similarly frame the debate as a profound impasse in a
joint vision of a national future. Outside the Knesset, religious demonstrators carried signs that decried the Sabbath-broadcasting decision
as "national suicide." Hundreds of religious high school students
marched in city streets in protest, and commentators warned that Sabbath broadcasts would "mean the nullification of Jewish identity as our
national identity."[51]

The conflict escalated further with the appearance of a cartoon on
the pages of *Ha'aretz* that depicted an Orthodox rabbi in traditional
garb and a flowing beard, protruding from a television screen into a living room, scolding finger wagging, as the caption orders "Shabbes!!!"
(see figure 6). The Yiddish word for "Saturday," pronounced with indig-
nation, was a familiar admonishment to secular Israelis, particularly
those who unwittingly found themselves on a Saturday drive through
an Orthodox neighborhood. For those unlucky drivers, the proclamation was accompanied by stone pelting—a practice that would become
routine by the following decade. Like the figure of the rabbi, the word
itself invoked both the old-world sensibility so many secular Jews disdained and the intrusive nature of the prohibition they so rejected.

The caricature, praised by some readers, was instantly inflamma-
tory, inviting accusations that the cartoon was anti-Semitic and drew
upon the imaginary storehouse of Nazi-era depictions of Jews. The
charges prompted *Ha'aretz* to publish a reply, accusing its critics of "a
peculiar sensitivity when it comes to representations of religious Jews"
and arguing that as part of Israeli society, the Orthodox and their leaders were legitimate targets of political skewering. Others, however,

הימים הללו

שאבסג!!!

FIGURE 6. Cartoon by Yosef Bas, *Ha'aretz*,
November 7, 1969.

feared it had gone too far: "The loud arguments circulating lately over the operation of television on Saturday contain worrying signs of a burgeoning culture war," warned one commentator.[52] By Thursday, as the controversy seemed to reach a peak with the IBA board decision, the television saga took another, more extraordinary, turn. Even as most dailies hailed the IBA decision and reported on public reactions and celebrations of the vote, Labor and Maphdal representatives spent the night in a tense meeting of their own. There was one more possible loophole, they found, buried in the IBA law itself—in subparagraph 12, to be precise (see chapter 3 for a discussion of the law). This clause allowed for government intervention in a committee decision if as many as ten of the thirty-one committee members submitted an official letter protesting a recent vote. Since nine members had already voted to suspend Saturday programming, government representatives rushed to contact the nine dissenters and find a tenth voice among the members who did not participate in the Thursday meeting. The agitated search yielded results, and, by morning, the government had enough names to legally suspend that evening's broadcast until the following week.[53]

With headlines announcing the coming Sabbath broadcast still on the newsstands, Israelis awoke Friday morning to radio reports that the evening broadcast would not take place. Not only was television becoming the most volatile election issue, but also the facts themselves seemed to shift from moment to moment. By midafternoon, the news that the government had found a way to circumvent the IBA circulated nationwide. A few hours later, however, everything would change again.

In the early evening hours, as the sun was setting to signify the beginning of the Sabbath, the prime minister and the minister of posts received a phone call informing them that, by order of the Supreme Court, that night's broadcast would go on the air as originally planned.

The unexpected IBA champions were two lawyers in their twenties who had filed a petition against the government only an hour earlier. The younger of the two, Adi Kaplan, himself an owner of a television set, had originally structured his argument around the issue of taxation, charging that he had been paying government taxes on his set, collected on the calculation—and promise—of a full week's broadcast. That afternoon, he consulted his brother-in-law, Yehuda Ressler, who decided to broaden the petition, charging illegal political meddling by the government in a public body for partisan ends. Further, in a hastily written six-page petition, Ressler added that the government suspension, granted through the letter of protest by ten committee members, was itself illegal: Since only nine of the undersigned were actually present and outvoted at the Thursday meetings, the outcome failed to meet the legal minimum of ten votes against the majority. Incidentally, Ressler's redirection of the petition was both a wise and lucky turn since, upon checking, Kaplan discovered that he had in fact neglected to pay his last television tax and, due to the lateness of the hour, could not post his payment before the following week.

With the petition completed too late to be officially filed at the court, Kaplan and Ressler resorted to less official methods and proceeded to drive to Jerusalem to the home of Judge Tzvi Bronzon, whose address they found in the local phone book. At 6:45 that evening, as a tired and defeated television crew was dispersing for the night, Judge Bronzon sat in his bedroom, pen in hand, quickly reviewing the IBA law and the Ressler petition. After some tinkering, the judge penned a court order for a thirty-day dispensation on government interference with IBA decisions, jotting it down on the petition itself. The young lawyers now raced to the Jerusalem home of an IBA official, who set off a chain of frenzied phone calls. It was now 7:20 PM. By 8:00, a skeleton crew was assembled back at the studios, along with the anchorman,

Haim Yavin; as the assistant director at the Independence Day broadcast, Yavin was now an old hand at this high-strung style of "instant television." More calls were made—to Galili, Meir, other ministers, and the Kol Israel news director. At 8:45, Kol Israel reported that a Sabbath broadcast would go on after all. By 9:07 Israeli television was on the air.[54] An instant celebrity, Ressler, the young lawyer, was too busy receiving congratulating well-wishers to watch that night's broadcast, but Golda Meir, a self-proclaimed television fan, did.[55]

In the wake of the first Sabbath broadcast (itself an unremarkable offering of a comedy-variety show and a sports program), the press overflowed with another celebratory wave of reporting on what had been dubbed "the Weekend Miracle."[56] Reports of Israeli festivities over Saturday television even drew comparisons to the outpouring of joy after the 1948 announcement of statehood.[57] Columnists titled their pieces "Bravo" and "Cheers," and Ha'aretz went so far as to publish the names of committee members who signed the government-penned vote dispute, calling their behavior a new "low in cynicism and careerism that a public figure can stoop to."[58] Profiles of Yehuda Ressler appeared in all the major papers, along with reports of phone calls, flower baskets, and wine bottles flooding his cramped Tel Aviv office. Television's victory—compared by one commentator to the Boston Tea Party—was widely hailed as a popular public victory over a powerful political machine. Television, despite its roots in governmental propaganda and national educational goals, had turned populist overnight. A handful of commentators again expressed dismay at the grand proportions the issue had taken on in the public imagination. One writer charged that the Saturday television affair was a political sham, an easy way for the public to raise the mantle of "individual rights" without a genuine struggle or the risk of opposition. Yet even for this writer, the affair was significant in crystallizing a struggle over a new Israeli identity, a contemporary, secular "identity of place" rising against the traditional Jewish identity of religion and shared history.[59]

Understanding the origins of Israeli television as primarily a function of national communication helps make sense of the Sabbath debate not only as a contest of wills between religious and secular communities, but as a broader debate about the collective identity of the state. Further, through staging this long-brewing conflict within the arena of television, what developed is a fundamental shift in understanding viewing practices (and, by extension, other domestic leisure activities) as individual and diverse. In the context of Israeli broadcasting history, however, this shift did not mean the relegation of the medium to a wholly private realm, but the freshly articulated differentiation between the broadcast's public point of origin (a national institution) and the private point of reception. It was here that the two spheres had acquired distinction.

Many commentators lamented the inexplicable ardor with which Israeli citizens asserted their "right" to watch seemingly inconsequential and "light" programming, but such readings failed to consider that the specific content of programming was immaterial, as the debate was precisely about the point of connection between official national institutions and private activity. It is tempting to read the Sabbath debate as a site of resistance and to characterize it as a popular rebellion that sought to throw off institutional control over private leisure. Such a reading, however, misses the mark by failing to consider the specificity of television's Israeli meaning in this period and its imbrication in a larger political debate. The Sabbath debate was not an attempt to sever the national sphere from private leisure, but rather a popular demand that public institutions express and endorse majority public experience. In this sense, the Sabbath television debate was primarily a struggle over representation.

As the past chapters have traced the history of television in Israel thus far, the symbolic projection of national ideals on the domestic screen emerged as a dominant paradigm for television's governmental founders. In the final chapter, television emerges in its full representational capacity to contest and disturb the very formation of a central national narrative.

6

GOOD FOR THE JEWS
Airing National Guilt and the Hirbat Hizaa *Affair*

In a land of immigrants like Israel, radio and television must be understood primarily as educational instruments that fulfill a national mission. Countries that posses a cultural tradition—like England—can permit themselves . . . a singing and entertaining box.

—Yitzhak Navon

If the nation is seen as a "body," an organism, then to take it apart and examine its history is to stop its heart from beating.

—Jonathan Boyarin, *Storm for Paradise*

Written in the spring of 1949, just as Israel's war of independence ended, S. Yzhar's (Yzhar Smilinsky) semi-autobiographical short story "Hirbat Hizaa" is the first-person account of a young IDF soldier who suffers a breakdown as his unit is ordered to evacuate a Palestinian village.[1] "This happened long ago," reflects Micha, the narrator, in the story's opening line, "but since then would not let go of me." A reluctant memoirist, Micha explains his attempts to submerge his traumatic experience, "to quiet it in the noise of days and dull it in the stream of things."[2] Yet the memory, like its consequence, will not stay buried. If, as Benedict Anderson famously proposed, nations are imagined through the printed word (and, as Homi Bhabha expounded, in and by literature), Israeli nationhood, so surefootedly developed and richly imagined in pre-1948 works of pioneering verve, found its coming into being ambivalently articulated in this piercing and melancholy anti-heroic war narrative.

The adaptation of the story for Israel's state television in 1977 precipitated the fiercest public debate about the nine-year-old service to date. The battle nearly caused the overhaul of the semi-independent structure of Israeli television and altered its status as a cultural medium. Moreover, the debate served as the definitive moment that polarized a newly identified cultural elite in opposition to government ideology, forever fractured a cherished mythology, and exposed a deep rift in the political foundations of the nation. All this despite the fact that the story itself, the purported center of the controversy, was widely read, had been taught in Israeli schools and universities for more than two decades, and was highly regarded as a founding canonical work of Israeli literature.

Tensions between visual and verbal representation, as W.J.T. Mitchell stresses, "are inseparable from struggles in cultural politics and political culture."[3] This power-inflected unevenness between modes of representation (primarily, for Mitchell, in terms of logocentrism) shapes the meanings proffered by the text—be it a representation of fiction, as in the novel-to-film narrative treatment, or news reports in print or on-screen. In such translations to other media, weaknesses and problematic noncorrespondence between narrative modes (word, image, movement, sound) are exposed as they produce different stresses, different experiences, and often different routes of meaning. Yet the disparities of media in and of themselves are not the only representational issues involved in political tensions over textual conversion: As the scandal over the televisual production of *Hirbat Hizaa* makes evident, the particular technological logic of media, along with their political contexts, renders certain translations problematic, volatile, and even dangerous.

The final case study in this book is, like that in the preceding chapter, a "bridge" incident, offered here as both a culminating example and a transitory moment. Much of what made the *Hirbat Hizaa* production so contentious offered striking parallels to the Shabbat controversy that kicked off a normalized television service (see chapter 5). Like the Saturday-broadcasting controversy, the *Hirbat Hizaa* production articulated a particular divisive version of national identity and gained poetic resonance as a victim of bad timing. Again, an IBA vote would come under extreme Knesset pressure during a government transition. Once more, that transition would denote a profound political shift. For a second time, television's fundamental tenet of independence would be challenged, and yet again, television would find itself in the midst of a stormy debate about the very essence of the Israeli national endeavor. This time, however, the controversy surrounded a particular text whose reincarnation from the written word to the television image would make all the difference.

Although the well-respected story had circulated widely, the 1977 attempt to adapt it for television became one of the most explosive controversies in Israeli television history. The "*Hirbat Hizaa* affair" served to highlight television's role in disturbing the complex interdependence of historical narratives, political ideology, and public consensus over memory in Israel's formative years. In doing so, it also illustrated the complex positionality of television in the middle register between culture and politics.

HIRBAT HIZAA AND NATIONAL MEMORY:
FROM STORY TO ADAPTATION

> S. Yzhar's "Hirbat Hizaa" is not Leon Uris' Exodus and Micha of "Hirbat Hizaa" is not Ari Ben-Cana'an of Exodus. Our wars cannot be packaged like bonbons.[4]

> I believe that the war of independence, like all other wars, was forced upon us . . . and that we acted, as a matter of course, with humanity, sympathy and consideration—perhaps more than any other nation. Aberrations sometimes occur, and it is necessary to eliminate and avoid them, but we must not turn them into a symbol and turn the occasional into the typical.[5]

The story, as literary critic Dan Miron describes it, was "a raging and pained protest" against the Zionist project, which seemed to have lost its way and turned its back on its principles. Deformed under the pressures of war, its senses had dulled as it twisted into a mask of harsh power.[6] As author S. Yzhar told an interviewer, the story emerged from his own war experience: "I didn't write ["Hirbat Hizaa"] as a Jew against an Arab, but as a person who has been hurt. Something materialized there that my consciousness would not accept. . . . In the expulsion of the villagers, . . . the destruction, . . . there was something in it that denied my whole worldview."[7]

Ordered to rid the newly won border area of "adverse forces" and "agents on enemy missions," a small unit of Israeli soldiers at the closing days of the 1948 war is dispatched in Yzhar's short story to assemble the inhabitants of a certain Arab village, arrest suspects, load the residents onto trucks that will transport them beyond the Israeli state line, and destroy the village site. Thus, armed with their convictions and their instructions to "burn-blow-arrest-load-send," the unit makes its way across the rich soil of the ancient hills to their target, the village of Hizaa.

As they await orders and boredom sets in, conversations turn from the callous arithmetic of the number of bullets it takes to kill a donkey to the possibility of planting mines to prevent Arab residents from escaping or crossing back into Israel. Entering the half-deserted village, the soldiers threaten an old man at gunpoint, shoot at men escaping in the distance, and round up the terrified residents. They repeatedly tell each other how much more ruthless and murderous the Arabs would be had their positions been reversed, and how, unlike the shocked and passive villagers, they would fight for their invaded homes. Micha, the narrator, is haunted by the abandoned feel of the empty streets. The unnatural stillness accusingly manifests itself as audible loss, and Micha imagines he can hear the vacant houses shouting at him: "You pass within them and suddenly, out of nowhere, hidden eyes of walls and courtyards and alleys speechlessly accompany you in the silence of abandoned desolation. . . . And suddenly, in the middle of the afternoon or before evening, the village that, just a moment ago was a rise of orphaned, silent and deserted huts, . . . this spacious gloomy village opens up and sings the song of objects whose souls have departed" (16).

Overcome by unease and then by guilt, Micha is taunted by an internal voice that mockingly repeats, "Beautiful soul, beautiful soul, . . . a gentle soul that leaves the distasteful work for others; that piously closes its eyes and averts its gaze to save itself" (pt. 3, 18). He begins questioning his platoon members about the orders to empty the village as a simultaneous argument rages inside him, with one side enunciating all the clichés of war and security, while the other, less articulate, can register only profound discomfort and a sense of growing moral outrage that has not yet fully formed in words or emerged into consciousness. The villagers—mostly old men, women, and children—are assembled and herded onto two flatbed trucks. They offer no resistance; the women cry and the villagers' attempts to plead or communicate with the soldiers are coolly rebuffed. As the day drags on, tensions surface and the soldiers begin to bicker over the treatment of the villagers. Micha watches as a mother and her young child, both enduring the "end of their world" with a quiet dignity that chills him, make their way to the Israeli truck that will transport them away from their home forever. As they pass, the woman looks at Micha with silent contempt; he averts his eyes in shame and meets those of her young son, and in an instant glimpses the boy's future—the trauma of this day imprinted on him as a legacy of hatred and violence. "Suddenly, like thunder, I knew it all at once . . . exile, here is Diaspora, this is Diaspora, this is what it looks like. . . . I couldn't stay in my place; . . . things gathered within me. I was never in exile, I told myself, I've never known it, but I've been told, spoken to, taught. It was repeated and drilled in my ears from every corner, in books and newspapers and everywhere: Diaspora. And it was in me, it seems, even then, with my mother's milk. What, in fact, have we done here today?" (19)

As Micha becomes increasingly agitated, his friends attempt to comfort him by describing how beautiful Hirbat Hizaa will become under the care of Jewish immigrants. "Of course," Micha thinks bitterly, "why couldn't I envision it before?"

> Hirbat Hizaa is ours. The question of housing and the problem of absorption; here we will house and absorb and how, . . . and who would imagine that there was once some Hirbat Hizaa here that we exiled and inherited? That we came, and shot and burned and blew up and pushed and banished. What in hell are we doing in this place? . . . Everything, everything for the refugees, their rescue and well-being. Our refugees, of course, those that we are ejecting, that's a completely different thing. Wait: a thousand years in exile. Killing Jews. Europe. Now we are the masters. And those who would live here: will the walls not shout in their ears? (pt. 3, 19)

Unable to act, Micha watches the trucks pull away, hauling their sobbing cargo from the village. As the platoon gets ready to leave for the night, Micha imagines the still, open landscape stretching in aching silence behind the departing group. As evening falls, Micha tells us, "All will be gone, God will descend and wander here, listening to the land as it screams" (pt. 3, 19).

As Yzhar himself described it, the story was not a political critique per se, but a meditation on the incongruity between ideology and the actual practice of war, between the purity of ideals and the brutal, often contradictory, actions taken in the name of their fulfillment. "The story is about guilt, . . . about an aberrant occurrence from classic Zionism. . . . I tried to describe a conflict between recognition or consensus that something must be done and . . . alarm at the results. . . . A man is sent to blow up a house, and when he receives such an order it sounds different than when he arrives and finds there people and children, that the house has life. . . . This conflict is also between this man's education, his worldview, his sense of Zionism that always said that we do not oust the Arabs but live with them in peace—and a different reality."[8]

Literary critic Nurit Gertz identifies the longing of the isolated narrator in Yzhar's work as a metaphysical rupture. The process of deportation, in Gertz's reading, stands for the internal Israeli process of disassociation from a historic past, from the possibility of a joint future with the Arabs, from the natural environment and human values they once held dear. More than a loss of innocence for Israelis just as the nation is coming into being, the story, for Gertz, depicts a process of isolation and loss: the loss of a connection with God, with the past, the Jewish continuum, the land, and finally, the very essence of the Jewish dream they had come there to recapture.

Gertz further suggests that it is Arab, not Jewish, life that is referenced in the story's evocation of both the Bible and nature: "[N]ature is eternal, Arab, and the Jew infiltrates it and violently destroys it; the future, too, is in the hands of the Arabs, and the God that appears at the story's end is a God that stands by the side of the Arab victim." "In practical terms," Gertz argues, "the story of Israeli literature in the '60s is the story of the results of 'Hirbat Hizaa.'"[9] This profound dislocation sends the next generation back to a metaphorical "Hirbat Hizaa," where that connection was lost through violence and destruction. The next generation of Israeli writers, she concludes, begins its stories at this point.

Initiated by the television director Ram Levi, the proposal to adapt the famous story was approved by the Israeli Broadcast Authority in 1976. As shooting began in March 1977, the project received some attention for its pedigree and ambitious scale. Starring several up-and-coming actors, a well-known Arab television personality, and an Israeli pop star, and shot on location in a Palestinian village with local residents in smaller roles, it was Israeli television's most expensive and lavish production to date. Scheduled to air in early 1978, *Hirbat Hizaa* was to mark a new era of cultural achievement for Israeli television at the close of its first decade and in time for the nation's thirtieth independence celebration. In May, while the film was still in production, the 1977 Knesset elections delivered the most dramatic results in Israel's political history. In a surprising landslide, the election of Menachem Begin's Likud Party had abruptly ended Labor's historic hegemony, undisputed since the state's 1948 inception. Fortified by plummeting confidence in Meir's cabinet after the surprise 1973 attack that began the Yom Kippur War, Begin's ascent was propelled by a powerful intersection of conservative religious factions and Likud's courting of disenfranchised Sepharadic voters, long resentful of Labor's policies and of the dominance of Ashkenazi elites. For Israel's political history, the election results ushered in what Leon Hadar has termed "the Second Republic," marked by Likud's staunch nationalism and right-wing politics that embraced religious conservatism and highlighted the ideology of "Greater Israel."[10]

By the time production wrapped in July, the political sea change brought new attention to *Hirbat Hizaa* and the IBA board's unanimous approval of the project. A sprinkling of reports and editorials began to suggest its "problematic" nature; the film's theme, shooting location, and ambitious scale all acquired a new political charge in postelection Israel. The story's critical introspection about Israeli treatment of Palestinians, its questioning of early land policies, and its indicting representation of a callous and desensitized army appeared in amplified incongruence to Likud's brand of nationalism. With its expansionist reworking of Zionist ideals, renewed emphasis on military might, open disdain for Arabs, and attitude of "matched belligerency" that saw power as Israel's only guarantor in regional politics, Likud's hawkish creed seemed to echo the very sentiments expressed by Micha's platoon members in response to his dovish qualms of conscience. As some early commentators suggested, the intended broadcast could appear as an airing of an ideological clash—a theme the new political majority might well find distasteful.

In a meeting that followed a screening of a rough cut in late August, only one member of the IBA board expressed opposition to the film. Nevertheless, the committee acknowledged the film's potential for controversy and considered that the IBA's decision to air it might be read as a tacit endorsement of *Hirbat Hizaa*'s critical perspective. This, it was feared, could attract unwanted political attention.[11]

Anticipating such criticism, it was decided to air the film not as a stand-alone feature—as initially planned—but as part of the discussion series *The Third Hour*.[12] To avoid "leaving the audience to confront the film on their own," the board announced in late August, *Hirbat Hizaa* would be broadcast as part of a public affairs discussion program where a bipartisan roundtable of "educators and writers" would follow the screening and discuss the "problems it raises."[13] No doubt intended as a precautionary measure, the recontextualization of the work was meant to create a structural distance between the programmers and the film. The placing of the narrative within the "brackets" of discussion acknowledged its provocative content while providing a televisual space in which to address and contain a critical backlash.

However, such framing did more than present the film as controversial, it defined its value (and broadcast worthiness) as sourced in its problematic nature and thus fundamentally relocated the presentation from the cultural sphere to a public affairs setting. Thus, the teleplay was reconfigured as airing not *despite* the controversy it might engender, but rather as a broadcast event *about* that controversy.

Nonetheless, the attempts to temper the film's sharp edges and preempt critical responses through containment went virtually unnoticed. In late January, two weeks before *Hirbat Hizaa*'s scheduled airing, the Knesset was called to discuss the upcoming broadcast. One coalition member, MK Kalman Cahane, opened the charged discussion by protesting that the IBA's independent status left the government helpless to intervene in broadcasts whose "permissive nature serves as a bad educational example . . . and deeply wounds the feelings of many Israeli viewers." Airing *Hirbat Hizaa*, the MK continued, would do "serious damage to the state of Israel" and bespoke nothing short of pathology. "I cannot understand the choice of this story as anything but 'Judeophobia,' self-hatred and [the desire for] self-destruction," charged the minister.[14]

For Cahane, the teleplay's danger lay beyond its mere "perversion" of history, and more crucially in its role in the formation of public opinion abroad:

> In all our battles, wars and clashes with the Arab population and Arab warriors—even the worst of them who came to murder and destroy—we tried to preserve . . . our and their humanity . . . [yet] we are represented in a twisted manner using all forms of mass communication all over the world. And to this purpose, Israel-haters will now add Israeli television itself. . . . We all know that we are not measured by the same standards as our enemies who are readily forgiven; . . . in all our actions, we stand as all the world's spotlight points at us—they search for sins among us with a magnifying glass—and at the same time, Israeli television presents—as if to the whole world—its soldiers as sadists. . . . This is a crime against the Jewish people.[15]

Notably, Cahane's condemnation did not focus solely on the film as singular or unusual. Rather, the MK directed his attack at the IBA as a whole, casting the film as extreme but indicative of a service whose flaw (and threat) lay in its independence from direct government control. Further, his emphasis on the film's "dangerous" selection as representative of a "self-destructive" attitude focused attention on both the IBA's governing structure and Israeli television's articulation of identity. By connecting programming back to television's old charge of education, morale upkeep, and cross-border communication, Cahane resuscitated the old tenets of the founding Israeli television discourse, with its twin anxieties of (internal) regulation and (external) observation. With this opening salvo, the parameters of the debate were set to include territory much wider than the film itself. Moreover, the attack positioned the issue not as a novel case that required official contemplation, but as yet another battle in a systematic struggle over television in total.

Cahane's vision of an unblinking, unforgiving world eye fixing Israel with its anti-Semitic glare can easily seem a mere paranoid projection, yet it readily fits into the historic pattern of telespeculation that saw television as Israel's face to the world—a vision that, as I have argued in earlier chapters, all but prompted its establishment.[16] In this sense, the program's fictional probing into the nation's darker past represented a direct violation of television's primary directive. Or, as one journalist later phrased it, "the Golem has turned on its makers."[17]

More immediately, concerns over world opinion were anchored in recent political developments that pressed on Israel's new conservative regime. By the late summer and early fall of 1977, a series of U.S.-facilitated encounters and secret meetings between Israeli and Egyptian representatives enlivened possibilities for peace negotiations. In November, Egypt's president, Anwar Sadat, had taken the remarkable step of publicly declaring his willingness to go to Israel and discuss a peaceful solution to the Palestinian problem and a long-term peace agreement.[18] In an ironic twist, it would be Begin, a heretofore steadfast opponent of land-for-peace concessions, who would host the Arab leader in this unprecedented visit on Israeli soil. Sadat arrived on November 19 and, in the glare of flashbulbs and countless TV cameras, shook hands with Menachem Begin, Golda Meir, Ariel Sharon, and other leaders and dignitaries. To many Israelis who watched the landing on their television sets, the visitor could not have produced more stunned responses had he traveled across the galaxy, and not the mere width of the Sinai Desert.

Sadat's overture, and the series of difficult ongoing peace negotiations that followed, had indeed thrust Israel and its recent military history into the world media spotlight. During the two weeks leading up to *Hirbat Hizaa*'s scheduled broadcast, negotiations with Egypt appeared at a standstill and Sadat was expressing frustration with the Israeli position—and with Begin's support for settlements in particular. On February 3, Sadat and U.S. president Jimmy Carter met in Camp David. Carter explicitly commented that the continuous Israeli encouragements of settlement and reluctance to withdraw from all occupied territories were an obstacle to peace.[19] As U.S. and Israeli insiders acknowledged, Sadat had appeared both courageous and gracious on the world media stage, despite enormous pressure and opposition in the Arab world. Begin's difficulty reciprocating in kind was equally apparent. As some in the coalition government argued, current political developments made *Hirbat Hizaa*'s timing inauspicious and particularly detrimental. "What is the point of screening this story, that has not a single positive word and all is negative? To broadcast it today, on the Israeli public screen, when we struggle for every drop of good will from those who do not already hate us? [In] better times, it would be possible to broadcast this film. . . . But to screen it today on national television—there is something dim-witted about that. It diminishes our stance to the outside during negotiations and inwardly, during—God forbid—a war."[20]

For director Ram Levi, the argument for delaying the broadcast for the duration of negotiations was disingenuous at best. "Those who argue this," he told a reporter, "surely assume that peace will never come, and thus we can avoid the unpleasant necessity of airing *Hirbat Hizaa* on television altogether." Yet the political significance of the program, and the symbolic punch of its chosen medium, were clearly aligned in the mind of Zevulun Hammer, the new culture and education minister. "It's inconceivable," declared Hammer, that a tax-supported service would air a program that depicted Israelis "as strangers in their own land."[21]

During that first Knesset debate, supporters of the broadcast invoked the examples of *Uncle Tom's Cabin, Roots, The Brothers Karamazov,* and *Gulliver's Travels* to argue for artistic freedom and the value of controversial works, yet opponents discounted the comparisons, contending that the film would surely influence world public opinion at the current delicate moment. Proponents of the broadcast argued that the film illustrated Israel's willingness to wrestle with difficult moral questions and represented the finest in its cultural achievement. "It would be better," Hammer countered, if the IBA were "to select another of our fine works of literature that does not carry self-accusations and is not as controversial."[22]

At the meeting's conclusion, members voted to refer the matter to an education subcommittee for further discussion. Infighting immediately began in the IBA managerial ranks as two members unsuccessfully appealed to the board, asking it to delay the February 6 broadcast and await the government committee's decision. The IBA board refused, but the committee soon declared it had no legal right to interfere with television programming; *Hirbat Hizaa* would be aired as planned.

Beginning with reports of the government's displeasure over the program and of the turmoil within the television management board, the buzz over the airing of *Hirbat Hizaa* was spreading quickly from the urban sidewalk cafes, where literati and journalists, fortified by Turkish coffee, cigarettes, and apple strudel, chewed over the day's events, to the critical attentions of columnists, magazine editors, and other opinion peddlers. In the week before the broadcast, columnists opposed to the film invoked impressionable youths (both Arab and Israeli), new immigrants, and an anti-Zionist European audience, arguing that the film pushed broadcasting independence to the absurd lengths of a state's financing its own undoing. Israel, argued one commentator, would face "a dreadful, worldwide loneliness." Reporting (inaccurately) that the film had already been purchased for exhibition in "the still pro-Israeli Holland," the author speculated that *Hirbat Hizaa* would quickly make its way far and wide, to "campuses, universities, youth camps—and not because the PLO cannot produce negative, much more negative, films about us, but since *Hirbat Hizaa* has the strength of the suspect's own confession."[23]

By the week's end, papers and call-in radio programs were teeming with supporters and opponents of *Hirbat Hizaa* debating the decision to air it, anticipating the film's proximity to the literary version, and exchanging jabs over television's power and responsibility. Cartoons in every daily recorded the level of anticipation and preoccupation with the film—depicting birds, animals, and even inanimate objects rushing to television sets in time for the 9:30 broadcast. Monday morning and early afternoon also brought hundreds of phone calls to the IBA office, requesting it reconsider and refrain from airing the film, as a small impromptu crowd demonstrated outside the Jerusalem studios. Hours before the February 6 broadcast was to start, an official request arrived from a Knesset Education and Culture Committee to delay screening. Again the IBA's governing body voted and, by a close margin, elected to turn down the request and instruct the crew to continue preparations for the evening program.

That night, Israelis tuning in for the evening's controversial offering were greeted with an unexpected development: An announcer informed the viewers that the scheduled screening of *Hirbat Hizaa* had been canceled by the culture and education minister. At the designated time, receiver screens went white as television workers expressed their protest by broadcasting forty-five minutes of "dead air." Reportedly, workers debated a national strike during this time, but the evening broadcasts concluded with a screening of the British production of Chekov's "Three Sisters." This "quality" replacement was rich in irony for one *Al Hamishmar* columnist, who recalled how the culture and education minister, when first stepping into his government post, emphasized the need to "even the scale between international and Israeli culture," and to include more of the latter in television dramas. "It seems he means to even the scales not so much between 'theirs' and 'ours' as for a Jewish offering of very particular tastes."[24]

As Hammer reasoned the following day, his action was necessitated by the IBA's refusal to consider Knesset requests, despite the "sensitive nature of the program" and the need for a "wider circle of public examination."[25] Insisting that he did not overstep his authority, the minister revealed that his intervention followed the expressed request of two IBA members—and was therefore perfectly legal.[26]

The last-minute cancellation of the much anticipated and much scrutinized film propelled the story to front-page status in virtually every newspaper the following morning. The striking parallel to the Sabbath programming scandal did not escape many commentators.

Some hinted, or openly speculated, that the two-member "request" was arranged with the minister well in advance as another attempt to squeeze government control through a deliberate legal loophole. "What happened yesterday—particularly in light of this precedent," wrote one columnist, "is simply unbelievable."[27]

"A SCORCHING OFFENSE": PUBLIC RESPONSE
AND THE "CENSORSHIP" DEBATE, ROUND ONE

It indeed requires a large amount of chutzpah to claim that at the nation's jubilee, in the midst of a desperate fight for lost world public opinion, a sacred mandate of freedom-of-opinion requires that we show, on our national airwaves, how cruel our soldiers were to the fathers of today's *Fatah*.[28]

The official dispute over the film received some attention in the press before the February 6 "whiteout." However, it was the cancellation that propelled the greater public reaction and led to several readings of the conflict—all of which found voice in the tumultuous debate that followed. For some broadcast supporters, the events were exactly akin to the Sabbath incident and represented government attempts to limit and control the independent broadcast agency. In this view, the content of the broadcast was thoroughly overshadowed by the danger posed to the institutional autonomy—mandated by the 1965 law—of the television authority. The IBA's legal representative argued the two cases' similarity in a view that was shared, at least informally, by a chief Supreme Court justice. "My impression," the judge observed, "is that the Minister stepped into the same trap as . . . Prime Minister Golda Meir during the case of Friday evening broadcasting."[29] A statement released to the press by the television staff the following day conveyed a "deep apprehension over the future of freedom of expression at the Israeli Broadcast Authority."[30]

For others on the side of the IBA, the conflict was between freedom of expression and governmental control. In this argument, the crux of the controversy was not in the government's legal violation of another agency's autonomy (as it had been in the Shabbat case), but a case of blatant, politically motivated state censorship of an artistic work. This was certainly the case for the story's author, S. Yzhar: "The worst aspect of what happened is that a Knesset committee appointed itself judge of an artistic work. . . . I want to emphasize the grave danger in violating the principle of separation between matters of politics and matters of art; the range of politics is very short and immediate while the range of art is infinite."[31]

Similarly, many critics and commentators decried what they saw as an inappropriate reduction of the cultural to political dimensions: "The Education and Culture Minister needs to see that the debate has deteriorated to such a low, painful level that Ram Levi's film (which none of us has seen) is no longer its subject; rather, it is the cultural shape of the nation. The damage done to the terms 'Culture' and 'Education,' by the defilement of this literary creation and by dragging it down with such provincial brouhaha and strategic tricks, is heavier than any film."[32] Several columnists who argued that Yzhar's story was a casualty of political art censorship employed the government's own rhetorical strategies that emphasized Israel's image on the world stage. Critics of the government argued that in designating the film a threat to Israel, forcibly removing it from the air at the last minute, and causing such a public stir, Hammer had visited on Israel precisely the kind of damage *Hirbat Hizaa* opponents had feared. "The incident," a typical liberal editorial went, "highlights artistic attempts to address this period in Israeli history and functions as a public indictment, in and outside Israel, of the government's swift attempts to obstruct its airing."[33]

The union of film and television directors fired off a telegram to Hammer calling his action cowardly and "typical of someone with shallow patriotic sentiments who is contemptuous of freedom of expression."[34] A call for Hammer's resignation came from a spokesman for the Labor opposition, who described the film as "not an expression of the Israeli society's weakness but of its moral strength" and denounced the minister's action for creating an "atmosphere of nationalistic hysteria."[35] Other organized responses soon followed, among them a petition by twenty-five well-known Israeli authors, Yzhar among them, calling for Hammer to reverse himself or resign, and an official statement from the Central Union of Israeli Writers declaring the cancellation "a dangerous precedent that could damage artistic and literary freedom, and requires artists to stand on the principles of freedom of expression."[36] On February 9, more than two hundred high school students in Jerusalem who had studied the story petitioned Hammer to resign over his "censorship of literature." Similar petitions were reportedly organized in Tel Aviv and other cities.

In the myopic view of history's rear-view mirror, the *Hirbat Hizaa* incident certainly appears just as many such critiques had deemed it: a cultural disruption, a case whose lingering interest lies in the atypical and startling collision between artistic freedom and government stricture. Indeed, as Yzhar himself declared in an early interview, such government intrusion into cultural matters was a "first" and a "dangerous precedent."[37] In surveying the groundswell of public response the controversy engendered, it is tempting to naturalize the supporters' claim for television as a cultural medium suddenly darkened by the vengeful cloud of conservative politics. Such a position, however, denies the particular history I have described in earlier chapters and ignores the consistent and predominant framing of culture *as* an ideological tool—and television as its superb conduit—an approach that both launched and defined Israeli television's establishment.

As television—unlike literature, cinema, or the independent press—emerged through its imagined suitability as an apparatus of national address and purported matchless facility in public education, the confluence of events presented the film as an ideological implosion. The complicated preexistence of Yzhar's story as a well-known cultural work and a contested piece of Israeli history made it an ideal test case, illustrating the depth of institutional meanings already invested in television and bringing these ideological expectations to the surface in a violent clash of political values. The traditional, "rooted" approach to Israeli television fastened the medium's (presumed) immense power to an ideological responsibility, while stressing that its independence was state granted. In this view, IBA's independence was designed to ensure commonplace political autonomy (freedom of the press) but could not extend to critiques of the state at large—making it fundamentally unlike other cultural outlets. "The State had bestowed on them a dangerous weapon, a unique and mighty instrument for dissemination, brain-washing, persuasion; for the birth of myths and the fortification of beliefs. And they decide that this is the time, and this is our generation's national and cultural imperative: to burrow in past wounds."[38]

As this editorial attack on the IBA makes plain, television's representational capacity is here defined solely as a means to an ideological end. Similarly, the minister of the interior, Dr. Joseph Berg, made a clear distinction between the text as literature and as a television program: "There's a difference between the appearance of a work in print and its screening in a such a powerful medium as television; . . . the broadcast of the film does not serve the public's interests and surely does not further the cause of peace." "It is unacceptable," added Hammer, the culture and education minister, "that certain people in television are taking advantage of the monopoly at their disposal and the great influential power of this communication tool to negative ends."[39] Many letters to the editor in support of Hammer expressed a similar position: "We seem to have forgotten that the place of films is usually in the movie theaters, where the public supports or rejects them there by its decision to pay the price of admission; . . . have we finished presenting to us and the world all of the horrors of the Arabs' war against us, so we can now show this film and balance the scales a bit? . . . [T]his is a classic example of frightful liberalism; . . . more power to Zevulun Hammer for blocking demoralization. It's not he who should resign, but those who provide our enemies with swords to destroy us."[40] As the progovernment position suggested, television's power was in its national significance and in the implicit mode of viewership and meaning making it elicited from audiences both in and outside Israel. The story, when read as literature or taught in schools, Hammer argued, was one of many cultural documents about the war and Israeli conduct. On television, however, *Hirbat Hizaa* was plucked out of this context and transformed into a single version of events. "Television has created only this one original film and it represents us as . . . cynical and ruthless." Thus, such a provocative selection removed the film entirely from a cultural realm, a disjointing made explicit by the minister's expression of appreciation for the film's artistic achievement. "From a professional and artistic point of view, [the film] was well-made and sensitive," Hammer observed. He added that on its artistic merits, it would have made a fine broadcasting choice "if it were not for its unjustified and scorching offense to us, if it were about an event far away from here."[41]

Israel's possible misconduct during its independence war was a raw nerve too tender to be touched in the face of Israel's instantly mythologized memory of nation building. It would be another decade before relevant documents were declassified, allowing Israel's "New Historians" to definitively puncture that myth, showing that many Palestinian villagers did not leave their land at the urging of Arab invading armies in 1948 but were in fact forced out by the Israeli army. Still, Yzhar's story of one such "relocation" mission during the 1948 war, while controversial in its historical claim, was embraced and widely praised as literature. The difference, then, lay in the selection process that transformed the author's voice into a collective address. As one critic argued, Yzhar's story may have been based "on his own personal truth," but its televisual adaptation transformed the work into a "public deception."[42] The deception lay not in the veracity of the event itself, but in the historical centrality it would acquire through televisual representation. Comparing the airing of *Hirbat Hizaa* to a screening of a film on Jewish Nazi collaborators on the Day of Remembrance, the critic maintained that not the truthfulness of the narrative would be in question, but its place of emphasis in the long view of history.

Television's representation of the story, in visual and thus concretizing terms, may well have given the narrative an uncomfortable material existence, moving it away from the shadowy, subjective realm of a memory play into the more explicitly confrontational register of a contested history. However, what touched off the firestorm was television's institutional presence, as well as the medium's meaning, in the context of the recent political upheaval. As Hammer observed after viewing the film, "It turned the incidental into the typical [and] could certainly be seen by the viewer as a documentation of blame about the ugly conduct of Israelis towards the Arabs during the war." What's worse, he cautioned, the film could raise doubts about "our fundamental right to the land."[43]

Whereas some arguments relied on the general notions of artistic freedom pitted against national responsibility, and others saw the controversy as an argument about representation of Israeli history, the public dispute quickly sharpened into a political, partisan battle. Several editorials suggested that the cancellation tactic was designed to delay the broadcast until March 12—when a new, Likud-appointed IBA board would begin its tenure, virtually guaranteeing the film's decisive elimination from the programming schedule. The ironic appearance of *Hirbat Hizaa*, a celebrated liberal critique, in the precise moment of conservative government transition raised the tenor of the debate to a political drama in which the IBA was cast as a Labor-led agency that posed a deliberate political challenge to the Right. To many opposed to the broadcast, *Hirbat Hizaa* was symptomatic of a television agency out of touch with national consensus and its own representative mandate: a "powerful and influential medium" that, as one typical letter argued, "has become the province of the political left [leading to] . . . a lack of balance . . . and systematic selectivity."[44]

To others, the stakes were even higher.

> The Likud party won the election, and we the voters believed that they will also do some checking into the IBA, which not just once served to fortify Israel-haters. To our disappointment, it turns out that the IBA are a supreme power and no one can hurt it. I was shocked to read . . . that despite the opposition of the Minister . . . and despite the knowledge that broadcasting *Hirbat Hizaa* will be a weapon at the hands of Israel-haters, the management decided to screen it. The question becomes: does the IBA control the Israeli government? Is it their aim to make our lives miserable and to poison the soul of our youths? Please! Shut their mouths before it's too late! The poison they introduce among our youth will bear rotten fruit in a short while![45]

BEAUTIFUL PEOPLE AND THEIR BEAUTIFUL SOULS: NEW POPULISM AND THE RECASTING OF THE CULTURAL ELITE

For many Israelis—and most readers who sent letters to various dailies—the *Hirbat Hizaa* affair was a political showdown. Yet the flare-up also exposed a fundamental rift in Israeli society and a new atmosphere of "political accounting" that tapped and transformed old

resentments and undercut the traditional coherence between the political leadership and the sphere of art and culture. Much as the seven-day
broadcasting schedule controversy provided a concrete catalyst for an
ongoing struggle between religious and secular visions of the Jewish
state, *Hirbat Hizaa* engaged the Israeli public not only through its challenge to artistic freedom, television's role in national culture, and the
government's political control of programming, but also and more fundamentally by linking the television version of Yzhar's story to a now
minority political viewpoint. For its opponents, the program epitomized the arrogance of the privileged class and the elitism of the cultural Left.

This new dynamic was first expressed at the very start of the controversy, when a newspaper opinion piece about the dispute intoned a
cultural stance that seemed to echo Begin's political revolution. Writing in a popular daily, the author invoked the liberal elite of artists,
literature professors, and political radicals (referred to here as "the
beautiful people," which would become a common term of derision)
whose obsessive insistence on public self-flagellation represented a
danger to morale and democracy itself. "There is no power in this
world, no sovereign or foundation, no flood or earthquake, no Knesset
discussion or public will that can delay the beautiful people from airing
Hirbat Hizaa. Our Shylocks demand their pound of flesh in democratic
freedom."[46]

Echoing the "self-hatred motif" already introduced in Knesset discussions, the author's Shakespearean reference here casually linked the
work's critical internal reflections with broad anti-Semitism and the
disparaging gaze of global viewership. Singled-out for the broadcast's
"brainwashing" were impressionable Israeli students and young Arab
men who "do not hide their desire to see Palestine rise on top of, and
not next to, the 'land of Robber-Jews.'" These, the column speculated,
would be joined by "new world order" journeymen from Europe, as
copies of the broadcast would be disseminated in "every international
forum."[47]

This early, explicit assault on the liberal elite (defined in the column as pro-Arab leftist intellectuals and media professionals) gave
voice to a long-fermenting cultural battle and a historical realignment
that could erupt only with the newfound power of the Right: "*Hirbat
Hizaa* does not appear in any map; it does not appear because it does
not exist. *Hirbat Hizaa* never stood and never existed. But this is so only
on the map. In conversation, in courses run by literature professors at
the Hebrew University, it is alive and well, it is larger than life."[48]

In a progressive, synecdochic chain, *Hirbat Hizaa* perfectly embodied television itself: Television stood for the IBA, the IBA for the Labor Party, the Labor Party for Israel's radical Left, and the radical Left for the elite classes. *Hirbat Hizaa*, then, served to demarcate a series of interrelated social, cultural, and political divisions. The text in this formulation, however, was itself not seen as a galvanizing divisive force; rather, it was symptomatic of a gaping schism. For conservative and progovernment voices, this widening gulf was fostered and nourished by television itself, "ever since," as one esteemed writer and commentator lamented, "the Six-Day war divided the populace into left and right in a completely artificial manner."[49]

For Ephraim Kishon, a hugely popular author and satirist, television's hostility to right-of-center politics was a given: "It is no secret that in the popular departments of television there is no foothold for the 'nationalistic elements'; . . . their work and opinion are systematically silenced . . . [by the] Leftist establishment . . . [who] divide among them all the committees, grants and prizes. . . . To belong to . . . the Right is to dig one's own grave in the media." But television's liberal political allegiances—along with the resentment they inspired—were indivisible from cultural tastes and class status: "Whoever wants to show his mug on television . . . must first recognize the legitimate rights of Arafat and applaud the garbage heaps at the Tel-Aviv museum."[50]

This explicit melding of liberal ideology with high-brow cultural pretension was a strategic coup for conservative rhetoric that joined ethnic tensions, religious practice, social conservatism, educational differences, and cultural tastes, folding these into "plain-speaking" populist nationalism to produce the precise opposite of the "cultural education" discourse that defined the Labor government's approach to both the original inter-Israeli social divide and the origins of television.

What is most important in understanding the formation of interlaced divisional discourses around the *Hirbat Hizaa* program is that the actual text was the trigger, rather than its substance. The controversy did erupt with the shift in government power and ideological bend— still, news of the broadcast would surely have caused some controversy even if the Labor Party had remained in power. The story's emphasis on Palestinian victimization and Israeli callousness would have been problematic for its challenge to the nation's foundation myth, the heroism of its soldiers, and its "purity of arms," a founding tenet in the establishment of the Israeli army, with its self-named emphasis on defense.

"Purity of arms," one of the most often invoked principles in Israeli discussion of military engagement, perceives combat as a necessary evil that can be employed only for the protection of human life—and thus is fundamentally defensive.[51] With its direct critique of

Israeli conduct and of the soldiers' cavalier attitudes, the broadcast would have doubtless generated angry responses and public protest in any context. The difference, then, was not in the text itself, but in what the text had come to mean in the unfolding debate. What emerged, over the course of the affair, as the differences in approaches toward television saw the nature of the national and representational quality of the service in the desire for "majority cultural uplift" and education on the one hand, and reflection of "majority politics" and nationalist values on the other. Labor's defeat, delivered by the very majority it targeted for cultural "correction" and brought on by a nationalist fervor born of recent military failures and perceived weakness, appeared to speak through Yzhar's controversial call for the recounting of conscience—particularly in its planned televisual address. In the gathering backlash against the Left's military and cultural stance, *Hirbat Hizaa*, with its institutional intrigue, textual provocation, and historical resonance, served as a potent irritant for a political frenzy. These divergent discourses, through their association with the broadcast, fused into a tight hard knot.

Whereas conservative rhetoric articulated the "liberation" of television from the grip of the liberal elite, for probroadcast proponents, government actions indicated new constrictions that sought to manipulate and control content for political gain. For both sides in this iteration of the debate, opponents' attitudes toward television texts, artistic freedom, and responsibility in expressions of national identity bespoke political extremism and stood for a general worldview that endangered the state. A rapidly coalescing set of descriptive shorthand characteristics in public discourse produced the archetypal "beautiful people" on the one hand, and the "fascists" on the other. The former were self-hating Jews whose radical politics matched their intellectual pedigree and elitist tastes and whose fetishistic obsession with others' victimhood displayed a dangerous "appetite for self-blame" (in Zevulun Hammer's words) and national destruction. These were poised against chauvinist boors whose utilitarian vision of culture matched their artless governance, betrayed a contempt for intellectual engagement and complexity, and endorsed a ruthless brand of thuggish nationalism.

Such historically resonant sketches abounded on both sides. In a mordant take on the program's replacement with the British production, one author adopted a note of mock alarm at the subversive messages contained in Chekov's tragedy, pondering how such an antiestablishment work could have made it past the tsarist censors in 1901, never mind the Israeli government in 1978. Turning to postrevolutionary Russia, the author concluded with a quote from a Soviet official, demanding from writers a primary engagement with Soviet politics. " 'Soviet' here could be changed to 'Israeli' and the picture will then be complete."[52]

Both depictions, while familiar and indeed common to the general spirit of culture wars, have specific reverberation in the Israeli case as, in their historical sweep, they evoked particularly painful periods in European Jewish history.[53] One such commentary equated the staunch nationalists who opposed the airing to "the Jewish equivalent of fascism . . . walking among us in brown shirts and black boots." The author further directed his wrath squarely at Begin's cabinet, "students and disciples" who "sit now on the throne of government and plan to brainwash us away from 'humanist garbage.' "[54]

STEWARDSHIP OR CENSORSHIP:
POLICY REVERBERATIONS AND ROUND TWO

> Today they worry about our image abroad, tomorrow about our mental health and the day after, they will guard our Jewish spirit. There's no need for a wild imagination to foresee [them] designing a nationalist-Jewish-religious culture for us all.[55]

> As someone who has seen the film I can say that if the film was done abroad, by a gentile, we would all say that he and the film are anti-Semitic.[56]

> This internal censorship is worse. . . . For many reasons, the stopped-up mouth is better than the lying mouth."[57]

Speaking to an interviewer immediately after the cancellation, Yzhar lamented that a debate about the film—after its screening— would have been *Hirbat Hizaa's* most important accomplishment: "This is what should have happened after the film, if it aired. It is a problematic film that will bring arguments; . . . this is not only legitimate, it's a desired result. To cancel the film is to close off a healthy, democratic public debate."[58]

Ram Levi, *Hirbat Hizaa's* director, told a reporter that Begin's self-professed "revolution of May 17 had, actually, begun right now" with the cabinet's active involvement in IBA's programming decisions. Well-known for provocative television documentaries and dramas that often portrayed Arab-Israeli relations, Levi expressed concern over "a new era in freedom of speech on television," as a new IBA board, reflective of the current political ideology, would replace the old. For Levi, his public clash with government authorities would prove unrepresentative of this new era. "What surfaced this week in all the front pages will be done quietly and internally, and there probably will be no more productions like *Hirbat Hizaa*."[59]

And, as indications immediately after the cancellation suggested, the "culture war" that erupted over the broadcast could have some real policy consequences. "Slowly we are getting used to a new reality," wrote one observer, "and the fears that flickered in the paranoids within us after May 17 of last year are being confirmed."[60] Signs of the "revolution" that Levi feared made news the very next day, when reports surfaced of a Likud proposal to amend the IBA law. The proposed change declared that the goal of television was not only to "foster good citizenship" (as stated in the old law), but also "to cultivate loyalty to the people and the state." "It is unacceptable," stated the amendment's authors, that the radio and television authority would air programs that "damage the well-being of the state and the feelings of the citizenry."[61]

Among other provisions, the proposal stipulated that no broadcast would "reflect in any way the personal views of the television staff or the presenters in controversial matters of national or social nature, or problems currently under public discussion. The Broadcasting Authority would promise that it would broadcast no material that harms the symbol of the state, its flag or its independence charter." The proposal further endowed the minister of education and culture with final discretion to direct the IBA to remove programs—or portions thereof—that appeared to violate these conditions. The IBA would be permitted to publicize such government directives, but the minister would also be granted the right to dismiss any IBA board member for noncompliance.[62]

In response to reports about the amendment proposal, the journalists union expressed its intent to oppose any attempts to change the IBA law; the union went further, circulating a petition in support of the IBA and against government involvement in broadcasting decisions as a fundamental free-speech principle.[63] On the following day, the daily *Ma'ariv* began printing Yzhar's story in a three-day series. Befitting the story's current status at the center of a political quake, the paper reprinted the entire text prominently in the paper's main section, rather than relegating it to the arts or literature section or the weekend special supplement. This well-known, much-reprinted thirty-year-old work of fiction was now today's political news.

Ma'ariv's decision to reprint Yzhar's story is curious considering how ubiquitous this work had been. More to the point, the reprint seemed to refocus the debate on the content of the story as the problematic element, whereas the controversy was not over the story itself but over its screen adaptation by Israel's national television service. As several government officials affirmed, there would be no controversy had the story been adapted as a commercial film for theatrical release (an idea enthusiastically supported by Israeli film producer Menachem Golan, who offered to show the film in his theaters, and emphatically rejected by Ram Levi, who insisted his adaptation was specifically televisual). Yet, in light of the nonbroadcast, the story was the closest material text available. In this sense, the paper's action might well be read as a defiant attempt to "air" the repressed text. Yet the reprinting also worked to support the interpretive stance that the controversy was about the story's content. By its placement in the political news section rather than in the arts section, however, the reprinting appeared to straddle both sides of the debate: the work of fiction *as* politics.

In this chapter, I have followed the structure of the debate by drawing some (albeit artificial) boundaries between the realms of politics and culture to emphasize television's odd perch in a blurry territory within. However, it is important to stress that Israeli literature and Israeli authors have long been highly visible in political discourse.[64] Moreover, it is precisely the discursive attempt to detach the two in the context of television that was so revealingly incongruous. As Smadar Lavie notes, Israel has one of the highest rates in the world for literary readership, and "literature plays a key role in forming Israeli national identity and culture. Hebrew literature . . . has been central to imagining the new Israeli national identity," and writers and poets have always been considered part of the "pantheon of Zionist pioneers." Far from marginalized or insular products for elite consumption, works such Yzhar's had been in active circulation. As Lavie reports, literary authors in Israel enjoy a high public status as artists, opinion makers, and popular celebrities whose personal trials and romantic entanglements are gleefully detailed in newspaper gossip columns. Many literati have opinion columns in Israel's major newspapers and literary debates are part of popular public culture. Canonical literature, Lavie adds, "is catalytic in transforming Israel's national ideology into practice—some prime ministers and Knesset members have been known to discuss with journalists what novels and poems they have been reading lately, and even to quote from them on the Knesset floor.[65]

It is in this environment that the culture war around *Hirbat Hizaa*'s airing developed, with its charges of liberal, out-of-touch elitism and cultural hostility. It is also in this atmosphere that *Ma'ariv*'s reprinting and placement of the story becomes fully legible, as few mainstream readers would see the controversy through the lens of artistic censorship alone.

While the proposal to amend the IBA law was ultimately unsuccessful, news of the attempt drew the sharpest fire to date from probroadcast commentators. One radio and television reviewer, Dorit Gefen, wrote:

"The attempt to turn the Knesset into a political and cultural censor raises shivers and constitutes a real and grave warning sign of what the future will bring, when commissars . . . will determine what is best for us, what we should watch and listen to, and perhaps also what we are permitted to read. Once the self-protective mechanisms of democracy are smashed through, there is no telling how far matters will deteriorate and what these new moral guardians have in store for us."[66]

In the following week, artists and academics, among others, held a public evening of protest in a prominent Tel Aviv theater. The unstructured evening included readings from Yzhar's story and speeches against Hammer and the Likud government, punctuated by calls from the crowd and political appeals that collapsed the somewhat delicate distinction between the battle over Yzhar's historical narrative and current political tensions. As the evening's speeches indicated, the *Hirbat Hizaa* affair became an easy metaphor for the state of the country in the Begin era. One typically impassioned speaker proclaimed the emergence of a "fascist faction" on the Israeli political landscape: "What has occurred after 1967 . . . is *Hirbat Hizaa* times one hundred."[67]

Throughout the *Hirbat Hizaa* scandal, news coverage of the television war shared space with reports about peace negotiations with Egypt, discussions over the ultimate fate of the occupied territories, and the Likud Party's "autonomy" proposal.[68] As pressures mounted over the nixing of the broadcast, one Likud official publicly announced his change of heart, stating that the controversy had placed his party members in "the unsympathetic . . . defensive position" and, since no substantive discussion could be maintained in such an atmosphere, it was now more important to allow the broadcast so that "Israel-haters will not claim we have something to hide."[69]

Petitions in support of both sides continued to pour into the IBA's Jerusalem offices. Notably, during the few days when government officials discussed the standstill and legal advisors declared the Broadcast Authority's legal independence from government influence, there appeared a discernible increase in calls to ban the broadcast altogether. A newly formed Public Alliance for a Change in the Face of Television claimed its petition against the broadcast had garnered 53,648 signatures; other petitions supporting the education and culture minister arrived from political organizations, artists and musicians, army veterans, and religious high schools. As *Al Hamishmar* revealed, Golda Meir herself attempted to influence the IBA board and to prevent *Hirbat Hizaa* from airing "so that we are not seen as terrorists."[70]

Counter-petitions and appeals in support of the broadcast also remained prominent. A group letter from communications scholars and renowned academics (Elihu Katz among them) argued against the claims that the broadcast would "damage" Israeli viewers.

By the end of the week, newspapers reported that the education committee was pulling away from involvement and allowing the IBA board full discretion over the decision to air the program. In a February 12 discussion that lasted five hours, the IBA board, in an eighteen-to-four vote, decided to air the program and scheduled it for the following evening.[71] Hammer reacted by stating that the specific matter of the broadcast was now closed, yet "I hope that we will soon have the opportunity to discuss the real, basic problem . . . of the correlation between conscience, authority and responsibility."[72]

On the evening of February 13, the night of the broadcast, the atmosphere at the Israeli television offices was tense. Several threatening phone calls prompted the stationing of security guards on the premises, the police were called after a reported bomb scare near the studios, and small groups of protesters continued to gather outside. The broadcast itself went as planned, airing as the first part of the discussion program *The Third Hour* and followed by a live studio debate about the program.

"DRUNK WITH GUILT": REACTIONS TO *HIRBAT HIZAA*

I am sorry that the film . . . has lost its human significance and has become . . . an Arab-Israeli problem.[73]

Who will guard the viewers' souls? This patronizing attitude towards the 'tv-watching masses' [has] reached new heights with the Hirbat Hizaa affair.[74]

As viewers familiar with the story could see, the film that finally aired in mid-February included a few changes that served to quell some of the story's more controversial moments, and to provide visual and external motivation for Micha's internal turmoil. The process of "softening up" the confrontational material began with Daniella Carmi's script and Ram Levi's direction, muting the cruelty and nihilistic brutality of both language and action in the original story. Carmi added dialogue by inserting friendly repartee between the soldiers from a different work by the author and, in the film's most extreme departure, included a love interest for Micha: a young, giggly communications officer ("the New Girl"), often at the receiving end of the protagonist's anxious brooding stares.

The tension of unrequited desire (the young woman appears barely to notice him) added new emotional motivation to Micha's point of view, locating it outside "natural" and physical events, and setting up his observatory position and despairing commentary as sourced (at least in part) in romantic longing. Unlike the story, which immediately identifies Micha as an outsider narrator damaged and altered forever by his experience, the film creates tension by suggesting the events of the day as a single recollection, opening on the fateful day—the first scene of the film—with the image of Micha cheerfully at play with his fellow soldiers. A close-up image of Micha's face, smiling broadly in midgame, is frozen on-screen, implying a flashback, as a voiceover intones Yzhar's opening line: "All of this happened long ago but it would not let go of me." In a shortened version of the original text, Micha tells the viewer of his attempts to bury his memories, of how every now and again he is tempted to think that this event was not so terrible. At other times, he is aware of the ease with which he can "join the large and general collective of liars." As the same young men are seen loading a truck with supplies, preparing for the day's orders, and engaging in friendly banter en route to the village, the temporal placement of the previous scene is thrown into question: Was the scene of Micha playing with his friends part of the same temporal logic as what follows? Did it take place after the event about to be portrayed, or before? This early moment of confusion, where the cinematic and narrative codes seem at odds, can easily be taken for the general clash of media transposition at the heart of the controversy, but more immediately, it points to important open questions: What *was* the impact of this event on the narrator? What would it be for the viewer? What should it have been for the state?

As the soldiers make their way to the Negev village, they sing (significantly, a Hebrew rendition of Cole Porter's "Don't Fence Me In"), joke, and share an easy, if bored, camaraderie. The camera lingers on landscape stretches, the imagery familiar to every Israeli viewer: rolling brown hills speckled with gray twisting stones, rows of olive trees, and long sweeps of green. In their short pants, olive caps, and playful manner, the young men resemble a group of day-trippers—their machine guns an odd incongruity—rather than soldiers on a mission of war. As a friend tells Micha, sensing his gloom: "Snap out of it. The war is over." When Micha replies, "So let's all go home, then," his friend explains, "I mean the kind of wars where people kill and die, big wars. Now we just have the little wars left." "I'm sick of it," retorts Micha. "If they want to go on, they should find other kids to play with."[75]

Assessed in terms of its mode of representation, the film can be said to fail perhaps due to the "smallness" of the incident it depicts. The power and horror of the event, as Yzhar describes it, lie not in what is done, but in the rage and longing it engenders: the most violence, in the melancholy that remains; the worst destruction, in the desperate absence that expulsion brings; and the extreme mutilation, in the moral transgression that cannot be revoked or put right. The film is unable to reproduce the metaphysical aspects of space, time, and judgment invoked in the story, nor can it emphasize and sensitize the viewer to the crucial significance of sound and stillness (the "scream of silence" Yzhar makes audible in his prose). Finally, once visualized by a nation so used to the sight of both olive-clad young men with Uzis and robed Palestinians, the sharp contrast that the story produces—between the Israeli figure and the Arab, uniforms versus tunics, Jeeps versus donkeys, and so on—is less prominent here. Similarly, the straightforwardness with which the soldiers are portrayed, despite its faithfulness to the story, adds a dimension of comfort and visual "fit" that resists their reading as intruders. Finally, the invaded landscape itself conveys little of the sense of foreignness or violation to contemporary Israeli eyes: Scenes where a couple frolics among the village olive trees, or soldiers lazily take repast in an orange grove, not only appear quintessentially local—from the vantage point of the Israeli living room—but also invoke all the romance of classic Israeli pastorals.

However, the most affecting feature of the visual adaptation of the story is in the role of the Palestinians themselves. In most aspects, the visual concreteness of the scene drains it of much of its emotional and suggestive power, once reduced to specificity. However, several scenes in which Palestinian villagers (all Palestinian extras and mostly nonactors) are herded in groups through shallow water, down muddy narrow village paths, and onto flatbed trucks gain emotional power through their multitextual reverberations. The images in and of themselves— women, old men, and children led away from their homes by stone-faced Israeli soldiers—utterly contradict bedrock imagery of the gallant Israeli defense fighter, of "purity of arms," and of Arab aggression, all indispensable in Israel's foundation mythology. The scenes so palpably challenge such ideologically reified imagery as to feel nearly heretical.[76]

Further, the resonance of such imagery with Jewish cultural memory—of diasporas, of pogroms, and even of Nazi death camps—is inescapable in its visual quotation here. In one such scene, a camera circles a truck cramped with crouching old men; their creased faces, fragmented through the barred truck walls, stare out impassively. This historical resonance is reinforced by Micha's increasing discomfort and protestation as the actual assembly and deportation of the villagers get underway. Finally, inescapably, the villagers are portrayed by nonactors and, as Israeli viewers knew, were actual Palestinian residents in and around the village where the film was shot. These old men, then, were playing out a tragedy that befell their own people only thirty years earlier, performing the trauma over again for the Israeli cameras. However unimaginable in the current second-intifada days, such a scene may not have been as shocking at the time, but still lingered in the uncomfortable middle place between fact and fiction, representation and memory. This shifting, unbalanced quality between past and present, reality and playacting, is accentuated by the inexperienced performances that grant the scenes a multiplying awkwardness, radiating outward from the screen as it already folds within it an acknowledgment of an implied uncomfortable viewer.

To actualize—and thus represent—Micha's growing unease, the film inverts and externalizes his misgivings into action and ongoing conversations. Through this process, Micha becomes a much more expressive, active agent. In one scene, he races to bring water to the villagers, only to find that he is too late—the truck has left without food or water. Winded, frustrated, defeated, Micha is further riled by the sight of the female officer in flirtatious, carefree play with another soldier. His disappointment fuels an outburst at his superior, to whom Micha breathlessly repeats: "We cannot do this."

In the last dialogue scene, Micha speaks what is only suggested in the story: that the Palestinian villagers are made into refugees so that Jewish refugees from Europe can be settled in their place. The next shot is of a small Palestinian boy being lifted onto the truck by his mother. The boy, who only minutes ago walked past Micha and met his glance, now looks abruptly back toward the village he is leaving—a point off-screen that coincides with the camera's location. In a moment of collapsed artifice, the boy glances directly at the camera, violating the logic of character location, and quickly turns away. Clearly an unplanned, raw impulse, the instance manages to redefine the space of action in an evocative way: Looking at his home, and simultaneously at the Israeli camera trained on him, the boy's open, unnerving glance extends directly to the audience, now placed precisely where his village once stood. This scene—the penultimate shot of the film—is particularly memorable: immediately, in midaction, as the boy is hoisted upward into his mother's arms, no longer on land and not yet in the waiting truck, the camera abruptly cuts to an extreme wide shot of the road to the village. The caravan of army Jeeps makes its way from the site, its job done. On the soundtrack, Micha narrates this moment of reverie, speaking the last paragraph in the story: "Everything suddenly became so open, so large, and we ourselves became tiny and insignificant. Around and around silence has fallen, and when the silence closes in on everything and no one disturbs the hush, and this stillness hums as something beyond silence. God will then appear, descend to walk in the valley, and witness its screaming."[77]

Angry reactions to the broadcast began almost immediately. Disapproving phone calls poured into the studio mere minutes after the film ended, with callers objecting to the portrayal that set mostly pitiless Israeli soldiers against innocent Arab victims. Whereas some protested the sympathetic depiction of Palestinian villagers in particular, most complained about a lack of "balance" in the program. Playing directly into widespread fears about the broadcast's portrayal, widely publicized accounts of viewer calls to the IBA office emphasized Arab callers who, it was said, asked the operators: "If it bothers you so much, why not just give us all of Palestine?"[78]

Reviews of the film were all but eclipsed by the controversy, and most articles in the daily press engaged with the film solely through the public debate over its airing.[79] In the leading mainstream daily, readers' letters turned largely angry after the broadcast. The tenor and theme of the debate moved away from the politics behind the program's suppression and from concerns over artistic freedom to livid reactions to the film's construction of audience sympathies and the narrative's relationship to Jewish history.[80] For many letter writers who decried the show, the injustice lay not in the representation of the work itself but in the lack of parity for such moral examinations. Typical letters in this vein often read as litanies of Jewish massacres: "Do we know of one Arab author that wrote one word of protest over the 1929 murders of the students in Hebron, or the murders of women and children in Tiberius in 1937, or the murder of the pupils in Shapir in 1955. . . . Must we justify protecting ourselves?"[81] One author provided a detailed list of Jewish exiles and pogroms in Europe, noting that, compared to these, the Israeli actions depicted in *Hirbat Hizaa* were mild and humane.[82] Others wrote in with their own accounts and family tales of violent encounters with Arab attackers, their tone of barely restrained outrage suggesting that the film was an attempt to erase their experience and present a national memory that both challenged and dismissed their own. A handful of positive letters congratulated the production, calling it a courageous drama and asserting that it demonstrated Israel's moral core and its refusal to flinch from a problematic history. Still, expressions of anger at the story and its selection for broadcast far outnumbered approving responses: "It's difficult for me to comprehend how, from all the horrors that our people have suffered . . . it is this incident that horrified S. Yzhar so. . . . We have been in this country from the early '20s, and we can tell of many terrible deeds done to the Jews by the Arabs, and not just during war. Why haven't any of these stories received the same publicity and attention?"[83]

One format employed by many letter writers was a sarcastic list of "suggestions" for future productions, including dramatized incidents of Arab attacks on Israeli villagers and the murder of Israeli athletes at the Munich Olympics in 1972, all told from the Arab point of view and in a manner that sympathized with and glorified the murders. Other suggestions included a fawning biography of Arafat, a suggested film entitled *Hirbat Israel* documenting the final destruction of the Jewish state, or a filmed version of the *Protocols of the Elders of Zion*.[84] Still other letter writers speculated that the IBA production offices were flooded with congratulatory telegrams from PLO and Arab leaders, or sardonically asked for a schedule of IBA's joint productions with Syria. All these viewers were clearly protesting what others had explicitly charged: that the IBA was aiding the enemy in the struggle over Israel's survival by both affecting world public opinion and eroding Israeli's own moral confidence.

Among public figures, the rancorous debate over the film's political meaning grew even harsher after its airing. The following morning, the commentator and future IBA director Joseph Lapid fired the first in a series of shots when he charged the film with portraying Israeli soldiers as Nazis and providing the "best possible service to our enemies." The program's damage to global public opinion, Lapid argued, was as nothing compared to its message about Israeli identity: "If there are still young and innocent among us who believe that Israel is their birthright, if there are still highschoolers who have not written to the Prime Minister about bloodied hands, if there are still soldiers who delude themselves into thinking they are called to a just flag, and if there are still citizens who do not doubt our right to exist, they have all been informed of their mistake last night. They have been exposed and left naked as the real face of our nation was screened in almost every Israeli home."[85]

For Lapid (and for the many readers who, in letters to *Ma'ariv* the following day, cheered his column), the program's demoralizing effect was most tangible when expressed through the discourse of national security and thus was legitimately read as a security threat. It bears repeating here that such an accusation, extreme as it may seem, readily conformed to the founding notion that aligned television messages with ideological imperatives and gauged the medium's success (or failure) through this evaluative dimension. For others, Yzhar's story—and by extension its dramatization—worked on precisely the opposite logic, one that viewed the moral grappling and thoughtful introspection it provoked as "a fundamental and distinguishing characteristic of Jewish cultural and philosophical tradition, and a source of strength."[86] Increasingly, the broadcast was characterized and understood as symptomatic of an Israeli—and more significantly, a Jewish—penchant for guilt. The social value in and political justification for its airing quickly became central themes.

Self-examination, wrote another critic, "does not weaken us." Rather, he argued, it reaffirms "Israeli conscience and sensitivity, and the ability to recognize suffering and reflect on consequence, even in the midst of justified fighting"—a quality unique to the Israeli nation and made possible through the Jewish people's own long history as victims. Responding to the charge that the film would be widely used by pro-Palestinian and anti-Israeli interests, he asserted: "The enemy has no use for *Hirbat Hizaa*; . . . the story had been translated to Arabic yet the enemy . . . probably understood what many of us refuse to understand, that the fact that we have the power to expose deviations . . . cannot help their cause."[87]

Yet another critic attempted to place Yzhar's story in the middle ground of the debate by stressing the distinction between "facts" and "truth" in the narrative. The story, he wrote, is about "the tears of the innocent," and so could not be taken to task for a lack in "balance" or historical truth. "No one doubted the justification of the war and no one feared that the story would shake students' understanding of that justification. . . . The story concerns primarily the interior-battle within the Jewish soldier, and this kind of interior battle is necessary and essential to the shaping of Israeli youth."[88] Just as critics on the Right accused the Left of a guilt fetish, liberal critics retorted that the Right exhibited a disregard for the consequences of morally questionable actions. It was this "dangerous, self-righteous absence of guilt," one critic asserted, that motivated the attempts to censor and then discredit the film. Claims that the film would endanger Israel in the eyes of world were but a cover, she argued. The film was a threat to the Begin government since it offered the nation time to think of peace. "Guilt," she wrote, "speaks to the world of a moral problem, on an act that stands in contradiction to the ethical understanding of the perpetrator; . . . such questions, while open, will be deeply influential when the time comes to make a decision and take action the next time an emergency situation arises. And perhaps this is the fear that bothers those who object to the screening of *Hirbat Hizaa*."[89]

As in the Letters to the Editor pages, devoted to (mostly negative) reader responses, many critics and editorials lambasted the production

as an expression of the liberal elite's blind investment in Arab victimization. As these commentators saw it, the show's producers and supporters valued the exorcism of guilt above the difficult work of
national security. For others, the choice of production was indicative
of a dangerous liberal detachment from the realities of Arab-Israeli relations and a political naïveté about their consequences. For many
conservatives, guilt in its thematic exploitation in narratives such as
Hirbat Hizaa amounted to self-hatred and a dangerous lack in national
confidence. "Even self-hatred must have its limits," Lapid had sniped
in his opening salvo.[90] And, as another critic saw it, the airing
amounted to a kind of private catharsis with grave public consequences: "The story of *Hirbat Hizaa* was written to expel the guilt complex of a sensitive author; the film should not have been made or
shown by a guilt-ridden handful who force their opinions on the nation's majority. What has been done on Monday is a stupid, evil act
that every man, woman and child in Israel will pay a price for in the
not too distant future."[91]

A petition from immigrants from the Soviet Union tied the production's airing more explicitly to anti-Semitism:

> The film has been screened and all "free speech" champions are
> happy. And we wonder, was this irresponsible innocence or premedi-
> tated sabotage? We . . . are sure that Russians won't miss the op-
> portunity and will screen significant portions of the film, especially
> those of Israeli soldiers mistreating the "poor refugees." . . . Here is
> the authentic (it was shown in Israel!) face of the Israeli. There's no
> better propaganda to confuse Russian Jewry, . . . and what great ma-
> terial for all Russian anti-Semites. All this yelling over freedom of ex-
> pression reminds us of the free expression of the tsarist Russian
> slogan, "Beat the Jews." This time, this slogan is brought to us cour-
> tesy of the "beautiful people" of Israel.[92]

Even Yzhar expressed reservations toward an Israel that was "drunk
with guilt" and pursues "peace by means of continuous and one-sided
concessions." Guilt, Yzhar argued, must be the root of action, not a persistent, passive state. Throughout the controversy, Yzhar had been active and visible in his support for the broadcast. Yet, in reflecting on the
thirty years that had passed since he wrote the story, the author
lamented what he described as an unbalanced cultural engagement
with the Arab-Israeli conflict. In this, Yzhar's comments came closest to
reflecting the feelings of a vast majority of letter writers: "In all these
long years, I've never heard about Arab guilt for slaughtering Jewish
communities thirty and fifty years ago. . . . Why don't the Arabs feel
guilty for what they have done to us?"[93]

GOOD FOR THE JEWS? FROM *HIRBAT HIZAA* TO CAMP DAVID

1967 . . . is Hirbat Hizaa times one hundred.[94]

> We could have congratulated Ram Levi on bringing this educa-
> tional story to the television age in such a decent way, if not for a
> group of dim and mean-spirited public figures and stupid government
> officials unleashing a wild attack on human values and national princi-
> ples . . . we got a fascinating lesson on how, in two hours of pseudo-
> educational and pseudo-analytical discussion, generations of labor
> movement Zionist values are erased as if they never existed.[95]

In the period that preceded the *Hirbat Hizaa* broadcast, as the fate
of the film hung in the balance of committee members, votes, and government delay efforts, the debate between advocates and detractors in
the pages of daily editorials circulated around issues of artistic freedom
and political control, the autonomy of IBA, the clash between the
Likud and its left-wing opposition, and the threat to world opinion. In
the broadcast's aftermath, contention over art and IBA authority—
while still fodder for discussion in literary journals—was largely abandoned as attention focused on the broadcast's political meaning.[96]

Describing the program as "a smashing blow" and a product of
"criminal inanity," one guest editorial accused it of endangering Israel
by undermining its Hasbarah efforts. These, he argued, were already
strained in fighting "a vast system, rich in resources to fund lies, fakery
and malice with one purpose: to build moral justification for the physical act of the destruction of Israel." "The Arab propaganda machinery
will make sure that the film will be screened on television stations on
every continent, with no post-film discussion by scholars and 'beautiful people' who know this is an aberration . . . PLO commentators will
sit there . . . and explain the film as they understand it; . . . in our eyes
this is a work of art about an anomalous incident, the abnormal nature
of which speaks to the purity of our aims and the clarity of our conscience but the world will see it as an admission of guilt by the accused
himself."[97]

An opposing editorial on the same page dismissed the claims about
the film's devastating effects on world opinion, arguing that, by itself,
the film offered no new revelations about Israeli history or conduct:
"Heaven help us, the danger that the French, Dutch, Americans, English, Mexicans, and maybe other, less sympathetic nations, should
watch *Hirbat Hizaa*. . . . What is the terrible secret that will be revealed
to all?" "Those who hate us" she argued, would refuse to believe in the
authenticity of a war film "in which no man is killed, no woman is
raped and no child is beaten." What was worthy of attention, this

editorial suggested, was the nature of Israeli concern with world public opinion and its obsession with representation rather than political action. "When you try to hint . . . about the negative attitudes of the world to things that happen here every day, they silence you with the crushing reply, 'Either way, the world is all against us.'" For those worried about world opinion, the article concluded, current Israeli settlements in the territories should prove more troublesome than a film.[98]

Overwhelmingly, three themes emerged in the postbroadcast critique: concerns over world public opinion (What will *they* think?), the value of guilt (What were they *thinking*?), and the question of parity in representation (a demand that can be placed in the meeting place between action and representation). In these, Israelis expressed their preoccupation with both the role of Israeli television in representations of history and politics, and the political consequences of such representations both domestically and internationally. As in earlier debates that centered on televisual articulations, the focused attention specified three points of reception (and impact): the internal Israeli viewing position, the foreign (in particular European, U.S., and Arab) evaluation of Israel based on its televisual output, and television's impact on the conflict itself—on the meeting place between Israel and its neighbors. Likewise, as in all previous television debates, the stakes were much higher than just television or representation, bespeaking fundamental national aspirations, and anxieties, and contemporary priorities. The *Hirbat Hizaa* controversy was, as one critic termed it, a "national seism" that left its marks on the Israeli social and cultural landscape.[99] What's more, in light of the recent election results, the affair exposed a fault line in Israeli politics and, in the postbroadcast shake-up, opened it to reveal a growing ideological chasm.[100]

Writing in the monthly magazine *Emdah* (Position), author and critic Pinchas Ginosar called the *Hirbat Hizaa* affair a "definitive experience for its generation." Yzhar's narrative retained its resonance, he argued, since it was constructed from the material of the Arab-Israeli conflict—a conflict that the state remained "up to its neck in"—and for its troubling relevance for the post-1967 reality.[101]

As my tracing of the debate thus far makes clear, the political undercurrents of the *Hirbat Hizaa* affair quickly surfaced in public exchanges over the program. Debaters relied on ideological and party divisions and located their own and opponents' positions about the broadcast within a political spectrum. Through this process, the television adaptation of *Hirbat Hizaa* quickly lost its status as a memory play about a past event and became instead a kind of theoretical public referendum about the framing of the past as a political foundation for current and future policies.

By mid-February, this discursive cohesion appeared all but cemented as the *Hirbat Hizaa* controversy was overwhelmed by a larger debate over the "held territories" when the Carter administration, encouraged by the start of negotiations between Israel and Egypt, pressed the Israeli leadership for territorial concessions. Articles about the postbroadcast debate, however, did not diminish and appeared in literal context to reports, editorials, and political cartoons that depicted the growing argument over territorial handovers and the concept of land for peace.

Not so much a sublimator of anxiety as a bellwether for moral positioning and identification, the debate around the show exemplified Israel's internal conflicts and the ambivalence that land concessions engendered.[102] Thus, in a startling coherence, television functioned to create public discourse and to carve out the contours of discussion.

What set the *Hirbat Hizaa* incident apart was sourced not in the claims for official Israeli culture or in the anxiety over world opinion, not in the invocation of "proper" representations of national character or in the government's active role in the attempt to shape such programming. All, as I've argued in previous chapters, not only manifested throughout television's Israeli history and prehistory, but also can be said to have structured that history. Rather, the incident's distinction was in the application of such ideological expectations to a particular and familiar text.

That the *Hirbat Hizaa* affair pitted a well-known story against the new problematic of television representation provides a potent example of the medium's central place in a crucial national debate. Yet again, television, much more than the object of struggle, provided the arena for the battle's enactment: an incident in which a thirty-year-old work of literature was reinvigorated with radical resonance in a new medium by a changing political context. In a parallel sense, however, the debate served to illustrate the contested nature of television's role in the cultural and political realm. Clearly, part of the anxiety *Hirbat Hizaa* provoked was in its inauspicious timing. Yet opponents insisted that television was different from literature in both its institutional makeup and its mode of address. The public outcry over this mode of institutional interpretation signaled both the growing regard for the medium and its shift in status, bringing to the surface a set of competing expectations that saw television not as an expression of national identity but as part of a cultural network of popular knowledge—a network through which national identity and its cultural expression were in continuous process of negotiation and remaking.

Yet, paradoxically, such a shift could not have occurred through this particular text if it were not for the earlier understandings of the medium. As I have shown throughout, the logic that fashioned television was its messaging capacity and its purported power of influence. This articulation precisely negated the notion of the broadcasting arena as a public sphere where ideas (however provocative) are raised for discussion. Here, *Hirbat Hizaa*'s eruption into public consciousness also appeared through this media logic. The disruptive power of *Hirbat Hizaa*, then, was not just in its political challenge but in television's collectivity that placed it precisely apart from the logic of cinema and print culture on the one hand, and from journalism on the other. Further, it rendered the text not as a mere note of dissent within the concert of consensus but as an expression of collective public discordance.

As the weeks went on, the *Hirbat Hizaa* debate slowly relinquished its hold on the front and editorial pages, slipped away from public attention, and was finally forgotten (perhaps an indication of the speed with which controversies rise and fall in Israel's news-dense environment), but aside from its political resonance, the affair left a lasting legacy for Israeli television. As one commentator speculated, "Maybe the controversy's greatest actual significance is that it was the opening shot in the media's struggle for independence."[103]

More than the tortured logic of "what will the world think" that had plagued most conversations about Israeli television well before its introduction, *Hirbat Hizaa* seemed to inflame the passions of objectors *not* because it was false, but precisely because—in its personal, abstract portrayal of a moral upheaval and in its demand for a just accounting of an unjust act—it evaded a historic or strictly factual framing. In its insistence on the poetic, it spoke to a larger sense of moral reckoning, and in its potential broadcast on Israeli national television, it appeared to demand such a reckoning not outside the discourse of official nationalism—where, as literature, it had existed since the nation's founding—but prominently within it. In its appearance on state television, Yzhar's narrative was oddly bifurcated, gaining a radical register just as it was inscribed into an official site of national representation. Thus, more than any other broadcast to this point, *Hirbat Hizaa* acknowledged a public divide and, by visually rendering its protagonist's morally pained paralysis, characterized so much of what would follow in the Israeli cultural engagement with "the Palestinian problem."

For a brief period after the program's airing, reports circulated about the government's intent to reform (or even eliminate) the semi-public IBA. These plans did not materialize but brought new (and lasting) public attention to the agency and its mission, programming, and structure.[104] One columnist mused that the struggle over *Hirbat Hizaa*'s broadcast might be over, but a larger battle over the continued independence of the IBA would go on.[105] Whereas the aftermath of the broadcast saw intensified government scrutiny of television broadcasts, it also marked a turning point for Israeli media: a legitimation of an ongoing tension between political interests and media programming. It was in this sense that the *Hirbat Hizaa* affair had put a definitive end to the official aspirations that brought television into being and confirmed it as a central and contested intersection that linked popular culture, public discourse, and official politics. Critic Pinchas Ginosar wrongly predicted that the *Hirbat Hizaa* controversy would be a defining and memorable moment in the minds of a generation of Israelis.[106] While this claim seems oddly bombastic in light of the momentous changes that took place in the same year (the first Arab-Israeli peace treaty, for one), Ginosar's forecast was perhaps less an indication of the importance of the television show and more a reflection of the compound meaning the controversy had come to represent. Despite the furor over the program at the time, it is a barely remembered footnote in a few current accounts of Israeli television. My aim here is not merely to resurrect a forgotten moment in television history. Rather, I argue that its near complete fade-out from national memory signals not its finally trivial value but its stature and function as a fully integrated cultural product.

CODA

In mid-December, nearly a year after its airing in Israel and three months after the signing of the Camp David Peace Accord between Israel and Egypt, *Hirbat Hizaa* was shown on Jordanian television. As the culture and education minister reported to the Knesset, the film was not, as feared, a sold or purloined copy, but a recording made directly from the live Israeli broadcast—evidenced by a snippet of the live Israeli studio feed that briefly followed. This item represents a fitting bookend to Israeli television's noisy start, marked by so much attention to its porous transmission borders. The unruly transmigrating signal that so preoccupied officials at the start of the Israeli television project had now seeped out in both directions. Yet discussion over the Jordanian broadcast lasted less than five minutes on the Knesset floor, and the news garnered a short paragraph in one daily paper; there were no subsequent reader letters, no debate or controversy. Television history had moved on . . .

CONCLUSION
On Televisual Imagination

As a single controversy, the *Hirbat Hizaa* affair is noteworthy for television's thorough implication (textually, legally, and rhetorically) in political struggles over cultural expression, history, and national memory. As a concluding case study in this book, however, the incident cannot be fully accounted for within the dimension of television itself and is wholly coherent only in the context of its local history, as the contours of the debate were completely proscribed by the particular meanings television occupied in the Israeli national and nationalist imagination. In this, the incident parallels my overall project in revealing how an imagined logic of technology both reflected and inflected a public process of discussion and local meaning making.

Writing about television in public settings, Anna McCarthy argues for the importance of considering viewership in the specificity of place: "Scale is central to the study of television because it generates much of the complexity of the medium itself, a complexity signaled in the tension between the placeless generality of the image and the specificity of its terminal forms. . . . To ask what the television screen is doing in the immediate space around it—in the 'microlevel' of reception—is to ask how these two scales are connected, to explore how a standardized 'elsewhere' of the image takes material form in a particular place."[1]

The Israeli television project, as imagined throughout its early history, can be understood as seeking to deny all individual specificity of locale and the "elsewhere" of the image, working instead to decisively fix the place of viewership within a national scale. In its ideological dimension, such a fantasy of television's omnipresence in everyday life is as a direct portal for communication between the state and the viewer's eye. It is a pipe in, an arena where the viewer directly partakes in a national imagination. If the first part of this book is, in total, an examination of the development of this telespeculating logic, the second part traces the process of its disintegration. As the escalating debates over Arab broadcasting, the Shabbat controversy, and the *Hirbat Hizaa* incident illustrate, this image of collective locale pixilated into ever-finer resolutions with public arguments that employed various constructions of identity, from the national to the ethnic, political, religious, and individual, to reposition television as a medium conflicted between collective address and private choice. The process by which this tight-weaved plan of national cohesion unraveled is hardly surprising when we recall that it was particular "problem" identities (immigrants, Palestinians, and neighboring Arabs) that were first construed as the targets of national narrowcasting.

Surely, the lack of capitalist investment in programming (and in commercial content) did much to deemphasize viewing as an activity that is largely domestic, personal, and familial. As we have seen in early chapters (recall MK Telmi's vivid radio description that so casually merged the domestic and political spheres), the home, in most Israeli broadcasting rhetoric, was both the site of national coherence and the (often endangered) point of penetration for cross-national and cross-cultural communication. These conceptions of domestic place, as I've noted earlier, are in no way unique to the Israeli experience of television formation yet represent an especially acute understanding of telecommunication in terms of offensive and defensive forms of collective address.

As we have seen throughout this account, the nature of the address imagined for television—and indeed, its sole call into existence—was sourced in the specific preoccupations that emerged from the core of the Israeli encounter with nation building, namely, security and cultural unity. Thus, the fabric from which the television argument was sewn had been cut to the measure of its national predicaments. Conversely, television anxieties and the arguments that sought to block (or delay) its introduction into Israel lay in the very same concerns. The role of television as an imagined technology in its prehistory was thus intertwined with the very grounding principles of national life in Israel. The pattern of assumptions, arguments, expectations, and fears that emerged as television was first considered, then rejected, reassessed, debated, and finally instituted, reveals how the fundamental concerns of border security, ethnic diversity, religious identity, Arab-Israeli relations, and immigration were constitutive in the formation of debates over Israeli national culture, and were conjoined in their consistent appearance in the Israeli television discourse.

These same fundamental notions, infinitely complex when viewed in terms of general national history, assume a particular clarity when reduced to their specific application to broadcasting. Thus, official and public debates over television's institution provide us with a privileged view into the anatomy of definitions: the meaning of culture, the constitution of citizenry, the stakes in national identity, and the mechanics of ideological power.

Further, as each chapter demonstrates, national preoccupations were not only revealed in concrete terms through the discussion over broadcasting, but also, in a process of cross-pollination, were themselves shaped and rearticulated through their association with the technology and its imagined dimensions—exposure, for example, emerged as the "cure" for cultural difference.

While the rhetorical employment of television in the service of Israeli national priorities had been particularly widespread when no "real" television service existed, this process did not come to an end with the first broadcast of Israeli television. The productive tensions between these various imaginings, attempts at control, and practical adaptations suggest that media histories require multiple vantage points that can account for industrial, institutional, and public encounters with technology as *modes of thinking* as well as material realities.

In the summer of 1967, just as the Knesset debated the introduction of general television into Israel, economist Robert Heilbroner asked the vexing question: "Do machines make history?"[2] Indeed, the question of technological determinism deeply troubled those engaged in the Israeli television debate, particularly that of technological self-determinism—the idea that television would "naturally" evolve into a popular and "low" format despite efforts to guide and control it (see chapter 3 for a discussion of the "open technology" debate). Raymond Williams has argued that such fears for television's erosion of cultural norms always constituted a political position linked with anxieties over the loss of privilege and cultural authority. Thomas Streeter, Robert McChesney, and Susan Douglas, among others, have all refuted such deterministic assumptions in the U.S. case, where government policies and institutional interests played a vital role in shaping the U.S. broadcast media as a private, commercial industry.[3] It is conventional to think of each discrete technology as posing a set of new questions for social practice. However, the focus of technological specificity often obscures the recurrent nature of some questions. As this historical work suggests, recirculations of common anxieties, power struggles, and negotiations for control are not the occasional by-products of technological development but are their structuring force.

However, as Claude Fisher, Daniel Czitron, and others have shown, the interaction between technological possibilities, official imaginings, and public practice can yield often surprising and unexpected results.[4] Here I want to distinguish my focus from claims for the resistant potential in technology's possibility, assertions over its apparently self-contained ability to transform social life, and arguments that regard technological developments as direct extensions of institutional power. Indeed, as tracing the struggle over broadcasting makes clear, political attempts to shape and control media are often far from univocal or consistent.

Instead of focusing on the results of efforts to steer television, I wanted to highlight various attempts to do so with the contention that it is not their ultimate success or failure that makes these efforts relevant in the medium's history, but their active and constituent participation in a public debate. As each case study herein illustrates, earlier discursive formations are always present and active in contemporary understandings of technology in the national context, and their deployments at the site of television are meaningful precisely because of their resonance and relevance far beyond the specific concerns over the medium. The recent attention to globalizing television, the concentration of corporate ownership, the disquieting popularity of ultraconservative media in the United States, new media technologies, and the rise of the Al Jazeera network in the Middle East all benefit from such contextual and historically informed approaches that consider not only the material facts of programming itself, but also the discursive and social processes that bring them into being and dynamically endow them with meanings.

As for Heilbroner's question, Israel's television history suggests that machines do not so much make history as reveal the forces that do.

In the post–*Hirbat Hizaa* days, Israeli broadcasting would undergo another seismic shift as discussions turned again to the implications of a one-channel monopoly over Israeli television. In the Eighties, the issue had become a full-fledged public debate, while Israelis were subscribing in large numbers to various illegal cable services that provided broadcasts from Europe and Russia (a service much desired by a rapidly growing post-Soviet immigrant population). In a striking and instructive parallel, another decade would pass in argument until new broadcast provisions would open the door to legal cable in 1989, a second commercial television channel in 1992, and regional (and private) commercial radio in 1996. Currently, Israelis enjoy a vast array of local and foreign broadcasts, making Israel's television environment one of the most diverse in the world.

Surely another volume could begin where this work ends, detailing the wide-ranging debates that took place as Israeli television expanded to include foreign and commercial broadcasts. As might be expected, much of the debate centered on anxieties over the loss of a distinct Israeli culture to Western (and particularly U.S.) popular and commercial influences. In addition to cultural imperialism, other issues included the validity of competition in news reporting, the influx of European and U.S. news, ownership structures of cable franchises, and the general fear of a changing Israeli society that so enthusiastically embraced U.S. popular entertainment. This next phase in Israel's television history clearly brings it more thoroughly into the current global conversation about media, dominated by notions of national culture, identity, and anxiety over foreign—largely U.S.—programming. As this study seeks to demonstrate, however, the parallel and nearly global nature of these anxieties should not be taken as a sign of their fundamental correspondence, since each society experiences cultural anxiety as the sum of its distinctive political, cultural, and discursive histories.

In focusing on particular discursive clusters and pattern formations as developing around and through the idea of television, the six chapters here are less a history in and of themselves and more a selective exploration of historical trajectories. Doubtless, other histories and scholarly examinations are needed to illuminate important patterns and events then and since that are outside the scope of this work: the history of Arab-language broadcasting in Israel, issues of military censorship, ongoing ethnic tensions within Israeli media, broadcast policy, the privatization of Israeli commercial media, locally produced popular media texts—and, which surely deserves its own scholarly attentions, the formation of the Palestinian Broadcasting Corporation (PBC) in 1994.

My overall purpose in this book, however, has been the examination of key ideas—what I have called preoccupations and telespeculations—that have guided original engagements with notions of broadcasting, and have developed in distinct and significant ways through their incorporation and relationship with a television logic. In this sense, I hope this book contributes not only to an Israel-specific field of scholarship but also to the study of this very broadcasting logic:

the conceptual grammar of media, and its development and uses in broader social, cultural, and political spheres.

The clichéd notion that we live in a "media-saturated" society, for one, reveals a tendency to think of media presence in our daily lives through a series of rarely analyzed but formative relationships and "commonsense" assumptions about representation, politics, popular tastes, and mass influence. Critical engagements with television, for the most part, have been interested in the linkages between representation and their "effects" (or the slightly softer "impact") on what we occasionally call our "culture" or, more broadly, real life. These constructions lead to compartmentalized approaches that see analysis of political content and opinion making as separate from the study of popular texts and meaning making and that hail endless explorations of media-induced (mostly violent) behavior and wholesale critiques about the role of television in a seemingly always-recent deteriorating and homogenizing popular culture. In total, this logic endorses a tacit understanding of television as an entity apart from the culture or daily life it so relentlessly dominates.

This rough sketch of tendencies does not mean to suggest that such approaches are necessarily wrong or irrelevant, but that they partake in a specific and narrow television logic of influence and maintain it as a primary—even singular—preoccupation.[5] As I've suggested in the Israeli case, understanding such preoccupations as themselves historically evolving and contextually dependent clusters of meaning helps broaden the field of media studies by offering new modes of engagement and approaches that account for the complexities of meaning-making systems, institutional pressures, and public use. Further, they seek to ask how much of contemporary television (as an industry, a business model, a symbolic language, and an information system) is shaped by the same impulses that frame its "effects."

Television is a daily practice, a technology, an international industry, and a cultural system of signs and narratives. It is constitutive in all these concrete ways, but also in less tangible modes of being. Television, as I suggested in the introduction, is a compound concept (often nestled in that other compound entity, "the media") whose presence in our daily life (as at once a system of production and consumption, creation and recreation, work and leisure, fact and fiction, now and then, here and elsewhere) derives its power precisely from a seductive opaqueness: assumptions about its "effects," anxieties over its influence, and excitement at its borderless possibilities. It is too broad, too amorphous, and yet, with our attentions directed to global pathways and media practice in the international and transnational context, appears close to the root of public as well as private means of trans-forming the world. In this sense, "television history" is a necessary fic-tion of classification that obscures a fundamental dependency.

Finally, debate over media texts within the social realm, however fervent and high-pitched in the accounts herein, is a rather typical and ordinary process. This, in essence, is what popular culture is about. The mechanics of media culture necessarily have their moorings and pur-pose in their contextual value. It is not in the parallel (one-to-one) rela-tionship between textual representation and "real life" that the work of culture is most potently observed or is most prominently influential. Rather, it is the process of meaning negotiation and continued discur-sive reworking that our so-called diversions draw from and activate.

Notes

INTRODUCTION

1. Epigraph: Tsvi Gil, *House of Precious Stones* (Tel Aviv: Sifriat Hapoalim, 1986), 33.
2. NBC's exploratory offer actually came early in the global history of television. By 1952, only fourteen nations had a national television service in place. By 1966, when Israel introduced its educational service, that number had swelled to ninety-eight.
3. Tefael Man and Tzipi Gon-Gross, cited in Dan Caspi and Yehiel Limor, *The Mediators: The Mass Media in Israel, 1948–1990* (Tel Aviv: Am Oved, 1992).
4. Izhar Smilinsky, January 1, 1963, Knesset Minutes, Meeting #200, Fifth Knesset, 668, Knesset Archives, David J. Light Law Library, Tel Aviv University, and Beit Ariela legal library, Tel Aviv. Hereafter, the Knesset Minutes will be cited as KM, followed by the meeting number and session number, and, where applicable, notebook and volume number.
5. Michele Hilmes, *Radio Voices: American Broadcasting, 1922–1952* (Minneapolis: University of Minnesota Press, 1997).
6. Among the countries in Israel's vicinity to establish television before Israel did were Iraq in 1956, Lebanon in 1959, Egypt and Syria in 1960, Kuwait in 1961, Sudan in 1963, Yemen in 1964, Cyprus in 1964, and Saudi Arabia in 1965. Iran began broadcasting in October 1966 and Jordan introduced general programming in 1968, only three months before Israeli general programming began.
7. Raymond Williams, *Television: Technology and Cultural Form* (London: Fontana 1974; reprint, Middletown, Conn.: Wesleyan University Press, 1992), 8. Citations are to the Wesleyan edition.
8. As Thomas Streeter and Robert McChesney have pointed out, commercial broadcasting systems, far from representing the absence of political or social attentions and interests, are the result of particular configurations of such controls. In this sense, it would be misguided to deem the state-sponsored alternative as somehow inherently *more* political or more "pure" in its ideological transparency. My assertion that the Israeli case presents itself as ideally fitted to an intentionality analysis refers rather to the relatively uncomplicated (and presumably singular) source of such intentions. See Thomas Streeter, *Selling the Air: A Critique of the Policy of Commercial Broadcasting in the United States* (Chicago: University of Chicago Press, 1996); Robert W. McChesney, "Conflict, Not Con-

sensus: The Debate over Broadcast Communication Policy, 1930–1935," in *Ruthless Criticism: New Perspectives in U.S. Communication History*, ed. William S. Solomon and Robert W. McChesney (Minneapolis: University of Minnesota Press, 1993).

9. Tony Bennett, *The Birth of the Museum: History, Theory, Politics* (London: Routledge, 1995), 6.

10. Steven Mullaney, "Strange Things, Gross Terms, Curious Customs: The Rehearsal of Cultures in the Late Renaissance," *Representations*, no. 3 (summer 1983): 40–67.

11. Toby Miller, *The Well-Tempered Self: Citizenship, Culture, and the Post-Modern Subject* (Baltimore: Johns Hopkins University Press, 1993).

12. See Paddy Scannell and David Cardiff, *A Social History of British Broadcasting*, Oxford and Cambridge, Mass.: Basil Blackwell, 1991; McChesney, "Conflict, Not Consensus"; and Nilanjana Gupta, *Switching Channels: Ideologies of Television in India* (Oxford: Oxford University Press, 1998).

13. Lynn Spigel, *Make Room for TV: Television and the Family Ideal in Postwar America* (Chicago: University of Chicago Press, 1992); Streeter, *Selling the Air*; Anna McCarthy, *Ambient Television: Visual Culture and Public Space* (Durham, N.C.: Duke University Press, 2001).

14. Streeter, *Selling the Air*.

15. Virginia Dominguez, *People as Subject, People as Object: Selfhood and Peoplehood in Contemporary Israel* (Madison: University of Wisconsin Press, 1989).

16. Benedict Anderson, *Imagined Communities: Reflections on the Origin and Spread of Nationalism* (London and New York: Verso Books, 1991.

17. Jonathan Boyarin, *Storm for Paradise: the Politics of Jewish Memory* (Minneapolis: University of Minnesota Press, 1992), xv.

18. As I show in chapter 3, an educational-television service meant for classroom use was introduced in 1966. By contrast, the often used term "general television" refers to a national service planned and offered for the general public and domestic use.

19. Raymond Williams, *Keywords* (New York: Oxford University Press, 1976).

20. Eugene Halton, "The Cultic Roots of Culture," in *Theory of Culture*, ed. Richard Munch and Neil J. Smelser (Berkeley: University of California Press, 1992).

21. Miller, *The Well-Tempered Self*, 174.

CHAPTER 1. MERE GLINTS AND REFRACTIONS

1. Epigraphs: Knesset members Ytzhak Ben-Aharon, July 27, 1959, and Menachem Parosh, November 21, 1962.

2. Papers in Yiddish, Polish, Rumanian, and Russian followed, after 1948, mostly as public, party-related ventures.

3. Dan Caspi and Yehiel Limor, *The Mediators: The Mass Media in Israel, 1948–1990* (Tel Aviv: Am Oved, 1992), 94–101.

4. See Ella Shohat, *Israeli Cinema: East/West and the Politics of Representation* (Austin: University of Texas Press, 1989).

5. *Hatzofe* (late December 1962), cited by Israel Yeshaayahu-Sharabi on the Knesset floor.

6. George Palash, January 16, 1952, KM, #43, 2d Knesset, 1008.

7. David Ben-Gurion, January 16, 1952, KM, #43, 2d Knesset, 1009.

8. Caspi and Limor, *The Mediators*, 97.

9. Quoted in Tsvi Gil, *House of Precious Stones* (Tel Aviv: Sifriat Hapoalim, 1986), 32.

10. Howard Sachar, *The History of Israel: From the Rise of Zionism to Our Time* (New York: Knopf, 1976).

11. Yehuda Gothelf, "The Problem of Leisure in Past Times and Today," in *The Cultivation of Leisure* (Tel Aviv: Histadrut, the Center for Education and Culture, 1962), 1.

12. Ibid.

13. Quoted in Gil, *House of Precious Stones*, 19.

14. Television Club directory cited by Gil, *House of Precious Stones*.

15. Quoted in Gil, *House of Precious Stones*, 19.

16. Gil, *House of Precious Stones*.

17. "Manufacturers Get Ready for Television," *Ha'aretz*, October 3, 1962, 4.

18. "On Television in Israel," *Ha'aretz*, October 26, 1962.

19. In his proposal, Aviv took care to mention that no broadcasts would take place on the Sabbath and holidays, so as to avoid a possible conflict with the religious party. It is not clear

whether Aviv proposed to pay all the costs of such a project or simply offered to volunteer his services to the endeavor free of charge.

20. Aharon Jacob Greenberg, July 27, 1959, KM, #680, 3d Knesset, 2693.
21. Babah Eidelson, July 27, 1959, KM, #681, 3d Knesset, 2706.
22. MK Carmel, June 12, 1962, KM, #141, 4th Knesset, 2278.
23. MK Greenburg, ibid., 2274–2275.
24. Shmuel Mikonis, January 1, 1963, KM, #200, 5th Knesset, 679.
25. In 1948, European Jews made up 75 percent of the population, compared to 55 percent in 1961.
26. Sachar, *The History of Israel*, 531.
27. Quoted and translated by Sachar, ibid., 413.
28. Nurit Gertz, *Captive of a Dream: National Myths in Israeli Culture* (Tel Aviv: Am Oved, 1995), 39, 38.
29. Amnon Raz-Krakotzkin, "Exile within Sovereignty: Towards a Critique of the 'Negation of Exile' in Israeli Culture," *Teoria Ubikoret* 4 (1994): 23–55; 5 (1994): 113–134.
30. Shohat, *Israeli Cinema*, 3.
31. Sachar, *The History of Israel*, 427.
32. Ibid.
33. Joseph Yambor, "Talk and Action in Integration," *Al Hamishmar*, November 28, 1962, 2.
34. Yagil Levi and Yoav Peled, "The Fracture That Wasn't: Israeli Sociology in the Mirror of the Six Day War," *Teoria Ubikoret* 3 (winter 1993): 115–128.
35. Daphna Golan, "The 'Border' in Israeli Discourse," *South Atlantic Quarterly* 94, 4 (fall 1995): 1060.
36. Shlomo Fisher, "Two Types of Modernization: On Examining the Ethnic Problem in Israel," *Teoria Ubikoret* 1 (summer 1991): 1–22.
37. Abraham Knani, "The Road to Integration," *Al Hamishmar*, November 16, 1961, 2.
38. Jacob Nizani, July 27, 1959, KM, #680, 3d Knesset, 2702.
39. Ibid.
40. Ibid.
41. Shlomo Jaacob Gross, July 27, 1959, KM, #680, 3d Knesset, 2696.
42. Givton letter cited by Gil in *House of Precious Stones*.
43. Joseph Yambor, "Television, Advertising, and Propaganda," *Al Hamishmar*, March 9, 1962, 44.
44. Babh Eidelson, July 27, 1959, KM, #681, 3d Knesset, 2706.
45. Joseph Tamir, *Survey of the Minister of Post*, June 7, 1966, vol. 45, 1670, Beit Ariela Law Library, Tel Aviv.
46. Yambor, "Television, Advertising, and Propaganda," 8.
47. Menachem Parosh, November 21, 1962, KM, #183, 5th Knesset, 235.
48. Emma Telmi, KM, July 15, 1959, 3d Knesset, 2561–2562.
49. Gilaad Haim, from a letter to Ben Gurion, cited in Gil, *House of Precious Stones*, 21.

CHAPTER 2. BROADCASTING THROUGH THE BACK DOOR

1. Epigraphs: Menachem Parosh, January 1, 1963, KM, #200, 6th Knesset, 679; Nathan Baron, "Television Will Enter through the Back Door," *7 Days*, September 9, 1962, 1.
2. Henry Cassirer, a television expert with UNESCO, and a representative from the Australian Broadcasting Service were the first international experts brought in to assess Israel's "television situation." Their document, which recommended the establishment of an Israeli television service, was written shortly after the two had visited Israel and was known as the Cassirer Report.
3. Tsvi Gil, *House of Precious Stones* (Tel Aviv: Sifriat Hapoalim, 1986).
4. Howard Sachar, *The History of Israel: From the Rise of Zionism to Our Time* (New York: Knopf, 1976).
5. Gil, *House of Precious Stones*, 21.
6. Eli Noam, *Television in Europe* (Oxford: Oxford University Press, 1991).
7. Eddie L. Soffer, *In the Image of the BBC* (Ettilngen: Alb-Verlag, 1985).
8. Moshe Ben-Ephraim, "Broadcasting Service—A Public Service," *Al Hamishmar*, January 24, 1962, 3.
9. Levi Eshkol to Levi Ytzhak Hayerushalmi, quoted in Dan Caspi and Yehiel Limor, *The Mediators: The Mass Media in Israel, 1948–1990* (Tel Aviv: Am Oved, 1992), 99.

10. Joseph Yambor, "Television, Commercials, and Propaganda," *Al Hamishmar*, March 9, 1962, 8.
11. Ben-Ephraim, "Broadcasting Service," 3.
12. Yambor, "Television, Advertising, and Propaganda," 8.
13. Arie Avneri, "A Television Center, Cable Cars, and 'National Days' Will Be Part of the Main Attraction to the Fair," *Yediot Ahronot*, May 20, 1962, 4.
14. For fear of Arab sanction, not every participating country had an "official" presence.
15. Yehuda Kastan, "The Eastern Fair, an Opening to Future International Fairs," *Ha'aretz*, June 7, 1962, and Tzvi Algat, "The Flying Camel," *Ma'ariv*, June 5, 1962, 3.
16. "Space Flights and Games from Chile Will Be Flown for Oriental Fair's Television," *Al Hamishmar*, June 1, 1962.
17. This particular lineup was advertised on June 7, 1962, in *Ha'aretz*.
18. "American Satellite Broadcasts Television to Europe," *Ma'ariv*, July 12, 1962.
19. Benjamin Shachor, January 1, 1963, KM, #200, 5th Knesset, 672.
20. Natan Ronvitch, "Television on Allenby Street," *Ha'aretz*, May 19, 1962, 6.
21. G. Shtrasman, "Regulations in the Matter of Television Receivers," quoted in *Ma'ariv*, May 29, 1962, 11
22. Sachar, *The History of Israel*, 384.
23. Emanuel El-Nekveh, "Arab Television Feeds Poison and Increases the Nationalism of Israel's Arabs," *Yediot Ahronot*, September 2, 1962.
24. Moshe Zak, "On the Baron's Account," *Ma'ariv*, September 21, 1962.
25. Menachem Parosh, November 21, 1962, KM, #183, 5th Knesset, 234.
26. Ami Assaf, Deputy Minister of Education and Culture, November 21, 1962, KM, #183, 5th Knesset, 238.
27. Menachem Parosh, November 21, 1962, KM, #183, 5th Knesset, 235.
28. "Manufacturers Get Ready for Television," *Ha'aretz*, October 3, 1962.
29. Joseph Harif, "The Rothschilds Are Willing to Finance Television in Israel," *Ma'ariv*, September 10, 1962, 1.
30. The announcement was a follow-up to an April Knesset agreement concerning a two-person Israeli delegation—Dr. Meir Shapira, an Israeli high-school principal, and Max Rau, Rothschild's Israeli representative—who were sent to study the question of educational television all over the world. Rothschild proposed that if the delegation's report were favorable, he would help finance such a service.
31. Arie Tzimoki, "The Creation of Television Will Cause Wild Competition and Snobbism," *Yediot Ahronot*, September 10, 1962.
32. "Television, on the Baron's Account," *Yediot Ahronot*, September 10, 1962, 1.
33. Tzimoki, "The Creation of Television."
34. Yambor, "Television, Commercials, and Propaganda."
35. Harif, "The Rothchilds Are Willing," 1.
36. Y. Ben-Porat, "Moshe, Our Father, Did Not Frequent the Cinema . . ." *Yediot Ahronot*, September 13, 1962, 7.
37. Moshe Zak, "On the Baron's Tab," *Ma'ariv*, September 21, 1962.
38. "Manufacturers Get Ready for Television," *Ha'aretz*, October 3, 1962.
39. Harif, "The Rothchilds Are Willing," 1.
40. Nathan Baron, "The Price of a Set Manufactured in Israel," *Yediot Ahronot*, September 23, 1962, 5.
41. Series of ads in *Yediot Ahronot* and *Ma'ariv*, September–November 1962.
42. "B.G. Agrees to Television, There Will Be No News Broadcasts," *Yediot Ahronot,* November 7, 1962.
43. Lea Porat, quoted in Aharon Doleb, "The Lord Giveth and Takes Away," *Ma'ariv*, November 23, 1962.
44. "Main Points Agreed Upon in Negotiations for Educational Television," *Ha'aretz*, November 8, 1962.
45. Gil, *House of Precious Stones*.
46. Hannoch Givton, quoted in ibid., 23.
47. Doleb, "The Lord Giveth."
48. Boaz Evron, "What Kind of Television, and When?" *Ha'aretz*, November 3, 1962, 5.
49. Quoted in Gil, *House of Precious Stones*, 25.
50. S. Arnon, "Television's Turn, When?" Letter to the editor, *Ma'ariv*, October 3, 1962.

51. "Kollek Wants Approval for Television Before Eshkol Departs to Brussels," *Yediot Ahronot*, November 18, 1962.
52. "The Government Will Discuss Television Today," *Ha'aretz*, November 18, 1962, 1.
53. Ibid.
54. "Kol Israel Workers Demand Delay in the Television Decision," *Al Hamishmar*, November 18, 1962, 1. The conflict hit its lowest point when Kol Israel's public struggle turned personal for Hannoch Givton. Even before the full details of the Rothschild plan were made public, a feud was reportedly brewing between Givton and Tzvi Zinder, a former Kol Israel manager and current head of the Government Information Center (known as the Hasbarah, the "explanation," Office). Both men had served on the Avidor Committee and were known as enthusiastic supporters of television. However, as *Yediot Ahronot* noted in September, each man perceived television as an extension of his own domain and was poised to battle over who would be named to oversee the television project (see Nathan Baron, "Television: How and When," *7 Days*, September 21, 1962, 5). Zinder's training and position as head of the information office raised further suspicions in the press over the propaganda uses of Rothschild's television project and its ideological purpose (see Evron, "What Kind of Television"). In December, Zinder was named administrative manager of the educational television service. Givton announced his upcoming resignation, only to reverse himself a few days later, telling the press, "I have no intention of becoming Kol Israel's undertaker" (see Arie Tzimoki, "Not Kol Israel's Undertaker," *Yediot Ahronot*, December 10, 1962). Despite the aversion of an all-out strike and Givton's retraction of his initial resignation, the crisis forever damaged Givton's standing with government representatives.
55. "Government Will Discuss Television," 1.
56. Emma Telmi, November 21, 1962, KM, #183, 5th Knesset, 236.
57. Nakdimon report quoted by Eli Eyal, "The End of a Fundamental Argument," *Ha'aretz*, November 2, 1962.
58. Here Rogel implicitly suggested what Givton and others in Kol Israel had already expressed, that television would succeed only as a continuation of radio—not as a separate and limited project—and that it would require the experience and expertise of Kol Israel staff.
59. Quoted in "Kol Israel Workers Demand Their Inclusion in Television Plans," *Al Hamishmar*, November 22, 1962.
60. Boaz Evron, "By the Receiver," *Ha'aretz*, November 3, 1962
61. Doleb, "The Lord Giveth."
62. Porat quoted in ibid.
63. Ibid.
64. Shmuel Shnizer, "Too Dangerous and Too Expensive," *Ma'ariv*, November 16, 1962.
65. David Ben-Gurion, quoted in Yosef Harif, "Ben Gurion Was Silent in Television Discussion," *Ma'ariv*, November 19, 1962.
66. Eldad Amita, letter to the editor, *Ha'aretz*, November 12, 1962.
67. Even educators appeared split on the question of television. A group of about fifty teachers, university professors, and intellectuals organized against television, publishing pamphlets and giving interviews to the press about television's dangerous effects on Israeli youth and the population at large. Among the most commonly cited reasons for resisting television were the lack of human contact it would foster (both between teacher and student and among students), its passive and superficial nature, the medium's tendency to discourage creativity and collective problem solving, and the possible health risks children might incur from sitting in place for prolonged periods of time (damage to neck and spine were often highlighted).
68. Menachem Parosh, November 21, 1962, KM, #183, 5th Knesset, 235.
69. "The Known Benefactor," *Ma'ariv*, November 30, 1962.
70. Moshe Koll, November 21, 1962, KM, #183, 5th Knesset, 236. Aharon Jacob Greenberg, January 8, 1963, KM, #203, 5th Knesset, 739.
71. T. Meiri, letter to the editor, *Ma'ariv*, September 12, 1962.
72. Izhar Smilinsky, January 1, 1963, KM, #200, 5th Knesset, 668.
73. Esther Raziel-Ne'or, January 1, 1963, KM, #200, 5th Knesset, 666.
74. H. Naftali, "Television, the New Worship Object," *Al Hamishmar*, December 28, 1962, 7.
75. Abba Eban, January 1, 1963, KM, #200, 5th Knesset, 661.
76. "Educators Warn against the Dangers of Television," *Ha'aretz*, November 12, 1962.

77. Menachem Parosh, November 21, 1962, KM, #183, 5th Knesset, 234.

78. Emma Telmi, KM, January 1, 1963, #200, 5th Knesset, 672.

79. Jody Berland, "Cultural Technologies and the 'Evolution' of Technological Cultures," in *The World Wide Web and Contemporary Cultural Theory: Magic, Metaphor, and Power,* ed. Andrew Herman and Thomas Swiss (London: Routledge, 2000).

CHAPTER 3. THE BELLY-DANCER STRATEGY

1. Epigraphs: Allon is quoted in Tsvi Gil, *House of Precious Stones* (Tel Aviv: Sifriat Hapoalim, 1986), 83; Perosh and Telmi quotes are from January 1, 1963, KM, #200, 5th Knesset, 681, 672. The cartoon is by S. Ben-David, letters to the editor, *Davar,* January 30, 1966.

2. Aharon Jacob Greenberg, January 8, 1963, KM, #203, 5th Knesset, 740.

3. Joseph Yambor, "Television, Advertising, and Propaganda," *Al Hamishmar,* March 9, 1962, 8.

4. Haim Mass, "Television Is Coming," *Ma'ariv: Days and Nights,* March 18, 1966, 8.

5. "The Other Side of the Coin: Educational Television," *Yediot Ahronot,* September 14, 1962.

6. Ibid.

7. "Boredom Isn't Necessary in Our Television," *Yediot Ahronot,* September 25, 1962, 5.

8. Yair Kotler, "Television Does Not Compete with Newspapers," *Ha'aretz,* October 15, 1962.

9. Ytzhak Goldstein, "For Television," *Ma'ariv,* November 25, 1962.

10. Ytzhak Goldstein, letter to the editor, Ma'ariv, November 25, 1962. Arie Goldbloom, "Pro (Non-Educational) Television," *Ma'ariv,* December 6, 1962.

11. Dan Margalit, "Television: Classroom or Marketplace?" *Herut,* November 23, 1962, 7.

12. Mikonis Shmuel, January 1, 1963, KM, #200, 5th Knesset, 678.

13. Izhar Smilinsky, ibid., 668.

14. Dan Margalit, "In the Showdown on Television, a Hesitant Draw," *Herut,* November 30, 1962.

15. Harif, "Ben Gurion Was Silent."

16. Shmuel Shnizer, "Beggars Will Institute Television?" *Ma'ariv,* December 13, 1962.

17. Nathan Baron, "Rothschilds Have Enough . . ." *Yediot Ahronot,* November 30, 1962, 5.

18. Ibid., "Television Will Enter through the Back Door," *7 Days,* September 9, 1962, 1.

19. Eli Ayal, "The End of a Fundamental Argument," *Ha'aretz,* November 2, 1962.

20. Meir Roth, letter to the editor, *Ha'aretz,* November 11, 1962.

21. "Educators Warn against the Dangers of Television," *Ha'aretz,* November 12, 1962.

22. S. Gelbert, "The Educational and the General," *Al Hamishmar,* November 30, 1962.

23. Joseph Boki, letter to the editor, *Ha'aretz,* November 7, 1962.

24. Yehoshua Bar-Joseph, "In Praise of Entertainment Television," *Yediot Ahronot,* November 23, 1962.

25. Israel Punt, quoted in "Film Owners Make Peace with Television but Want Compensation," *Yediot Ahronot,* September 20, 1962.

26. Izhar Smilinsky, January 1, 1963, KM, #200, 5th Knesset, 669; Shnitzer, "Beggars Will Institute Television?"

27. Izhar Smilansky, January 1, 1963, KM, #200, 5th Knesset, 670.

28. Esther Raziel-Ne'or, January 1, 1963, KM, #200, 5th Knesset, 665.

29. Yehoshua Bitzur, "Anti-Television Majority in the Knesset," *Ma'ariv,* November 22, 1962.

30. Government decision quoted in Tsvi Gil, *House of Precious Stones* (Tel Aviv: Sifriat Hapoalim, 1986), 25.

31. Abba Eban, January 1, 1963, KM, #200, 5th Knesset, 660. Succeeding quotes from this speech are cited by page number in the text.

32. Emma Telmi, ibid., 673.

33. "Television's Thrown into Doubt" *Ha'aretz,* February 26, 1963, 1. The reports noted that the recent redrafting of the proposal for the creation of the Israeli Broadcast Authority eliminated all reference to television, despite the explicit assurances the government had made to Kol Israel, promising to include television with radio as part of the agency's area of operation. For many, this erasure surely indicated complications for, if not the demise of, the television plan. The legal disassociation of Kol Israel and the educational service is important to note, since it was the government—specifically the Office of Education and

Culture—that would maintain content control over television. In one sense, this separation worked to keep each medium under discreet authority, but it also highlighted the difference in purpose envisioned for each service as the government labored to distance the coming of educational television from the problematic aspects of Kol Israel—namely, the presence of its commercial channel (the Light Wave), the criticism over its political coverage, and its association with entertainment and news. Thus, as the previous chapter details, the national broadcasting service (Israeli radio) was defined as an information and entertainment mass medium, while television was carefully designated an educational, high-cultured, institutional, and strictly nonentertainment utility. Moreover, while radio was widely perceived as a domestic leisure technology, government officials were careful to insist that educational television was a classroom technology to be used in a communal instructional setting.

34. Abba Eban, March 6, 1963, Knesset speech cited in "Educational Television Approved," *Ha'aretz*, March 7, 1963, 2.
35. In the aftermath of the Lavon affair, Ben-Gurion was opposed by the so-called Old Guard led by Golda Meir and other party veterans. Lavon himself was promptly expelled from the Mapai Party after Ben-Gurion threatened to resign in 1961, yet the ideological battle between Ben-Gurion's "New Guard" protégés (led by Moshe Dayan) and the traditional labor leaders within the party only intensified as the party was weakened with the 1961 election and as the Old Guard realigned itself with the ousted Lavon.
36. Ben-Gurion would return to politics, briefly forming a new party with Moshe Dayan, which was subsequently reabsorbed into Labor. However, Ben-Gurion's popularity and influence within Israeli politics would never match his pre-Lavon days.
37. Broadcasting was not altogether absent from press reports, as the government was busy crafting and reworking what would be become the IBA (Israeli Broadcast Authority) law in 1965.
38. Sarnoff-led NBC had long expressed interest in Israeli programming, yet I have found no indication that the network was approached. A possible explanation for this is that NBC had invested in broadcasting in the Arab world.
39. Tzvi Lavi, "Television in Israel—From Plan to Execution," *Ma'ariv*, July 21, 1965, 3.
40. Ibid.
41. Quoted in Gil, *House of Precious Stones*, 31.
42. Unlike his predecessor, Eshkol was not a firebrand visionary, a charismatic ideologue, or an awe-inspiring intellectual. Known primarily as a talented manager and a master of conciliatory politics, the new prime minister appeared, for the time being, to regard television with a singular, uncomplicated vision: Excited by its informational capacity and motivated by its practical deployment, he made no secret of his interest in exploring general television from the very start.
43. Menachem Barash, "Eshkol Calls for a Practical Discussion in Instituting General Television in Israel," *Yediot Ahronot*, March 24, 1965.
44. Gil, *House of Precious Stones*, 31.
45. Eddie L. Soffer, *In the Image of the BBC* (Ettilngen: Alb-Verlag, 1985), 68.
46. In particular, the government pointed out that the plenum committee would be selected from public figures in Israeli art, literature, and education and would not answer directly to the government. Also, the BBC charter required the agency to renew its license every ten years; the IBA required no such license.
47. From the February 1963 IBA law proposal, cited in "IBA Law Proposal on the Knesset's Table," *Ha'aretz*, February 26, 1963, 6.
48. Soffer, *In the Image of the BBC*.
49. Moshe Oneh, discussion on broadcasting service law, March 8, 1965, KM, #456, 5th Knesset, 1460.
50. *State Education Law* (5713-1953, section 2), Knesset Archives, Jerusalem.
51. *Broadcasting Authority Law*, 5725-1965, part 1, "Basic Provisions," section 3, subsection 1, Knesset Archives, Jerusalem.
52. Ibid., subsections 2–5.
53. Ibid.
54. Levi Eshkol, *Survey of the Prime Minister's Office*, May 25, 1965, vol. 43, 1936. Succeeding quotes from this document are cited by page number in the text.
55. Gil, *House of Precious Stones*, 31.
56. Abraham Rotem, "Kol Barama," *Ma'ariv: Days and Nights*, June 23, 1965, 15.

57. Joseph Charif, "Israeli and Arab Television Channels," *Ma'ariv* July 23, 1965.

58. Lavi, "Television in Israel," 3.

59. "Television," *Ma'ariv*, July 21, 1965.

60. This model, originally proposed as a money-saving device, was drawn from the examples of Scandinavia, Algiers, and Poland, which all experimented with dual-language programming.

61. Opponents of the dual-language plan dismissed assumptions about the intellectual level of the general populace and the supposition that "programs that were good for the Jews were good for the Arabs" (Gil, *House of Precious Stones*). For this faction among television proponents, television's capacity for targeted narrowcasting, not mass broadcasting, was its chief political utility and raison d'être. What made Israeli television seem palatable was precisely the argument that Arab television, in Jewish and Arab homes alike, was decidedly *not* good for the Jews.

62. Menachem Barash, "Receivers in Israel May Not Be Suitable," *Yediot Ahronot*, July, 15, 1965, 19.

63. Arie Tzimoki, "General Television—In Two Years," *Yediot Ahronot*, July 19, 1965, 3.

64. Izhar Smilinsky, January 1, 1963, KM, #200, 5th Knesset, 669.

65. "Television," *Ma'ariv*, June 23, 1965.

66. "Television," *Ma'ariv*, July 21, 1965.

67. Ranvit Importers advertisement, *Ma'ariv*, July 23, 1965.

68. Westinghouse (Electra importers) advertisement, *Davar*, June 1965.

69. Menachem Barash, "Eshkol Calls for a Practical Discussion in Instituting General Television in Israel," *Yediot Ahronot*, March 24, 1965.

70. Gid'on Raicher, "What's New in Kol Israel," *Yediot Ahronot*, March 30, 1965.

71. Rotem, "Kol Barama," 15.

72. David Lifkin, "Experimental Television in December," *Davar*, July 27, 1965.

73. In retrospect, that the Ministry of Post was entrusted with the first television transmission may seem puzzling, but it fit the notion of Israeli television as a utility and a delivery channel.

74. Menachem Sla'ee, "First Broadcast in Educational Television," *Yediot Ahronot*, January 4, 1966.

75. Tzvi Lavi, "The Fly Threatened the Television Screen," *Ma'ariv*, January 7, 1966, 9.

76. First Pilot ad, *Ma'ariv*, January 7, 1966.

77. "How to Buy a Television Set," advertising supplement, *Davar*, January 1966.

78. "Television in Israel," advertising supplement, *Davar*, January 1966.

79. "Shwab-Lawrence Television in Israel," advertising supplement, *Davar*, January 1966.

80. "The Figure behind the Beard: Perma-Sharp Quiz," *Ma'ariv*, January 1966.

81. Mass, "Television Is Coming," 8.

82. Editorial cartoon, *Ha'aretz*, January 5, 1966.

83. Eitan Habar, "The Level of the First Broadcast Was Too High," *Yediot Ahronot*, March 25, 1966.

84. "The Government Approves, in Principle, of Creating General Television," *Davar*, July 19, 1965, 2.

85. Joseph Charif, "Israeli and Arab Television Channels," *Ma'ariv* July 23, 1965, 15.

CHAPTER 4. CLENCHED FIST AND OPEN PALM

1. Second epigraph quote from *Bunker Archeology* (New York: Princeton Architectural Press, 1994), 19.

2. Anthony Giddens, *The Nation-State and Violence* (Cambridge: Polity Press, 1985).

3. Yoram Peri, "Media, War, and Citizenship," *Communication Review* 3, 4 (1999).

4. Hillel Nossek and Yehiel Limor, "Fifty Years in a 'Marriage of Convenience': News Media and Military Censorship in Israel," *Communication Law and Policy* 6 (winter 2001): 1–36.

5. Benjamin Shachor, November 13, 1967, general-television discussion, KM, #215, 6th Knesset, 136–137.

6. Uri Avneri, *Survey of the Minister of Post*, June 7, 1966, vol. 45, 1677, Beit Ariela Law Library, Tel Aviv.

7. Joseph Tamir, *Survey of the Minister of Post*, June 7, 1966, vol. 45, 1670.

8. Aharon Yedlin, November 13, 1967, general-television discussion, KM, notebook 3, vol. 50, 131.

9. Tamir, *Survey of the Minister of Post.*
10. Avneri, *Survey of the Minister of Post.*
11. Tamir, *Survey of the Minister of Post.*
12. Galili immediately antagonized both the Rothschild Fund and Kol Israel Radio workers—and Hannoch Givton, the news head, in particular. He opposed the independent educational operations of the Rothschild Fund and quickly proved a bitter enemy to Givton's vision of a popular broadcasting medium—and to Givton himself. Shortly following his appointment as liaison to the government on television matters, Galili moved to dispose of Givton—whom he successfully ousted soon after—and to pressure the government to end the Rothschild Fund's television agreement and subsume it under the IBA. Tensions between Galili and Rothschild's representatives reached a boiling point, prompting the Rothschild family lawyer to pen an angry private letter to Eshkol demanding that the government maintain its promise of independence to the education service.
13. Shnei-or Zalman Abramov (Nachal Party), *The Budget Law of 1967/1968,* February 13, 1967, 1253, David J. Light Law Library, Tel Aviv University.
14. Ibid. As MK Abramov noted, this was the first time an army employee was appointed to a civilian task without retiring from his army duties.
15. Israel Galili, February 21, 1967, KM, 6th Knesset, 1393.
16. Although, as in the previous vote for educational TV, the implementation of the plan still required a Knesset-wide debate, the approval did tilt the weight toward general television within the coalition and communicated a favorable government view.
17. *Knesset Report on General Television in Israel,* January 1966, cited in Tsvi Gil, *House of Precious Stones* (Tel Aviv: Sifriat Hapoalim, 1986), 34.
18. Shmuel Mikonos, March 8, 1965, KM, #456, 5th Knesset, 1458.
19. Avneri, *Survey of the Minister of Post.*
20. For a detailed account of this "drift toward belligerency" and the military tensions that led to the war's outbreak, see Benny Morris, *Righteous Victims: A History of the Zionist-Arab Conflict, 1881–2002* (New York: Vintage Books, 1999).
21. Martin Van Creveld, *The Sword and the Olive: A Critical History of the Israeli Defense Force* (New York: PublicAffairs, 1998), 172.
22. While Arab goals seemed to center on avenging the outcome of the 1948 war and on the recapture of Israeli-held land, Israel's defensive position as a lone David under Goliath's surprise attack has recently been questioned by military historians who argue that Israel's military capability was largely underestimated and unknown by the public, the press, and even some government officials. Whereas standard histories insist that the Israeli public, despite its anxiety, was not aware of how perilous its position really was, recent accounts like Van Creveld's insist that Israel deliberately exacerbated the conflict with Syria and, despite diplomatic attempts to avert the war, intended to engage the Arabs in a military conflict all along.
23. From Nasser's address to the Egyptian Parliament, May 25, 1967, cited in Howard Sachar, *The History of Israel: From the Rise of Zionism to Our Time* (New York: Knopf, 1976), 633.
24. Van Creveld, *The Sword and the Olive,* 176.
25. Sachar, *The History of Israel.*
26. Reuven Lavitan, "Tzahal Explains Its Deed to the World," *The Reporters' Yearbook* (Tel Aviv: Association of Israeli Journalists, 1967), 50.
27. On April 7, 1967, when the Israeli army shot down six Syrian planes, and later two Egyptian MiG planes, the information office moved swiftly to publicize the incident, characterizing it as purely defensive and successfully evoking sympathy and even admiration around the globe.
28. Lavitan, "Tzahal Explains Its Deed," 55.
29. Ella Shohat, *Israeli Cinema: East/West and the Politics of Representation* (Austin: University of Texas Press, 1989), 67.
30. Edward Said has written extensively on this general tradition, as have Homi Bhabha and Ella Shohat, among others.
31. Ygaal Lossin, "The War on the Ether Waves," *The Reporters' Yearbook* (Tel Aviv: Association of Israeli Journalists, 1967).
32. Despite the news reports, the country remained largely ignorant of the extensive damage the Israeli unit had inflicted on the Egyptian Air Force in its opening strike. Perhaps the most decisive blow of the war, the Israeli surprise attack on the Egyptian air force (timed

to occur immediately as planes returned to their base) left the most powerful single force in the entire united Arab army in ruins. As some military historians argue, this first mission, combined with Egyptian radio's proclamations of victory, left all other forces ill-prepared for the Israelis' rapid advance and, more than did any other battle, determined the outcome of the war.

33. Lossin, "The War on the Ether Waves," 58.

34. Other backup plans included the splitting of the unified service (Jerusalem–Tel Aviv) into three local broadcasts (Jerusalem, Tel Aviv, and Haifa) in case the major service was disabled.

35. Children's programming was initially suspended but was reintroduced after repeated requests by listeners.

36. Lossin, "The War on the Ether Waves."

37. Ibid, 60, 58.

38. Women had always been subject to the IDF's mandatory service provision, and while they had taken active part in live-fire battles in the 1948 war, female soldiers were subsequently barred from combat in the infantry, airborne, and armored divisions. This gender-based exclusion was successfully challenged in the Israeli courts and was overturned in 1995.

39. A meticulously coordinated surprise Israeli attack on the Egyptian air force managed practically to demolish Israel's most daunting enemy in one day. In the five days remaining, Israeli brigades repelled the Egyptians and, despite Dayan's initial appeals to caution, captured the Sinai Peninsula down to the embattled southernmost tip and the Strait of Tiran. Meanwhile, on the eastern border with Jordan, the Israelis captured the West Bank and East Jerusalem, and, in the northeast, Israel ended the war by pushing back the Syrians and capturing the strategic Golan Heights.

40. Lossin, "The War on the Ether Waves," 61.

41. Reportedly, Radio Cairo had announced that Tel Aviv was in flames by the second day of fighting; when the truth of the Egyptian loss became clear, Nasser was shocked.

42. Gertz, *Captive of a Dream*, 21 (my translation).

43. Van Creveld, *The Sword and the Olive*, 199.

44. In the aftermath of the war, newfound Israeli arrogance and shortsightedness, coupled with Arab steadfast refusal to accept or negotiate with the Jews, led to the most costly mistake in Israeli-Arab relations in the Middle East. While initially Israel had been fully prepared to use many of its territorial gains (with the noted exception of East Jerusalem) as bargaining chips for peace agreements, the Arabs were, at the time, unwilling to negotiate. As many accounts reveal, Dayan, Eshkol, and most other military and political leaders did not consider the newly won territories permanent. Most strategic reports envisioned the quick return of the Golan Heights and the Sinai in exchange for peace treaties with Syria and Egypt, and autonomy or a Palestinian statehood agreement for the Gaza Strip. While Jerusalem and the West Bank were more problematic due to their religious significance, some reports proposed a Jordanian agreement that would allow Palestinian autonomy in the area.

45. Gabriel Cohen, November 14, 1967, KM, #216, 6th Knesset, 156.

46. Asher Hassin, November 13, 1967, general-television discussion, KM, #216, 6th Knesset, 137.

47. Van Creveld, *The Sword and the Olive*, 197.

48. Ori Ram, "Memory and Identity: The Sociology of the Historians' Debate in Israel," *Teoria Ubikoret* 8 (summer 1996): 21.

49. Shohat, *Israeli Cinema*.

50. Shmuel Glodsmidt, "TV and the Press: A Few Observations in Light of the Western Experience," *The Reporters' Yearbook* (Tel Aviv: Association of Israeli Journalists, 1968), 138.

51. Benjamin Shachor, November 13, 1967, general-television discussion, KM, notebook 3, vol. 50, 136.

52. Israel Galili, "Government Announcement on the Establishment of General Television," November 13, 1967, KM, notebook 3, vol. 50, 126.

53. Shachor, general-television discussion, 136.

54. Galili, *House of Precious Stones*.

55. Galili, "Government Announcement on General Television," 125.

56. Yedlin, general-television discussion, 132.

57. Shmuel Mikonos, November 14, 1967, KM, #216, 6th Knesset, 151.

58. Amnon Lyn, November 14, 1967, KM, #216, 6th Knesset, 153.
59. Israel Galili, "Government Announcement on the Founding of General Television (the Minister's Response)," November 28, 1967, KM, #222, 6th Knesset, 268.
60. Uri Avneri, November 14, 1967, KM, #216, 6th Knesset, 149.
61. See Shohat's discussion of the films *Rebels against the Light* (Alexander Ramati, 1964), *They Were Ten* (Baruch Dienar), and *Sinaia* (Ilan Eldad) in Shohat, *Israeli Cinema*.
62. Eliezer Smoli, quoted in ibid. (translated by Shohat), 89.
63. Galili, "Government Announcement on General Television," 265.
64. Kol Israel was broadcasting seven and a half hours of Arabic radio programs daily beginning in 1962. More than half that time was dedicated to "news, commentary and programs in different national dialects," the rest to music and entertainment (David Ben-Gurion, February 25, 1963, budget law for 1963–1964, KM, 5th Knesset, 1234). According to Ben-Gurion, the emphasis of the broadcasts was to serve the internal Arab population, yet Arab newspapers and radio, as well as Arab leaders' speeches, indicated that Kol Israel had a large listenership in neighboring nations as well. In the following year, Kol Israel had widened its programming scope for Israeli Arabs, adding programs for women, youth, farmers, laborers, and Bedouins. Some programs were targeted specifically to refugees, and one program featured Arab listeners' greetings to their relatives outside Israel. The programs enjoyed a wide audience, as evidenced by approximately a hundred thousand listener letters received by Kol Israel's Arab-language division in its first year alone.
65. Lossin, "The War on the Ether Waves," 62.
66. Ibid.
67. *Al-Jundi Al-Lebnani* (Lebanese military monthly publication), July 1967, cited in ibid.
68. Cited in ibid.
69. Aharon Yedlin, November 13, 1967, general-television discussion, KM, #215, 6th Knesset, 132.
70. Uri Avneri, November 13, 1967, KM, #216, 6th Knesset, 148.
71. Galili, "Government Announcement on General Television," 126.
72. Elad Peled's letter is quoted in Gil, *House of Precious Stones*, 44.
73. As Gil and others have observed, Galili's actions were largely motivated by his desire to oust Hannoch Givton, the popular head of the Israeli Broadcasting Authority, and to insure he would have no part in the emerging television service. Galili thus sought a figurehead whose expertise and authority would make Givton superfluous.
74. Elihu Katz, "Television Comes to the People of the Book," in *The Use and Abuse of Social Science*, ed. Irving Horowitz (New Brunswick, N.J.: Transaction Books, 1971), 254.
75. Galili quoted in Gil, *House of Precious Stones*, 131.
76. Israel Galili, interview by Gil, ibid., 46.
77. Galili, "Government Announcement on General Television," 127.
78. Committee Guidelines, cited in Gil, *House of Precious Stones*, 131.
79. Many opposition Knesset members viewed the language distribution with some suspicion, speculating that the Hebrew hour was part of the government's attempt to begin general broadcasting without the passing of the broadcasting law, thus allowing a precedent of general-television broadcasting under the direct supervision of a government office. This anxiety alone pointed to a clear, publicly held distinction between Arabic-language and Hebrew broadcasts: While most Knesset members and public opinion makers agreed that general television, like radio before it, must operate outside the government as an independent agency, few expressed the same requirements for Arabic-language services.
80. Ytshak Navon (Raphi Party), November 14, 1967, KM, #216, 6th Knesset, 142.
81. Emil Habibi, November 14, 1967, KM, #216, 6th Knesset, 145.
82. Navon, ibid., 142.
83. Avneri, ibid., 148.
84. Ibid.
85. Hassin, November 13, 1967, general-television discussion, KM, #215, 6th Knesset, 138.
86. Baruch Kimmerling, "Militarism in Israeli Society," *Teoria Ubikoret* 4 (fall 1993): 124. The subhead quote "Finally, Something to Watch!" headlined Israel's first-ever television column: Gidon Raicher, "The Small Screen," *Yediot Ahronot*, May 5, 1968.
87. Galili, "Government Announcement on General Television," 125.
88. Nathan Ribon, "Television on an Iceberg," *Ha'aretz*, May 3, 1968.

89. Uzi Peled, "Memories from the Creation of Television," *Ottot '93*, 1993, 10–13.
90. Roman Prister, in "The Citizen and Taxes," *Ha'aretz*, May 18, 1968.
91. Ibid.
92. Yaron Zelig, "To Conquer the Screen," *Al Hamishmar*, May 13, 1986.
93. Reports that Galili was surreptitiously watching television while on the official podium appeared in several accounts of the events. My own viewing of the footage from that day does not decisively confirm this.
94. "Broadcasting the Parade—Survey Results," *Al Hamishmar*, May 23, 1968, 4.
95. Ibid.
96. Ran Perry, "Television's First Performance," *Ha'aretz*, May 10, 1968, 6.

CHAPTER 5. JEWISH TELEVISION OR MICKEY MOUSE CULTURE?

1. Second epigraph quote is from Eddie L. Soffer, *In the Image of the BBC* (Ettilngen: Alb-Verlag, 1985), 15, 42.
2. Quote and subhead quote from Paulina Shechter, letter to the editor, *Ma'ariv*, November 11, 1969.
3. Elihu Katz, "Television Comes to the People of the Book," in *The Use and Abuse of Social Science*, ed. Irving Horowitz (New Brunswick, N.J.: Transaction Books, 1971), 258 (emphasis in original).
4. Israel Galili, August 13, 1968, KM, #323 of 6th Knesset, 3263.
5. Ytzhak Navon, August 13, 1968, KM, #323 of 6th Knesset, 3270.
6. Even the emergency plan drew some fire from Orthodox MKs, who sought, unsuccessfully, to limit Hebrew programming.
7. Various speakers, question-and-answer period, January 5–February 25, 1969, KM, vol. 53, 1780, 2908–2912.
8. Tsvi Gil, *House of Precious Stones* (Tel Aviv: Sifriat Hapoalim, 1986).
9. Center for Social Research survey results, cited by Gil, *House of Precious Stones*, 69.
10. "Lawless and without Conscience," *Ha'aretz*, November 5, 1969, 9.
11. Golda Meir had assumed government leadership in March 1969 after the death of Prime Minister Levi Eshkol, who did not live to see Israeli television go beyond its initial experimental phase. Significantly, his February funeral would be one of the last "experimental phase" broadcasts before television assumed its daily schedule.
12. "Bitterness at the IBA," *Ha'yom*, May 5, 1969.
13. Various speakers, "Prof. Elihu Katz's Decision to Step Down," March 19, 1969, KM, 7th Knesset, 2054–2060.
14. Katz, "Television Comes to the People."
15. The 1969 election saw a slight decrease in the support for the left-wing Labor Party, and a rise in votes for both the religious Maphdal and right-wing Gachal Parties. The growing strength of these was attributed in part to the uncertainty over the fate of the captured territories, to resentment over the total control of the Labor-centered workers' union, and to the vote of so-called Oriental Israelis and Middle Eastern immigrants. Many in these traditionally religious and working-class communities were reacting to the historically discriminatory policies of the elitist left wing—along with its secular politics. Others were echoing solidarity with conservative Orthodox values of Maphdal and the hard-line anti-Arab platform of Gachal.
16. Nachum Barneah, "Why There's No Giving Up to Maphdal on the Television Question," *Davar*, November 5, 1969.
17. Cited in Dan Caspi and Yehiel Limor, *The Mediators: The Mass Media in Israel, 1948–1990* (Tel Aviv: Am Oved, 1992), 117.
18. Arie Tzimoki, "Conciliation to Maphdal in the Television Matter," *Yediot Ahronot*, November 5, 1969, 4.
19. Amnon Rubenstein, "The Matter: A Question of Conscience," *Ha'aretz*, November 6, 1969, 9.
20. "A Forthright Victory and the Continuation of the Plot," editorial, *Ha'aretz*, November 7, 1969.
21. Ze'ev Price, "Television on Saturday. Pro and Con: Letters to Editor—Labor's Surrender..." *Yediot Ahronot*, November 19, 1969; Moshe Lex, letter to the editor," *Ma'ariv*, November 6, 1969; Reuven Haimovitz, letter to the editor, *Ma'ariv*, November 7, 1969.

22. Gidon Raicher and Arie Tzimoki, "Ma'arach and Maphdal Ministers in Last Effort to Prevent Saturday Broadcasting," *Yediot Ahronot*, November 7, 1969, 1.
23. *Hatzofe* Survey, *Hatzofe*, November 10, 1969.
24. "A Majority Is for Saturday Television," *Ha'aretz*, November 5, 1969, 9. "The Price of Coalition," *Davar*, November 5, 1969.
25. Nathan Ribon, "IBA Rejects Government Request," *Ha'aretz*, November 7, 1969, 1.
26. The decision was difficult since several members were implicitly threatened that a vote against the government could weaken the IBA law and reverse the proceedings. Moreover, the current Labor government had proven more generally supportive of the IBA, and, by all accounts, many on the voting committee were themselves Labor supporters and feared that Labor policies might well be compromised if the IBA stood firm.
27. An open election for the principle of seven-day broadcasting was opposed by only five votes.
28. "A Forthright Victory and the Continuation of the Plot," editorial, *Ha'aretz*, November 7, 1969.
29. Efraim Lamka, letter to the editor, *Ha'aretz*, November 11, 1969, 16.
30. "A Shameful Decision," *Hatzofe*, November 7, 1969.
31. Sara Rozenberg, letter to the editor, *Hatzofe*, November 10, 1969; Y. M. Grinitch, letter to the editor, *Ma'ariv*, November 10, 1969.
32. Shlomo Shmagar, "A Small and Noisy Group That Wants to Awaken Hatred," *Yediot Ahronot*, November 14, 1969, 7.
33. Jacob Edlestein, "Other Aspects in Israeli Television," *Hatzofe*, November 11, 1969.
34. "A Protest on the Abuse of Station" and "A Speech by Rabbi Lavian," *Hatzofe*, November 18, 1969.
35. David Telzner, "Mickey Mouse Enters the Culture War," *Hatzofe*, November 11, 1969.
36. David Richardo, "Television Broadcast on Saturday: Readers' Commentary," *Hatzofe*, November 11, 1969, 3.
37. Edlestein, "Other Aspects in Israeli Television"; Jacob Abraham Barur, letter to the editor, *Ha'aretz*, November 17, 1969; Head Rabbi Nissim, quoted in "Anger in Government Circles," *Ma'ariv*, November 11, 1969.
38. Edlestein, "Other Aspects in Israeli Television."
39. M. Friedman, cited in Yehiel Limor and Hillel Nossek, "The 'Monkey Trial' in the Land of the Bible: Modern Techniques of Religious Censorship," International Communication Association conference paper, June 2000, Acapulco, Mexico.
40. Howard Sachar, *The History of Israel: From the Rise of Zionism to Our Time* (New York: Knopf, 1976), 1976.
41. Limor and Nossek, "The 'Monkey Trial,'" 13.
42. Moshe Bikler, letter to the editor, *Ma'ariv*, November 7, 1969.
43. Ze'ev Herring, "The Birthing Pains of Government and the Television Polemic," *Davar*, November 1969.
44. Abbah Norok, letter to the editor, *Ha'aretz*, November 24, 1969; Herring, "The Birthing Pains."
45. G. Yehuda, "The Choice: Maphdal or Gachal," *Davar*, November 5, 1969.
46. Mark Tavor, letter to the editor," *Ma'ariv*, November 11, 1969; Ron Shapiro, letter to the editor, *Ma'ariv*, November 7, 1969; Ilan Strashnov, letter to the editor, *Ha'aretz*, November 11, 1969, 10.
47. "This Is the Situation When There Is No Majority," Labor Party ad published in national dailies, November, 6, 1969.
48. Haim Romo, letter to the editor, *Yediot Ahronot*, November 19, 1969; Paulina Shechter, letter to the editor, *Ma'ariv*, November 11, 1969; Shaul Pinchassi, letter to the editor, *Ha'aretz*, November 11, 1969, 10.
49. Zohar Golan, letter to the editor, *Ma'ariv*, November 14, 1969.
50. Can'anim ad, *Ha'aretz*, November 11, 1969, 11.
51. "Saturday and Entertainment," *Hatzofe*, November 3, 1969, and "Demonstration against the Operation of Television on the Sabbath," *Hatzofe*, November 8–12, 1969.
52. "On Caricatures in Ha'aretz," *Ha'aretz*, November 11, 1969; Arie Tzimoke, "The Saturday Television Affair: The Start of a Culture War?" *Yediot Ahronot*, November 16, 1969, 4.
53. Raicher and Tzimoki, "Ma'arach and Maphdal Ministers."
54. Nathan Ribon, "A Citizen's Plea to Supreme Court Made Saturday Broadcast Possible,"

Ha'aretz, November 9, 1969, 1; Gidon Raicher, "The Dramatic Race," *Yediot Ahronot*, November 9, 1969, 3.

55. Gil, *House of Precious Stones,* 79.
56. Yehuda Bachar, "The Two Cousins and the Weekend Miracle," *Yediot Ahronot*, November 9, 1969, 3.
57. Haim Liberman, "Saturday Broadcasting," *Ha'aretz*, November 24, 1969, 15.
58. "Disgraceful Behavior," *Ha'aretz*, November 9, 1969, 8.
59. Gidi Yatziv, "The Noise over Religion: Opium for the People," *Ha'aretz*, November 25, 1969, 13.

CHAPTER 6. AIRING NATIONAL GUILT AND THE *HIRBAT HIZAA* AFFAIR

1. Epigraphs: Yitzhak Navon, quoted by Shlomit Toib, "Who Will Guard the Viewers' Souls?" *Al Hamishmar*, February 17, 1978, *Channels and Wave* supplement, 20; Jonathan Boyarin, *Storm for Paradise: the Politics of Jewish Memory* (Minneapolis: University of Minnesota Press, 1992), 118.
2. S. Yzhar, "Hirbat Hizaa," *Four Stories* (Israel: Merchavia Press, 1949); my translation, here and throughout, is from the *Ma'ariv* reprint, February 9–11, 1978, pt. 1, 16. Hereafter, page numbers appear in parentheses in the text.
3. W.J.T. Mitchell, *Picture Theory* (Chicago: University of Chicago Press, 1994), 3.
4. Yossi Sarid, January 25, 1978, "The Plan to Broadcast *Hirbat Hizaa* on Televsion," KM, vol. 81, 1410.
5. Zevulun Hammer, quoted in Avraham Tirosh, "Hammer to *Ma'ariv*: In the Film *Hirbat* Hizaa the Occasional Has Been Turned into the Typical," *Ma'ariv*, February 10, 1978, 3.
6. Dan Miron, "Bein D'mama LeZeaka" (Between silence and the cry), *Dappim: Research in Literature* (Haifa: Haifa University Press, 1992).
7. S. Yzhar, interview by Haim Nagid, *Ma'ariv*, February 10, 1978, 37.
8. Ibid.
9. Nurit Gertz, "Generation Shift in Literary History: Hebrew Narrative Fiction in the Sixties," *Literature, Meaning, Culture* (Porter Institute for Poetics and Semiotics, Tel Aviv University) 15 (1983): 77.
10. Leon Hadar, "The 1992 Election Earthquake and the Fall of the 'Second Israeli Republic,'" *Middle East Journal*, no. 4 (autumn 1992).
11. These fears were grounded in the Likud's contentious relationship to broadcasting in general and to political reporting in particular: As the opposition, the Right had originally opposed the creation of a television service and repeatedly accused both radio and television of extreme political bias.
12. Jacob Cohen, "The Hirba and the Debate," *Ma'ariv*, February 6, 1978, 30.
13. "*The Third Hour* with *Hirbat Hizaa*," *Chotam Weekend Supplement: Al Hamishmar*, February 3, 1978, 22.
14. Kalman Cahane, "Agenda Item 4: The Plan to Broadcast the Play *Hirbat Hizaa*," January 25, 1978, KM, vol. 81, 1406.
15. Ibid.
16. Israeli anxiety over world public opinion and over its media representation abroad was a perennial preoccupation and served to bring media repeatedly to the fore in political discussion.
17. Ydov Cohen, "The Golem Turns on Its Maker," *Ma'ariv*, February 6, 1978, 5.
18. As Benny Morris documents, a solution to the Palestinian problem was initially first on Sadat's mind, yet Palestinian representatives refused to meet with him during his November visit and his overture to Israel was called "treasonous" by Yassir Arafat. Following the PLO response, Sadat shut down the PLO's Cairo office and limited his Israeli negotiation efforts to Egyptian land returns. For a detailed discussion of the process leading up to the Egyptian-Israeli peace agreement, see Morris, *Righteous Victims: A History of the Zionist-Arab Conflict, 1881–2002* (New York: Vintage Books, 1999), 444–494.
19. Howard Sachar, *The History of Israel: From the Rise of Zionism to Our Time* (New York: Knopf, 1976); Morris, *Righteous Victims*.
20. Amos Hadar, "Agenda Item 4: The Plan to Broadcast the Play *Hirbat Hizaa*," January 25, 1978, KM, vol. 81, 1407–1408.
21. Ram Levi quoted in *Al Hamishmar's Chotem Weekend Supplement*, February 3, 1978,

22. Zevulun Hammer, "Agenda Item 4: The Plan to Broadcast the Play *Hirbat Hizaa*," January 25, 1978, KM, vol. 81, 1408.

22. Ibid.

23. Cohen, "Golem Turns on Its Maker," 5.

24. Jacob Ravi, "Who Will Benefit from Delaying *Hirbat Hizaa*," *Al Hamishmar*, February 8, 1978, 3.

25. Joshua Bietzur, Joseph Waxman, and Amos Lebav, "Supreme Court to Discuss Petition against the Minister Hammer," *Ma'ariv*, February 7, 1978, 4.

26. Reports named two board members, Eli Tavin and Yitzhak Meir, affiliated with the Likud and the Orthodox Parties respectively, who facilitated the minister's intervention. According to the IBA law, such intervention was permissible once a minimum of two voting board members expressed a principled objection to a majority decision.

27. Hannoch Bartov, "Hirbat Hammer," *Ma'ariv*, February 7, 1978, 5.

28. Ephraim Kishon, "The Fake Magnifying Glass," *Ma'ariv*, February 10, 1978, 14. Fatah is the Syrian-based PLO's Arab Liberation Movement.

29. "The Case of *Hirbat Hizaa* in the Supreme Court," *Al Hamishmar*, February 10, 1978, 12.

30. Shlomit Toib, "Delay in Screening *Hirbat Hizaa* Angers the Public," *Al Hamishmar*, February 8, 1978, 1.

31. S. Yzhar, interview by Aharon Priel, *Ma'ariv*, February 8, 1978, 17.

32. Bartov, "Hirbat Hammer," 5.

33. Ravi, "Who Will Benefit," 3.

34. Shlomit Toiv, "The Education Minister Cancels the Screening of the Film *Hirbat Hizaa* on TV Last Night," *Al Hamishmar*, February 7, 1978, 1.

35. Victor Shem-Tov, quoted in "The Minister Must Step Down!" *Al Hamishmar*, February 7, 1978, 1.

36. "Writers' Union: 'A Dangerous Precedent,' " *Ma'ariv*, February 10, 1978, 3.

37. Yzhar interview by Priel, 17.

38. Cohen, "Golem Turns on Its Maker," 5.

39. Berg and Hammer quoted in Yeoshua Bitzur, "Television Staff Refused to Screen *Hirbat Hizaa* to the Education Committee," *Ma'ariv*, February 8, 1978, 4.

40. Jacob Dovev, "More Power to Zevulun Hammer," letter to the editor, *Ma'ariv*, February 9, 1978, 23.

41. Hammer quoted by Tirosh, "Hammer to *Ma'ariv*," 1.

42. Kishon, "The Fake Magnifying Glass," 14.

43. Hammer quoted by Tirosh, "Hammer to *Ma'ariv*," 1.

44. Channan Abramson, letter to the editor, *Ma'ariv*, February 9, 1978, 23.

45. Lea Ganz, letter to the editor, *Ma'ariv*, February 8, 1978, 23.

46. G. Benjamin, "*Hirbat Hizaa*," *Ma'ariv*, February 3, 1978, 14.

47. Ibid.

48. Ibid.

49. Kishon, "The Fake Magnifying Glass," 14.

50. Ibid.

51. Yossi Beilin, *Israel: A Concise Political History* (New York: St. Martin's Press, 1992).

52. Moshe Dor, "Three Acts," *Ma'ariv*, February 8, 1978, 5.

53. For an account of the political and policy dimensions of culture wars, see Jim McGuigan, *Culture and the Public Sphere* (New York: Routledge, 1996).

54. Benzion Finklestein, "Hurbat Hazon—After the *Third Hour*," *Al Hamishmar*, February 20, 1978, 4.

55. Dorit Gefen, "A Stupid, Dangerous Decision," *Al Hamishmar*, February 10, 1978, 9.

56. Hanoch Kal'ee, quoted in "*Hirbat Hizaa* to Air Tonight," *Ma'ariv*, February 13, 1978, 4. Kal'ee was the sole member of the IBA board opposed to the film's airing.

57. Dan Miron, "In the Margins of the *Hirbat Hizaa* Affair," *Eta: The Independent Left Review* 6, 2 (June 1978): 3.

58. Yzhar, interview by Priel, 17.

59. Ram Levi, interview by Shulamit Toib, "The Revolution . . . Starts Now," *Al Hamishmar*, February 9, 1978, 8.

60. Dor, "Three Acts," 5.

61. "Television, Geula Cohen Style," *Al Hamishmar*, February 10, 1978, 12.

62. Ibid.
63. "Journalists to Discuss Political Intervention," *Ma'ariv,* February 9, 1978, 4.
64. S. Yzhar (the pen name of Yzhar Smilianski), like many other prominent Israeli artists, had been a political figure and a member of the Knesset.
65. Smadar Lavie, "Blowups in the Borderzones," in *Displacement, Diaspora, and Geographies of Identity,* ed. Smadar Lavie and Ted Swendenburg (Durham: Duke University Press, 1996), 59.
66. Gefen, "A Stupid, Dangerous Decision," 9.
67. Avraham Rotem, "Not a Lonely Battle," *Yediot Ahronot,* February 10, 1978, 3–5.
68. The autonomy proposal conceded self-rule in the occupied territories but limited Palestinian governance to municipal and local matters, precluding national independence and statehood status.
69. Moshe Kazav, quoted in Joseph Waxman and Yehoshua Bitzur, "IBA Officials Will Probably Permit Broadcast," *Ma'ariv,* February 12, 1978, 4.
70. Meir quoted in Toib, "Who Will Guard," 20.
71. Three of the members who voted against the screening expressed support for delaying it in light of the current political climate. Only one member argued for a complete cancellation of the film, citing its incendiary and possibly offensive content.
72. Joseph Waxman, "*Hirbat Hizaa* to Broadcast Tonight," *Ma'ariv,* February 13, 1978, 4.
73. Ram Levi, speaking on the morning after the screening, quoted in Joseph Waxman, "No One Objected to the Script," *Ma'ariv,* February 14, 1978, 17.
74. Toib, "Who Will Guard."
75. The next scene suggests the nature of the "play" Micha refers to. The soldiers, perched on a hill above the village, notice a few Arab men who are escaping. As a few of the soldiers shoot in the direction of the escaping villagers (without hitting a single one), the activity becomes a kind of frenzied sport in which the Israeli soldiers vie for the machine gun, competing to be the most accurate shots, mocking each other's skills and aiming ability.
76. It is important to note here that the film was not unique in its representation of Israeli aggression as such, but rather it was this image's televised materiality that made the staging so unusual.
77. Yzhar, *Hirbat Hizaa* (my translation).
78. *Hirbat Hizaa* survey reported in *Ma'ariv,* February 14, 1978, 2.
79. Twenty-four hours after the screening, youth groups were meeting to discuss the film and its impact. In one Tel Aviv meeting, the teenage MC began discussions by saying: "Now, after the broadcast, everyone is looking at us, the youth, to see how the film has affected those who are about to be drafted and possibly take part in the next war. When the politicians fought their own battles for and against the broadcast, no one asked for our opinion" (quoted in Smadar Shir, "Youth Converse about *Hirbat Hizaa,*" *Ma'ariv,* February 17, 1978, 25).
80. In this chapter, I focus on the most common and visible responses to the broadcast. For reviews that discussed the merits of the film as a work of art or a literary adaptation, see Pinchas Ginosar, "Hirbat Hizaa 1978," *Emda* 29–30, 3 (May–June 1978): 48; Miron, "In the Margins," 3; and Jacob Melchin, "A Bad and Harmful Script," *Ma'ariv,* February 17, 1978, 39.
81. Arnold Margalit, letter to the editor, *Ma'ariv,* February 15, 1978, 23.
82. Y. Levin, letter to the editor, *Ma'ariv,* February 19, 1978, 21.
83. Sima Figle, letter to the editor, *Ma'ariv,* February 16, 1978, 20.
84. See Letters to the Editor sections in *Yediot Ahronot* and *Ma'ariv,* February 14–19, 1978.
85. Joseph Lapid, "Herpat Hizaa," *Ma'ariv,* February 14, 1978, 5. Also quoted in Haim Shor, "Hirbat Hizaa and the Aftermath," *Al Hamishmar,* February 16, 1978, 3.
86. Dorit Gefen, "*Hirbat Hizaa*—Fate or Destiny," *Al Hamishmar,* February 17, 1978, 11.
87. Haim Shor, "Chapters from *Hirbat Hizaa,*" *Al Hamishmar,* February 16, 1978.
88. Pinchas Ginosar, "*Hirbat Hizaa,* 1978," *Emda,* May–June 1978, 48.
89. Aliza Amir, "So What Do You Propose? After *Hirbat Hizaa,*" *Chotam,* February 17, 1978, 3.
90. Lapid, "Herpat Hizaa," 5.
91. Yair Borle'a, "The Poisoned Orange: Television's Present," *Ma'ariv,* February 16, 1978, 5.
92. Readers petition in "Letters to the Editor—After the Screening," *Ma'ariv,* February 19, 1978, 21.

93. S. Yzhar, "On Not Being Drunk with Guilt," interview by Ychiel Hazak, *Al Hamishmar*, February 17, 1978, 4–6.
94. Rotem, "Not a Lonely Battle," 3–5.
95. Finklestein, "Hurbat Hazon," *Al Hamishmar*, February 20, 1978, 4.
96. At this later stage in the debate, the story would also be repeatedly interrogated and evaluated on its singular merits as a record and discursively positioned as an indictment of a particular incident, an approach that marked a considerable departure from its commonly received literary value and allegorical dimensions. For his part, Yzhar remained intractable in his refusal to answer questions about the factual incident that inspired his story. His insistence that the "real facts" of the case were immaterial and irrelevant infuriated opponents and encouraged speculation on the location of the real village raid. Several exposés by reporters and ex-military personnel attempted to pinpoint the village and to reconstruct military actions in the field. In one such article, a high-ranking officer recalled the author as a young soldier and adamantly insisted that the operation—if it happened at all—was "both irregular . . . and directly contradictory to express instructions . . . signed by my very hand" (Gil Ceisari, "I Was the Officer in the Hirbat Haz'az Operation," *Ma'ariv: Days and Nights*, February 17, 1978, 9).
97. Borle'a, "The Poisoned Orange," 5.
98. Ofra Yeshua, "What Will the Gentiles Say?" *Ma'ariv*, February 16, 1978, 5.
99. Ginosar, *"Hirbat Hizaa* 1978," 48.
100. It was in the wake of the debate (three weeks after the controversial airing) that the famous publication of the "officers' letter" on March 7 marked the formation of the Israeli peace movement, Peace Now.
101. Ginosar, *"Hirbat Hizaa,* 1978," 48–49.
102. Acknowledgment that the 1967 "land gains" were, in fact, occupations of foreign territories and wrongs that required righting was a moral equation difficult for many Israelis to accept. Repeated Arab attacks before and after the 1967 war had made it easy for Israelis to maintain the narrative of victimization and encouraged the logic that saw territorial possessions as necessary security measures. In its function as a political narrative, however, *Hirbat Hizaa* directly linked Israeli conduct in 1948 to land occupation in 1967. Although Sadat's attempts to include the Palestinians in a comprehensive peace treaty were unsuccessful (his overture toward Israel was widely regarded among the Palestinian leadership as a fundamental betrayal), discussions with Egypt did center on land captured by Israel in the 1967 war. After prolonged efforts and endless confidential meetings, a peace treaty was signed by the Egyptian and Israeli delegations at Camp David in September 1978.
103. Ginosar, *"Hirbat Hizaa* 1978," 48.
104. Several proposals were discussed in the Knesset about such reforms, and reports circulated that the government was seriously considering overturning the IBA law altogether and reintegrating Israel's sole broadcasting agency under government supervision. As the new IBA managerial board was appointed by April, commentators repeatedly emphasized the political leanings of the new members and observed that the board had taken a sharp turn to the Right. Editor and former IBA board member Chaim Shor noted that the new board was made up primarily of Likud supporters and very few moderate voices. Further, according to Shor, *Hirbat Hizaa* seemed to serve as a kind of litmus test; none of the members who had voted for the broadcast was reappointed. "It seems that the new ruling order are not at peace with the fact of the IBA's independence. And even if, at the moment, they do not dare to act on changing that law—as to not diminish, God forbid, the image of a supposed democracy—they do all they can to return us backwards . . . and change the authority to an agent-arm that aids [their] policies" (Chaim Shor, "A Hundred Days of Benevolence?" *Migvan*, July 1978, 28).
105. Haim Tzadok, "The IBA: Is Its Independence Assured?" *Yediot Ahronot*, February 17, 1978, 16.
106. Ginosar, " *Hirbat Hizaa,* 1978," 48–49.

CONCLUSION

1. Anna McCarthy, *Ambient Television: Visual Culture and Public Space* (Durham: Duke University Press, 2001), 11.
2. Robert L. Heilbroner, "Do Machines Make History?" *Technology and Culture* no. 8 (July 1967).

3. See Susan Douglas, *Inventing American Broadcasting, 1899–1922* (Baltimore: Johns Hopkins University Press, 1997); Susan Smulyan, *Selling Radio: The Commercialization of American Broadcasting, 1920–1934* (Washington, D.C.: Smithsonian Institution Press, 1996); Robert McChesney, "Conflict, Not Consensus: The Debate over Broadcast Communication Policy, 1930–1935," in *Ruthless Criticism: New Perspectives in U.S. Communication History*, ed. William S. Solomon and Robert McChesney (Minneapolis: University of Minnesota Press, 1993); Raymond Williams, *Television: Technology and Cultural Form* (Middletown, Conn.: Wesleyan University Press, 1992).

4. See Claude Fischer, *America Calling: A Social History of the Telephone* (Berkeley: University of California Press, 1992); Daniel Czitron, *Media and the American Mind: From Morse to McLuhan* (Chapel Hill: University of North Carolina Press, 1982).

5. For a developed critique of the domination of the "effects" approach to television, see Toby Miller, "What We Should Do and What We Should Forget in Media Studies," in *Global Currents: Media and Technology Now*, ed. Patrice Petro and Tasha Oren (New Brunswick, N.J.: Rutgers University Press, forthcoming).

Index

About the Author

Tasha G. Oren is an assistant professor of film and media studies in the English Department at the University of Wisconsin–Milwaukee. She is coeditor of *Asian American Popular Culture* (New York University Press, 2004) and of *Global Currents: Media and Technology Now,* forthcoming from Rutgers University Press.